CW00968552

The Economic History of Belize

From the 17th Century to Post-Independence

To Bob

Happy Xmas 2012

Love,

Barbara & Victor

The Economic History of Belize

From the 17th Century to Post-Independence

by
Barbara Bulmer-Thomas
Victor Bulmer-Thomas

CUBOLA BOOKS / BELIZE

Published by:
Cubola Productions
35 Elizabeth Street
Benque Viejo del Carmen
Belize, C.A.

First Edition, April 2012

ISBN: 978-976-8161-39-0

Printed and bound in Mexico

Copyright © 2012 by Cubola Productions

All rights reserved. No part of this book may be reproduced or transmitted in any form or by any means, electronic or mechanical, including photocopying, recording, xerography, or any information storage and retrieval system, without permission in writing from the publisher.

In memory of James Swasey

1912-1994

Contents

Foreword

It is common knowledge that the economy of Belize was driven for centuries and until the middle of the 20th century by forest products, that it then became dependent on sugar and other farm produce, and that at the turn of the century and into the 21st, services, primarily tourism, became dominant. What this exceptionally important book does is not only give us abundant details about the workings of each period, but also present convincing explanations about why things happened as they did; it helps us to understand the unfolding of the Belize economy over three and a half centuries, its intricate workings and its effects, like no other has even attempted to do. And it does so with a rare authority and erudition, while at the same time making it comprehensible to the layperson that shies away from the sometimes unintelligible jargon of economists, incisively explaining the interlocking effects of economics, politics, society and culture.

The first chapter has nothing to do with economics, but it will surely be one of the most avidly read and controversial sections of this outstanding work, as it compellingly debunks the myth that there was some legendary buccaneer called Wallace who gave his name to the country through some mysterious linguistic corrupting process, and goes on to just as convincingly conclude that "Belize" owes its origin to the indigenous Maya. This will not sit well with the few remaining "loyal and patriotic" Baymen, although they might be delighted with the authors' insistence that the Baymen were not all the "ungovernable Wretches" that historians have depicted, because a pew was reserved for them at a church in Boston, where most Belize logwood exports to the US went in the first half of the 18th century. Of course, history also teaches us that religion was no guarantee of morality or humanity: the missionaries came with the bible in one hand and the sword in the other.

The authors discredit a number of other myths, across the breadth of Belize's history, such as that the cutters did not have slaves before the 1720s, that the famous devaluation of December 1949 was all bad, and that Belize's education is superior to that of its Central American neighbours. Everywhere we find interpretations of economic phenomena that throw new light on our understanding of Belize's history. We all know, for example, about the 19th century entrepôt trade with Central America, but here we learn that in the years after 1820 it "dwarfed" the exports of logwood and mahogany together. We also learn that as early as then profits made from economic activities in Belize "tended not to stay in the country," a phenomenon that prevails until the present, in what the authors mischievously but accurately call "the Ashcroft effect".

And then there is the delightful chapter, which surely we owe to Barbara's indefatigable digging, on the Botanic Station established in 1892, a matter hardly ever referred to in general or economic histories of Belize, but which was important both as an indication of the colonial initiative to diversify the economy and as the precursor of both the Agriculture and Forestry Departments.

It is generally recognized that colonialism was bad for Belizeans, but here the authors show with cold economic facts just how bad it was for its economy, how badly it fared in the century after Belize was declared a colony in 1862. In 1900 domestic exports per head were about half of what they were in 1850, and by 1950 the economy was in an even worse state, prompting the authors to conclude that "independence for Belize may not have been a panacea, but it was a huge advance on the mean-spirited and short-sighted approach to development that had characterised colonialism".

It is undoubtedly the chapter dealing with the economy of Belize since independence that will be of greatest interest to students and general readers alike, not only because, for the first time, it lays out clearly what happened and why and with what consequences, but also because, along with the concluding chapter, it dispassionately points out where we made a few bad turns and what we can do to fix it.

Belize is indeed fortunate that a scholar of the calibre and breadth of Victor has decided to bring his sharp mind to bear on its economic history, having written authoritative works on the economic histories of Latin America, Central America and the Caribbean. This enables the authors to do something that is so very important for our understanding of Belizean history, economic or otherwise, which is to place Belize within a global and regional context. Belizeans tend to be much more insular than the islands themselves; our national media scarcely refer to such issues, yet we can never understand what is happening to us unless we know how and why the unfolding of policies and actions outside our country affect us. Indeed, the authors justifiably upbraid us for claiming to be a "bridge" between Central America and the Caribbean: "Belize has been more like an island separated from both". They conclude that Belize will need to devise a long-term development strategy that starts from the assumption that the growth model adopted since independence is seriously flawed, as evidenced by increased poverty, unemployment, inequality, violence and insecurity.

The authors firmly believe that a better future is possible for Belize and express the hope that this book will be seen as a contribution towards that important goal. It can, and should; it must become required reading for all secondary and tertiary students and teachers, and for all leaders and decision makers in the public and private sectors. Above all, its lessons must be learnt by workers, who have had to bear the brunt of the bad turns taken, and who alone, acting in unity and consciousness, can force the changes necessary to make Belize a more just and democratic society.

This collaborative work is a labour of love, forged in the love story that unfolded when the British Victor, whose first job was teaching in Belize in 1966-1967, met the Belizean Barbara at a Belize party in London in 1968. It is a concise, incisive, illuminating work not just on the economic history of Belize, but on its social, cultural and political framework as well. Of special assistance is the large number of tables, figures and graphs constructed by the authors from material unearthed by them, which, along with the book's thorough bibliography, will help enormously the student to understand the workings of the economy and their effects on the people.

No Belizean should fail to learn and act on its lucid and perceptive lessons.

Assad Shoman
Havana, January 2012

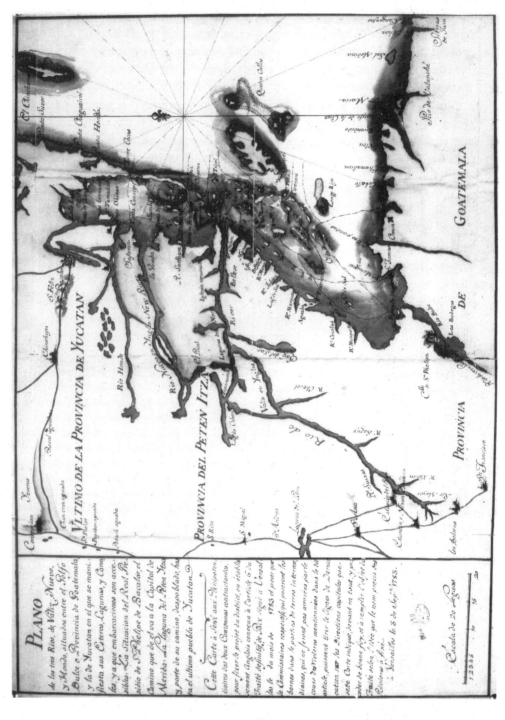

1783 map showing the Balyz, New and Hondo Rivers.
Source: Archivo General de Indias

Preface

While several good histories of Belize have been written from a diplomatic, political or social dimension, there has never been an economic history covering the whole period from its origins in the 17th century to the present day. This is the gap that this book seeks to fill. Each of the six chapters is divided into three or four parts, with a concluding chapter.

The period covered by this book is roughly 350 years. It starts with the arrival of the first British settlers and goes beyond independence. The British, of course, were not the first to settle in Belize nor were they the first Europeans to reach the country. However, the first Europeans—the Spanish—had only a military and religious interest in Belize when they challenged the long-established dominance of the Maya. Although the Spanish presence continued into the 17th century, it had ceased by the time the British arrived and therefore has no relevance for the subsequent economic history of the country. Meanwhile the economic system developed by the Maya over hundreds of years in Belize was undermined first by Spanish conquest and later by forced migration to other parts of Central America.

Belize underwent several changes of name during the period covered by this book. It only came to be called Belize in 1973. For simplicity we normally refer to the country as "Belize" regardless of the period, unless the context demands otherwise. Belize City also had other names in earlier periods. We normally refer to it as "Belize town" or "Belize City", although before 1973 it was just called "Belize".

In an economic history of this nature, it is customary to start with a chapter on "the land and the people". We have chosen not to follow this convention as there are already many good books on these subjects. The environmental resources of Belize are well described in Jolly and McRae (2003) and Bridgewater (2011). The Belizean people are central to Leslie (2008) and Shoman (2011). There are also general histories that cover both topics, such as Iyo, Tzalam and Humphreys (2007), as well as more specialized ones such as Bolland (1977) and Graham (2011).

Instead, we start in Chapter 1 with the foundations of Belize in the 17th century. It begins with the two "origin" myths that have proved so enduring in Belize regarding the mysterious figure of Peter Wallace on the one hand and the idea of settlement by shipwrecked sailors on the other. We then demonstrate that both myths are in fact fictions. The chapter also shows conclusively that there never was an historical figure called Peter Wallace. Since the name "Belize" cannot therefore be derived from "Wallace", the second part of the chapter explores the alternative possibilities and concludes that it is indeed derived from a Maya word. The third part of the chapter then considers the identity and location of the settlers who came before the establishment of the logwood trade.

Chapter 2 covers the century during which Belize was an illegal settlement based on the export of logwood. This period ends in 1763 with the Treaty of Paris. The four parts of the chapter deal with the foundation of the logwood settlement; its population–free and slave; the market for logwood; and the methods of production. The chapter emphasizes that Belize in this period was not subject to British Navigation Acts and was therefore able to sell its logwood all over the world. The trade with Boston, however, was particularly important.

Chapter 3 covers the century of the legal settlement from the Treaty of Paris to the establishment of the colony of British Honduras in 1862. During most of this time Belize was known as the British Settlement in the Bay of Honduras. It is during this century that the foundations of modern Belize were laid. Indeed, Belize was very prosperous for much of this period. The four parts of the chapter deal with the geopolitical rivalries between the United Kingdom and the United States that shaped British policy towards Central America in general and Belize in particular; the mahogany trade; the entrepôt trade; and the social relations that emerged with the abolition of the slave trade and the emancipation of the slaves.

Chapter 4 covers the period during which Belize was a British colony, this period ending in 1981. The chapter starts with the political economy of colonialism, as Belize was now for the first time a formal part of the British Empire. It then explores the decline of the Belize economy, which roughly corresponds to the period up to 1900. The next 50 years, representing the fall of the Belize economy, are the subject of the third part. The fourth part of the chapter looks at the recovery and diversification of the economy from 1950 to independence. There is an Appendix to this chapter on the Belize Estate & Produce Co., which we believe is the first attempt to use primary resources to study a firm that had such enormous influence on Belize.

Chapter 5 is a case study of the Belize Botanic Station that was established by the colonial authorities in 1892. It illustrates perfectly the dilemmas faced in seeking to diversify the Belize economy away from forestry towards agriculture as well as the tensions between different departments of the British government itself. The Botanic Station closed in the 1930s

14

and few people today know of its history despite the fact that it occupied a prominent position on the Belize River close to the Haulover Creek. This chapter also contains five short appendices, one of which lists the native plant specimens believed by officials to have commercial value.

Chapter 6 explores the Belize economy since independence. It begins with production, where Belize's performance–as measured by the growth of Gross Domestic Product per head–has not been as fast as might have been expected following the end of colonialism. The chapter then looks at the distribution of income in Belize starting with the division between residents and non-residents and then at the distribution among residents themselves. The third part looks at the labour market since independence and the problem of creating jobs of sufficient quantity and quality. The final part looks at macroeconomic policy in Belize since independence.

Chapter 7 contains the conclusions to the book, where we pull together the main threads in the economic history of Belize distinguishing between the "positives" and the "negatives". The book ends with a comprehensive list of references and several appendices.

This book's origins go back over 40 years to when we first met and started discussing Belizean issues. At that time, long before independence, there was no internet and no personal computers. Library material could only be consulted in the city where it was held, making research on Belize's economic history difficult since the relevant archives are scattered across many countries. Indeed, it would have been almost impossible to write a book such as this at that time.

All this has now changed and research has become much easier thanks to digital archives that are expanding constantly. Much of the British material relevant to Belize is now available online, although some can still only be consulted at the National Archives, the British Library or Kew Botanic Gardens in London. The Spanish material is increasingly accessible through the internet as a result of the ongoing process in Spain of digitising the colonial archives. The primary sources in North America, especially Boston, relevant to Belize's early economic history are not yet available electronically, but many secondary sources have made use of them and these are accessible online. There is also the Digital Library of the Caribbean (DLOC) that carries a wealth of material from across the region relevant to Belize. And in the post-independence period, almost everything of importance is available through the internet.

Many people have helped us in the preparation of this book. It is not possible to mention all of them, but we would be grossly negligent if we did not single out Assad Shoman for the numerous contributions he has made through challenging our ideas, suggesting new materials and reading draft chapters. The staff of the Belize Archives and Records Service in Belmopan, the National Archives in London and the Institute of Commonwealth Studies, London University, dealt with all our queries efficiently. One of us (Barbara Bulmer-Thomas) came across the materials for Chapter 5 in the archives at Kew Botanic Gardens while working as a scientific researcher with David Sutton, formerly of the Natural History Museum in London. The staff at the Kew Gardens Archives and Kate Manners in particular were very helpful–as was Johnny Searle, present owner of the land at Bolton Bank that contains the site of the Botanic Station.

Barbara and Victor Bulmer-Thomas
Basil Jones, Ambergris Caye

1. The Origins of the Belize Settlement

The Spanish reached Belize before the British, and the Maya were established long before either of them. Yet the history of Belize is intimately associated with the British because they were the first Europeans to establish a settlement that was more than transitory. It was this settlement that eventually expanded to reach the boundaries of modern Belize.

All Caribbean countries, with one exception, can document with some accuracy the date of the first permanent settlements by Europeans. For example, Cuba was first settled by the Spanish in 1511, Antigua by the British in 1632, Martinique by the French in 1635 and St. Eustatius by the Dutch in 1636. The one exception is Belize, whose British origins have been shrouded in a mixture of fact, myth, legend, naivety and dishonesty.[1]

All societies strive to establish a narrative about their origins. Some of these are creation myths that may once have been believed, but are now accepted as fable. An example is the Finnish myth about the origins of ancient Karelia, where the earliest inhabitants are said to have sprung from an egg.[2] Others have an element of historical truth that has been embellished over time to favor the founders. An example is the colony of Jamestown in Virginia, whose first British inhabitants were much more incompetent and disorganized than their subsequent sanitized image would suggest.[3]

The purpose of this chapter is to disentangle the facts from everything else in the stories about the origins of Belize. The chapter starts with two common myths that Belize was first settled either by a buccaneer called Peter Wallace or by shipwrecked sailors or–in some versions–both at the same time. These two myths can now be shown to be false despite the fact that they have been repeated *ad nauseam* in the secondary literature.

---

[1] Spanish *entradas* into Belize, however, have been reasonably well documented. See, for example, Means (1917), Stone (1932), Thompson (1988), Jones (1989) and Graham (2011).

[2] This story is told in an epic poem called the Kalevala written by Elias Lönnrot in the 19th century.

[3] See Elliott (2006).

Since Wallace never existed, the name of the country cannot be derived from his surname–as has often been suggested. Thus, the second part of the chapter looks at the etymology of the word "Belize". This is complicated by the large number of countries and publications in which places and people have been named "Belize". It is easier to say with certainty what words "Belize" is not derived from, although a strong case can be made for its derivation from a word or words in Yucatec Maya.

The third part of the chapter is concerned with the first British settlers before the establishment of logwood extraction as the main economic activity. This is the most problematic part of the chapter, as we will never know with certainty who the first settlers were. There is a certain justice in this, however, since we will also never know exactly who were the first Paleo-Indians or Maya in Belize–nor, for that matter, the first Africans, Garifuna or refugees from Yucatan.

The Wallace and shipwrecked sailors myths

A Google search using "Peter Wallace Buccaneer" as the keywords records over one million entries. This is an astonishingly high number. Most of these repeat the claim that Wallace, Wallice or Willis[4] came to Belize in either 1638 or 1640, that he founded a town at the mouth of the Haulover Creek that is today called Belize City and that he was a buccaneer of Scottish origin. Many also claim that he came from the island of Tortuga, off the coast of Haiti, where the British had established a foothold until they were driven off by the French in 1640.

Strangely, however, there is no mention of "Wallace" in the literature on Belize before 1827. In the first book devoted exclusively to the Belize settlement, written by Captain Henderson and published in 1809, there is no mention of his name.[5] Nor is he mentioned by Nathaniel Uring, who visited the settlement in the early 18th century.[6] Even more surprising is that he is not listed by Alexandre Exquemelin in his exhaustive study of buccaneers first published in 1678.[7] Furthermore, when the *Honduras*

[4] As the name is not spelt consistently, we will refer only to "Wallace" unless it is absolutely necessary to use a variant spelling in order to avoid confusion.

[5] See Henderson (1809). The second edition in 1811 also makes no reference to "Wallace".

[6] See Uring (1726) and Uring (1928).

[7] This book has been published in many languages and editions with considerable variation in content as each country sought to portray "its" buccaneers in the most favorable light. However, no edition in any language refers to "Wallace". For a relatively recent English edition, see Exquemelin (1976).

Almanack–a quasi-official record of the settlement–was first published in 1826, there was no mention of Wallace and the authors stated cautiously that the "British settlement of Honduras, of which Belize is the capital, cannot be traced to be of any greater antiquity than from the administration of Oliver Cromwell."[8]

This understandable caution was thrown to the wind in the second edition of the *Honduras Almanack* published in 1827.[9] This states that "Wallice" was "Lieutenant among the Bucaniers who formerly infested these sea...he first discovered the mouth of the River Belize."[10] This was then repeated in subsequent editions, with the 1829 edition stating that "The town of Belize, situated at the mouth of the river of the same name, was so called after its first discoverer, Wallice, a noted Bucanier who made this, the place of his retreat."[11]

More information on "Wallace" was provided by the final edition of the *Honduras Almanack* in 1839 where we learn that "Belize owes its origin to a Scotch Corsair Chief of the name of Wallace, a native of Falkland in Kinrosshire. At the time that these formidable pirates were driven from Tortuga, a small island situated a few miles north of St. Domingo [Haiti], Wallace, to escape from the just vengeance of the Spaniards, fled for security amongst the numerous islands on the coast of Yucatan and finally settled at the mouth of the River Belize. Here after many vicissitudes both by sea and land Wallace fixed his residence, erected a few log huts and a small fort alice [fortaleza], which stood on the site now occupied by the handsome premises of Messrs. Boitias and Delande."[12]

This edition of the *Honduras Almanack*, in addition to reasserting that "Belize" is derived from "Wallace", gives an interesting insight into Wallace's *modus operandi*. Wallace, we are told, was joined from time to time by other "restless spirits" who "made repeated incursions upon the Spaniards....It does not appear whether this small but formidable band of Settlers were received with encouragement by the natives or treated as

---

[8] See *Honduras Almanack* (1826), p. 5. Cromwell was Lord Protector from 1649 until his death in 1658, although it could be argued that his "administration" included the years of the Civil War that began in 1642.

[9] The *Honduras Almanack* was at first supported by funds from the public assembly in Belize and there were annual editions between 1826 and 1830 inclusive. The quality was superb and these early editions sometimes included colour prints as well. There was then an edition in 1839, which is of a very inferior quality. The 1829 edition is available digitally as a Google book (http://books.google.com/) and the 1839 edition can be found in the Digital Library of the Caribbean (http://www.dloc.com/).

[10] See *Honduras Almanack* (1827), p. 5.

[11] See *Honduras Almanack* (1829), p. 5.

[12] See *Honduras Almanack* (1839), p. 2.

enemies,–they formed however a close alliance...with the fierce and indomitable Indians of the Mosquito Shore; by arming these new allies with fire arms they carried on a series of hostilities of the most destructive kind with the Spanish forces by whom the Settlement was surrounded on all sides."[13]

This version of the Wallace myth was then reproduced faithfully by John Lloyd Stephens, who visited Belize during his exploration of Maya sites in Central America (Stephens cited the *Honduras Almanack* as his source).[14] Since this book was immensely popular, going into many editions, the Wallace myth acquired an international following that would never have been possible if it had remained confined to publications in Belize. As a result, the story was repeated in many other secondary sources.[15]

By now the careful reader will have noted that Wallace may have been a "noted" buccaneer, but he appears not to have had a first name. This omission was made good by Justo Sierra, a Mexican author, who wrote a series of articles about Belize in the magazine *El Fénix* published in Campeche in 1849. Sierra, whose ten articles were entitled "Ojeada sobre el establecimiento británico de Belice y reflexiones sobre su futura influencia", not only claimed that Wallace's first name was "Peter", but also that he landed in Belize with 80 companions.[16] In addition, Sierra claimed that Wallace did not settle until the Spanish fort at Bacalar had been destroyed by a group of buccaneers. Bacalar was attacked by Abraham Blauvelt in 1648 and again in 1652,[17] so this places Wallace's arrival in the 1650s–not 1638 or 1640s as implied by the *Honduras Almanack*. Sierra therefore added three elements to the Wallace myth and it is worth quoting him in full, as the article is not often cited these days:

Dícese que un bucanero escocés, atrevido y emprendedor, llamado Petter [sic] Wallace, movido de la fama de las riquezas que se ganaban en aquellas expediciones infames, y asociado de los más resueltos de sus camaradas, determinó buscar un sitio a propósito en que colocar perpetuamente su guarida, a fin de salir a sus piraterías en la mejor ocasión y volver con toda seguridad. Como ésto ocurría a mediados del siglo XVII, la costa de Yucatán bañada del golfo de Honduras, se hallaba totalmente deshabitada de españoles, pues el único establecimiento que allí había, el de Bacalar, había sido aniquilado por la irrupción del filibustero Abraham y por la sublevación de los indios de aquel distrito. Wallace hizo un perfecto reconocimiento de aquellos bajos y

---

[13] See *Honduras Almanack* (1839), p. 3.

[14] See Stephens (1841), Vol.I, pp. 14-15.

[15] See, for example, Squier (1858), pp. 576-77.

[16] Hubert Bancroft, in his three volume history of Central America, repeats Sierra's account almost word for word, although he gives as his sources Peniche (1869) and García Pelaez (1851). See Bancroft (1883), Vol. II, p. 624.

[17] See final part of this chapter.

arrecifes…y desembarcó allí con unos ochenta piratas, que desde el momento mismo construyeron unas cuantas chozas, circunvaladas de una especie de empalizada o ruda fortaleza.[18]

Various authors, Belizean or based in Belize, then consolidated the myth over the next eighty years without adding much of substance. Archibald Gibbs, for example, mentions Wallace, but treats him more as a figure of legend and does not give a first name.[19] The *Handbook of British Honduras*, the successor to the *Honduras Almanack* and published three times between 1890 and 1892, also mentions the "celebrated buccaneer" Wallace, although without much conviction and again without giving a first name.[20] On the other hand, the next edition of the *Handbook* in 1925 was much less circumspect, since the authors included a chronology in which it is stated that in 1638 "Wallace, or Willis, a Scotch Corsair Chief, the Buccaneer of historical fame, to escape from the just vengeance of the Spaniards, established his rendezvous at the mouth of the Belize River, where he erected a few log huts. He came from Hispaniola."[21]

The next development in the Wallace legend can be traced to a Guatemalan historian, Francisco Asturias. Writing for the first time in 1925, Asturias claimed that Wallace was Sir Walter Raleigh's "primer oficial" and that he accompanied him on his voyage of 1594 intended to discover El Dorado. After the death of Queen Elizabeth I in 1603, Raleigh's fortunes declined and Wallace is said to have left his service and "se dedicó a correrías por su cuenta". Asturias claims that Wallace set sail from England on May 14th 1603 and arrived at the mouth of the Belize River, where he established a settlement. He then became disillusioned by squabbling among his companions and returned to England in 1617 where he died in 1621.[22]

Sir John Burdon, editor of the three-volume *Archives of British Honduras* and governor of the colony at the time of publication of the first volume in 1931, was sufficiently intrigued by Asturias' claims that he started a correspondence with him in 1930. This exchange of letters was then reproduced by Asturias in the second edition of his work on Belize, published in 1941.[23] The correspondence makes clear that Asturias had no primary sources for

---

[18] See Sierra (1849). The quote is repeated in Ancona (1889), Vol. 2, pp. 367-68. Both Sierra and Ancona give "Petter" for Wallace's first name, but this is presumably a misprint for "Peter". See Appendix 1 for English translation.

[19] See Gibbs (1883), pp. 21-22.

[20] See Bristowe and Wright (1890), p. 25.

[21] See Metzgen and Cain (1925), p. 1. In fairness to the authors, the historical sketch (p. 31) is more cautious, repeating almost exactly the words of the earlier editions of the *Handbook*.

[22] See Asturias (1925).

[23] See Asturias (1941).

his claims about Wallace, even repeating his statement from the first edition that he had no proof ("sin tener ningún comprobante, me imagino que es en esta expedición cuando él llega a la desembocadura del Rio Viejo, que desde entonces comienza a llamarse de Wallace o Belize").

Unfortunately, instead of quietly burying this nonsense, Burdon repeated some of it in his Introduction to the *Archives of British Honduras* as if it had some authenticity.[24] Even worse, Burdon misquotes Asturias by stating that Wallace arrived in Belize in 1617, when Asturias actually said he had arrived in 1603 and left in 1617.[25] Thus, a new layer was added to the Wallace myth, which has been repeated in numerous secondary sources.

Many of these elements of the Wallace myth were conveniently summarized by José Antonio Calderón Quijano, who is most famous for his attempt to derive the name of Belize from Wallace.[26] However, the high point of the Wallace myth was provided by E. O. Winzerling in 1946, when he devoted a whole chapter of his book on the origins of Belize to "Captain Willis". We now learn that "Willis" set sail (from where is not stated) in 1639 for Tortuga with a group of adventurers "drawn mostly from those expelled from Nevis" and became master of the island. He was then driven off by the French in August 1640 and set sail for the mouth of the Belize River where he founded a settlement "approximately in September 1640."[27]

The publication of Winzerling's book was followed soon after by the rise of the nationalist movement in Belize.[28] This played down the European origins of the settlement and emphasized instead its African and Maya roots. Understandably, there was little room in this new narrative for "swashbuckling heroes" such as "Wallace". Assad Shoman, for example, does not mention him in either the first or second edition of his *Thirteen Chapters of a History of Belize* nor does the quasi-official *A History of Belize: Nation in the Making* that is widely used in schools.[29]

The legend, however, has refused to die despite the lack of interest of most contemporary Belizeans. A recent history of Belize, for example, states: "The 'Wallace Legend' suggests that a Scottish buccaneer or pirate, Peter Wallace, first settled at the mouth of the Belize River, possibly in 1638. The

---

[24] See Burdon (1931), p. 3.
[25] This mistake is all the more extraordinary as Asturias had corrected Burdon's error in their correspondence during 1930. See Asturias (1941), p. 14.
[26] See Calderón Quijano (1944), Lámina II.
[27] See Winzerling (1946), Chapter 4.
[28] The Wallace myth was, however, kept alive by Caiger (1951) and all editions of the *Brief Sketch of British Honduras* published between 1927 and the 1960s. Even Humphreys (1961), Waddell (1961) and Dobson (1973) devote some space to it.
[29] See Shoman (1994), Shoman (2011) and Leslie (2008).

Spaniards supposedly misspelt his name until it changed into the word 'Belize'. So far, there is not enough historical evidence to prove this legend."[30]

This agnosticism with regard to the historical evidence is fortunately incorrect. We can in fact demonstrate that [Peter] Wallace never existed and therefore cannot have been the founder, or one of the founders, of Belize. The key is what persuaded the authors of the *Honduras Almanack* to change their story between 1826, when there is no mention of Wallace, and 1827, when there is. The answer, curiously, is found in the two-volume *Annals of Jamaica* written by the Reverend George Wilson Bridges and published in 1828.

In the second volume, Bridges appends a "supplementary note on the history of Honduras."[31] Here we learn that his information on the Belize settlement came from "two highly respectable and well-informed inhabitants of Honduras, George Westby and Thomas Pickstock, Esquires." These two Baymen,[32] both of whom were members of the Public Assembly in Belize and the second of whom was a well-known merchant, can be presumed to be the source for Bridges' claim that:

> Willis, the notorious Buccaneer, was the first Englishman [sic] who settled on the banks of the river to which he gave his name. The Spaniards called it Walis, and the corrupting influence of time has softened it to Belize. The ex-governor of Tortuga sought his retreat on the shores and isles of Yucatan, where a multitude of his subjects or friends, who preferred a distant fortune to a narrow home, quickly joined him.[33]

Bridges had access to the *Honduras Almanack* for 1827, as we learn from his note on mahogany,[34] and his account of Wallace is similar to that of its Belizean authors (possibly Westby and Pickstock).[35] However, it is not exactly the same. First, Bridges spells the name "Willis" not "Wallice" and, secondly, Bridges claims he was an ex-governor of Tortuga–a claim not made by the *Honduras Almanack* until 1839 (see above).

The reference to Tortuga and the spelling of "Willis" by Bridges turn out to be crucial. Unlike the origins of the Belize settlement, the origins of the Tortuga settlement are well documented.[36] Tortuga was claimed by the Providence Island Company, established by the Earl of Warwick and

---

[30] See Iyo, Tzalam and Humphreys (2007), p. 287.

[31] See Bridges (1828), Vol. II, pp. 497-505. Both volumes are available digitally as Google books.

[32] The settlers in the Bay of Honduras were known as Baymen; those on the Mosquito Shore were known as Shoremen.

[33] See Bridges (1828), Vol. II, p. 134.

[34] See Bridges (1828), Vol. II.

[35] It is almost certain that Pickstock was one of the authors. See Cave (1976).

[36] See, for example, Newton (1914) and Kupperman (1993).

other leading Puritans in 1629, and named Association Island. The Spanish had succeeded in driving off the British and French settlers in December 1634,[37] but they drifted back and by the end of 1639 its population was around 300 (mainly British). They chose as their governor Captain Roger Floud, who had at one time been sheriff of Providence Island.[38] The settlers, however, were dissatisfied with Floud, who was forced to return to London to clear his name.

The remaining British settlers elected a Captain James as their leader (called in the Providence Island records "President James").[39] By now, however, the French on the island had fallen out with their British colleagues and a plan was hatched to overpower them. An expedition was sent from the French half of St. Kitts in 1640 and the British were driven off. The British then left for Providence Island, which would be captured by the Spanish in 1641.[40]

The history of Tortuga was first recorded by three French authors, although unfortunately none of them had access to the documents of the Providence Island Company. The first, J. B. Du Tertre, uses information based on the testimony of the French governor.[41] Writing in 1667, Du Tertre stated that the 300 French and British buccaneers in 1640 chose an Englishman ("un anglais") as their chief. This presumably is Captain James. However, Father Charlevoix writing in 1733 repeated essentially the same story, but gave the name as "Willis" ("Parmi les Anglois...il y en avoit un, nommé Willis, qui étoit homme de tête & de résolution").[42]

We will never know why Charlevoix chose to call Captain James "Willis". It is possible, as surmised by Arthur Percival Newton, that his first name was "William" and Charlevoix confused his first and second name.[43] However, there can be no doubt that the "ex-governor of Tortuga" referred to by the French writers, the *Honduras Almanack* and Bridges was none other than Captain James. This man never went to Belize, although he does appear in 1663 in a list of buccaneers operating from Jamaica and Tortuga.[44] Intriguingly, he is also cited in the apocryphal story by Gibbs as the sea captain who discovered the value of logwood in 1655.[45]

[37] See Haring (1910), p. 60.

[38] See Newton (1914), p. 280.

[39] See Haring (1910), p. 64, note 1, and Newton (1914), pp. 280-81.

[40] See Haring (1910), pp. 63-65.

[41] See Du Tertre (1667).

[42] See Charlevoix (1733), Vol. II, pp. 10-11. This work is available digitally on the website of the Bibliothèque Nationale Française (http://gallica.bnf.fr/). "Among the English... there was one, named Willis, who was a leader and decision-maker" (authors' translation).

[43] See Newton (1914), p. 281, note 10.

[44] See Haring (1910), p. 273.

[45] See Gibbs (1883), p. 24, who quotes the *Honduras Almanacks* of 1826 and 1827 for this story, which is demonstrably false (see Chapter 2). The original source is Dampier (1699).

An extensive search for a buccaneer called "Wallace", "Wallice" or "Willis" in the 17th century reveals not surprisingly that there was no such person. The original mistake was made by Father Charlevoix in 1733 and we will never know whether the authors of the 1827 edition of the *Honduras Almanack*, nearly a century later, deliberately or accidentally repeated the error. The Reverend Bridges, who almost certainly had access to Charlevoix's work, at least spelt "Willis" correctly, but he must also take some of the blame for spreading the Wallace legend.

If "Wallace" never existed, the first of the foundation myths can be laid to rest. However, what of the second (the myth of shipwrecked sailors in 1638)? This first makes its appearance in the 1829 edition of the *Honduras Almanack* that contains a chronology. This states: "1638–this year a few British subjects first inhabited Honduras, having been wrecked on the coast."[46]

This story was then repeated in most subsequent editions. It resurfaces in Gibbs, who states, "In 1638 a few British sailors were wrecked on the coast of Yucatan and would appear to have settled."[47] It was then repeated in all editions of the *Handbook of British Honduras* with the 1925 edition going so far as to claim that 1638 was the year both of the shipwrecked sailors and the arrival of Wallace![48]

The shipwrecked sailors myth has never enjoyed the popularity of the Wallace myth, but it still has its supporters. One of these, perhaps surprisingly, is the Belizean newspaper *Amandala*. In an article in 2011, introducing its readers to the complexity of the territorial dispute between Belize and Guatemala, the newspaper stated:

Our history began when English and Scottish sailors (buccaneers) landed at the mouth of the Belize River in 1638. They were the first to do so and might have claimed the land in the name of the sovereign, except for the fact that this land, our land, by an accident of history was from 1494 a part of the Spanish Main.[49]

Shipwrecks are common in foundation myths, as indeed in literature (*Robinson Crusoe* being the most famous example). There were, however, many shipwrecks off the Central American coast in the first half of the 17th century and it is possible that the Belize shipwrecked sailor myth is based loosely on one of these. In 1642, for example, the *William and Sarah* was wrecked 20 to 30 leagues from Providence Island and four or five leagues from the Moskito Keys off the coast of modern Nicaragua with 50 or 60

---

[46] See *Honduras Almanack* (1829), p. 40.
[47] See Gibbs (1883), p. 23.
[48] See Metzgen and Cain (1925), p. 1.
[49] See *Amandala* 6 May 2011.

being saved.[50] Even more intriguingly, a slave ship, in which the slaves had overpowered their Portuguese masters, was wrecked to the south of Cabo Gracias a Díos in 1641 and the survivors were captured by the Miskitos.[51]

What is certain, however, is that shipwrecked British sailors cannot have founded Belize in 1638. First, the Spanish fort at Salamanca de Bacalar was fully operational at this time and the Spanish would not have tolerated a foreign presence in such close proximity. They did not tolerate it in Providence Island in 1641 and Roatan in 1642, so they would certainly not have ignored "80 sailors" at the mouth of the Belize River in 1638. Second, this was the period when the Providence Island Company was flourishing with monopoly rights over privateering along the whole Central American coast. Any shipwrecked British sailors would have therefore made their way back to Providence Island or to the small British settlement at Cabo Gracias a Díos. Third, the Providence Island Company records are silent on both such a shipwreck and also on a British presence anywhere in Belize, whereas they provide considerable details on the attempts to colonise the Mosquito coast and the Bay Islands.

The two myths about the origins of Belize are therefore without foundation. They do, however, have a common source (the *Honduras Almanack*) which was written at a time when the Baymen craved respectability and hoped to become a British colony. It is understandable that the settlement's elite should create a narrative that put them on a par with other British colonies in the Caribbean. This is no excuse, however, for modern historians who have a duty to put the record straight. There was no Peter Wallace and no shipwrecked sailors established a settlement at the mouth of the Belize River in 1638.

The etymology of "Belize"

If Wallace never existed, then the word "Belize" cannot be derived from his name. By the time the Wallace myth was created in 1827, the settlement was already starting to be called Belize and the word, or close versions of it, had been in existence for a long time as the name of the country's main river and the town at the mouth of the Haulover Creek. The heroic efforts of Calderón Quijano and many others to establish the derivation of "Belize" from "Wallace" were therefore all in vain.[52]

---

[50] See Kupperman (1993), p. 340.
[51] See Conzemius (1932), p. 17.
[52] In fairness to Calderón Quijano (1944), his book is still worth reading for other reasons, particularly his treatment of diplomatic history.

The word "Belize" must therefore have a different provenance. Since the Maya had been in possession of Belize for thousands of years, we can be sure that they had named all the rivers, main geographical features and many of the islands long before the arrival of Europeans. The Maya texts, however, were largely destroyed, so we are forced to rely on the Spanish chroniclers for second-hand information about these names. The chroniclers, in turn, relied on the priests, soldiers and adventurers who carried out the first *entradas* into what is today Belize.

Among these first Spaniards to enter Belize were some good linguists. Nevertheless, it was often a struggle for the Spanish to write down the sound of the Maya words in Spanish letters as the orthography of [Yucatec] Maya and Spanish were so different. The Maya, for example, had a letter that sounded like "w", although this letter is rarely used in the Spanish language. It is not surprising, therefore, that we find among the chroniclers many variant spellings of the same Maya words.

By way of illustration of the etymological problem, we may consider in 1525 the first Spanish *entrada* that took Hernán Cortés across the Maya Mountains and down to the Sarstoon River. The first attempt at orthography by the Spanish had rendered the Maya word for the river as "Zac-tun", which would go through many variations before being anglicized to "Sarstoon". However, the evolution of the word is fairly clear and the Maya origin has never been in doubt.

The second *entrada* brought Alonso Dávila to Belize in 1531.[53] It is possible that on his retreat southwards from Villa Real, the town he founded near modern day Corozal, Dávila may have entered the Belize River.[54] However, he and his followers were fleeing from their Maya pursuers and were in fear of their lives. There was no meaningful contact with the villagers on the river and no opportunity to learn its Maya name. The Spanish chroniclers of Dávila's failure are remarkably silent on place names in Belize and dwell more upon his safe arrival in Honduras.

The third *entrada* brought the Pacheco family to the northern half of Belize in 1545. The three members of the family were exceptionally cruel, even by the standards of the day, and certainly did not win any hearts and minds with their barbarous behavior. However, they were the first Spaniards to reach Tipu, one of the most–if not the most–important Maya settlements in Belize at that time. They "converted" the Maya to Christianity and paved the way for the visit of numerous Spanish priests, soldiers and administrators in the following decades.[55]

---

[53] This ignores the failed attempt by Francisco de Montejo to subjugate Yucatan in 1527-29, when the conquistador may have briefly reached modern day Corozal.
[54] See Chamberlain (1948), Thompson (1988) and Graham (2011).
[55] See Jones (1998).

Tipu, as we now know thanks to recent archaeological work,[56] was on the eastern branch (the Macal) of the Belize River. The Pacheco family reached it by taking the New River as far as the southern end of the New River Lagoon. They then travelled overland to reach the Belize River, probably around Banana Bank, crossing Labouring Creek on the way before proceeding upstream to Tipu. Over time, this would become the favoured route of the Spaniards for reaching Tipu, although on occasions they used the Hondo River as far as navigation permitted before marching southwards to Tipu. What is clear is that they did not go south down the coast of Belize and enter the Belize River from the sea.

The chroniclers are all in agreement that the river on which the village of Tipu was located was called the Tipu. Indeed, it was standard practice for the Maya to name their towns and villages after the rivers on which they stood. However, some chroniclers were confused about the location of Tipu and often assumed it was on a branch of the Hondo River such as Booth's River or River Bravo. This has caused great confusion, as any user of early maps of Belize will know, and the mistake was repeated by Doris Zemurray Stone in her important article on Spanish *entradas* published as late as 1932.[57]

Now that the mistake has been corrected, we can say for certain that Tipu was the Maya name for the Belize River. However, no one has ever claimed that "Belize" is derived from "Tipu", so the problem of etymology remains despite the fact that the Belize River is the most important in the country and that the town of Belize stands close to its mouth.

Fortunately, the mystery can be solved by reference to a much later *entrada* in 1677. This was undertaken by Father José Delgado with the purpose of exploring an overland route from Guatemala to Yucatan in anticipation of the Spanish military campaign to defeat the Itzas in Peten. Father Delgado, a Dominican priest, travelled with Maya interpreters from Alta Verapaz in Guatemala to the Belizean coast, hispanicizing all the Maya names for the towns, villages and rivers along the route.

Father Delgado is most famous for having been captured by settlers close to the Manatee Lagoon and providing the first direct evidence of a permanent British presence in Belize. However, he deserves to be more famous for what followed. After his release, he was allowed to proceed northwards along the coast of Belize back to Yucatan. Although the settlers kept one of his Maya entourage, he was allowed to retain the services of others and with their help carried on naming the rivers along the coast.

---

[56] See, for example, Pendergast, Jones and Graham (1993).
[57] See Stone (1932).

If we pick up his story at the Texach (Manatee River), he says[58]:

From here to the river of Xibum four leagues.
From here to the river of Balis two leagues.
After these two leagues one enters in the river of Tipu.

Delgado wrote four different accounts of his journey and his spelling of Xibum varies. Thus, it is also written as Xilam.[59] However, all are agreed that this is the Sibun River. Since two leagues is roughly eight kilometers, the next river is the Haulover Creek–today a canalized branch of the Belize River. Delgado calls this "Balis" and "Baliz" in different versions of his story, but it is clear that this must be the "river" that flows through modern Belize City. Delgado never had a chance to enter this water system with his Maya guides, so he probably did not realize that the Haulover Creek is not strictly speaking a river. Nevertheless, he was quite correct when he said that the next river was Tipu, as this is of course the Belize River.

It is now clear why the Spanish chroniclers did not use the word "Balis" or "Baliz" at first. The river that mattered for the Spanish was the Tipu, as this led to their missions in the heartland of Belize. The Balis was a minor waterway that they would never have had occasion to use. Even if they had reached the Belize River from the sea, they would not have used the Balis–preferring instead the main artery that reaches the coast just north of the Haulover Creek.

For the British, however, it was a different story. The Balis would become a crucial part of their history and economy. It was a tributary by which they could reach the Belize River from the cayes and its mouth would in due course become the site of their main town. And although they probably never read any of Delgado's accounts of his journey, they had access to all the same Maya informants for the name.

"Balis" or "Baliz" is no doubt a corruption of the original Maya word brought about by Delgado's hispanicization.[60] Thompson has claimed that it means "muddy" or "muddy waters" in Yucatec Maya.[61] Using modern Maya-Spanish dictionaries, this cannot be proven.[62] However, "Ba", "Baal" and "Bal" are very common prefixes in modern Maya and "Ba" is even a

---

[58] See Thompson (1972), p. 29. See also Ximenez (1930).

[59] See Stone (1932), p. 268.

[60] One should note that Delgado used Maya words as the basis for his name of every river without exception during his *entrada*. See Thompson (1972), pp. 28-29, and Ximenez (1930).

[61] See Thompson (1972), p. 31.

[62] See the website of the Foundation for the Advancement of Mesoamerican Studies (http://www.famsi.org/reports/96072/index.html), which contains the most up to date Maya-Spanish dictionary currently available.

word in its own right.[63] Thompson may be correct, but this is something where modern scholarship may yield dividends in the future.[64]

The word "Balis" then underwent two different evolutions–one in Spanish and one in English. The one in Spanish is relatively simple, as the Spanish would regularly replace the first letter with "V" and/or the last with "z" or even "x". Thus, the title of a map in 1751 is given as:[65]

Plano de los tres Rios de Balyz, Nuebo y Hondo cituados entre el Golfo dulze o Provincia de Goatemala, y la de Yucatan, en el que se manifiesta sus Esteros, Lagunas y Canales y a que Embarcasiones son aseccibles; la cituacion del Real Precidio de S. Ph. de Bacalar, el camino que de el va a la capital de Merida, la Laguna del Peten Itza y parte de su camino, despoblado hasta el ultimo Pueblo de Yucatan.[66]

However, 25 years later in 1776 the title of a map of the region is given as:

Mapa del Ceno de Honduras, Establecimientos de Ingleses, havitaciones de Indios Caribes en la Costa de Valis, navegacion de esta para Navios y Balandras con sus principales fondeaderos, abrigos, aguadas y escollos, estendida de orden de el Muy Ylustre Señor D. Martín de Mayorga, Presidente Gobernador y Capitan Gral. de este Reyno de Guatemala.[67]

The Spanish were also prepared to write it occasionally as "Walis", "Waliz" or "Walix". Thus, the title of a communication from the Governor of Yucatan to Spain in 1733 states:[68]

Expediente sobre el permiso del corte del palo de tinte concedido a los ingleses en los ríos Walis, Nuevo y Hondo, provincia de Campeche; providencias para impedírselo en los parajes a que se extendieron y nueva concesión por los últimos tratados de paces.[69]

---

[63] There are 34 entries for "Ba", 92 entries for "Baal" and more than 200 for "Bal" in the Maya-Spanish dictionary.

[64] It has been suggested that "Balis" cannot be a Maya word because it does not appear in any Maya dictionary. See Encalada and Awe (2010), p. 34. However, there is also no reference to "Xilam" or "Xibum", which all are agreed are Maya words from which the present day 'Sibun' is derived. Encalada and Awe (2010), p. 35, then argue that it must be derived from the old Spanish word "valiza" meaning a buoy or marker. However, there is no evidence to support this hypothesis.

[65] Many old Spanish maps and documents of Central America, including Belize, can now be accessed through the Portal de Archivos Españoles (http://pares.mcu.es/).

[66] See Appendix 1 for English translation.

[67] See Appendix 1 for English translation.

[68] See Portal de Archivos Españoles (http://pares.mcu.es/).

[69] See Appendix 1 for English translation.

This demonstrates at the very least that the word cannot be Spanish in origin, since "W" is not a letter used in this language.[70] This again strongly suggests that it is of Maya origin.[71]

The Spanish were in fact fairly consistent in the way they wrote the name. A search on the Portal de Archivos Españoles, where much material has now been digitalized and more is being added all the time, shows that the name was almost always given as "Balis" or "Valis" with some variation in the final letter.[72] This can also be seen in the splendid cartographic catalogue of Belize compiled by Alain Breton and Michel Antochiw.[73] However, as the British presence became more established, the Spanish cartographers would give the English name as well. This was not a variant Spanish spelling, but an attempt to understand English usage.[74]

The British, never very good linguists, had much more trouble with the name "Balis". As early as 1705 it was written "Bullys".[75] By the middle of the century it often appeared as "Bellese".[76] This was still in use in 1775 in the famous Jefferys map of that year, where the river is named "Rio Baliz or River Bellese". By the time of Henderson,[77] it had become "Balize"[78] and the final step was taken in the *Honduras Almanack* when it became "Belize".[79]

The evolution from "Balis" to "Balize" is straightforward, but why did the Baymen feel it necessary to change the name from "Balize" to "Belize"? This could simply be normal linguistic corruption of a kind that is common in all languages. However, there is another intriguing possibility. The name "Belize" or "Bélize" was in common use in French literature from the mid-17th century to describe a mythical female figure. This name has nothing to do with the Maya word "Balis", but it was used by the French author Gombauld in 1657 in his

---

[70] Today there is still a Maya village near Merida in the Yucatan peninsula called Walix.

[71] Diehards will no doubt argue that it could be derived from a different non-Spanish European word other than Wallace. The only serious candidate is "balise", the French word for beacon. This hypothesis, almost certainly incorrect, will be examined below.

[72] See Portal de Archivos Españoles (http://pares.mcu.es/).

[73] See Antochiw and Breton (1992).

[74] This is one of the reasons for the confusion in Calderón Quijano (1944), since his Lámina II (reproduced in Dobson (1973)) gives both names in some cases without explaining that one is the name the Spanish thought the British were using for the Belize River.

[75] See Burdon (1931), p. 60.

[76] See Burdon (1931), p. 75.

[77] See Henderson (1809) and Henderson (1811).

[78] This was still being used thirty years later. See Stephens (1841), Chapter 1.

[79] Even here there was not complete consistency, since the 1826 edition of the *Almanack* has a print of St. John's Cathedral at "Belise".

book of epigrams, where a short poem describes the love of Cosme for Belize.[80] A few years later in 1672, Molière would include a female character, Bélise, in his play *Les Femmes Savantes*. There would be many other such examples in French literature.[81]

By the beginning of the 19th century Belize had become officially a British settlement and there was a yearning among some of the Baymen for imperial trappings. The images in the *Honduras Almanack*, especially of the Supreme Court, make this clear. Many travelled to Europe as a result of their commercial interests. We will never know for sure, but the Baymen may have been unintentionally influenced by French literature in the transition from "Balize" to "Belize".

In any case, the popularity in French literature of the character "Belize" helps to explain the use of the name in different places around the world. There is a river named Belice in Sicily. Since the island was taken by the French-speaking Normans from the Arabs in 1072, it is probably of French origin. There is a town called Belize in the Republic of Congo. This French-speaking country was colonized by France in the 1880s before winning its independence in 1960.

There is also a river and town called Belize in Cabinda, the Portuguese-speaking enclave that belongs to Angola but is separated from it by the Democratic Republic of the Congo (DRC). This has excited the interest of Belizean scholars and even raised the possibility that the slaves brought the name with them.[82] However, the truth is rather more prosaic. The DRC was a Belgian, and therefore French-speaking, colony while Portugal disputed ownership of Cabinda with the French for many years. The Cabinda Belize and the Republic of Congo Belize are quite close geographically and they are therefore likely to have a common French linguistic heritage.

The French literary character "Belize" may well be derived from the French word "balise" meaning "beacon". This is certainly the origin of the name of the island at the mouth of the Mississippi River, which owes its derivation to the time before 1763 when Louisiana was a French colony. It is almost certainly the reason why Ephraim G. Squier, a US citizen familiar with all the area around the Gulf of Mexico, preferred "balise"

---

[80] See Gombauld (1657).

[81] These include a famous love story, written in the 1680s, between Cléante and Bélise by Anne de Bellinzani, whose *nom de plume* was Presidente Ferrand. See Ferrand (1880) and Langlois (1926).

[82] See Iyo, Tzalam and Humphreys (2007), p. 99.

to "Wallace" as the origin of the name "Belize".[83] Nevertheless, although ingenious, it is incorrect.[84]

Although "Belize" is almost certainly derived from "Balis", there have been attempts to derive it from other Maya words. The most important of these was the claim by George Price in 1958 that it was derived from "Belikin"–two Maya words meaning "road towards the east".[85] Price gave as his source a book by Alfredo García Bauer published in the same year.[86] However, García Bauer had in fact lifted the idea from Gabriel Angel Castañeda, who had published an article to this effect the previous year.

Castañeda subsequently developed his ideas more fully in a book published in 1969 and appropriately entitled "Belikin".[87] Castañeda was a Guatemalan nationalist, who believed passionately that Belize belonged to Guatemala and that the British had no right to be there. One of the targets of his book is the (mis)derivation of "Belize" from "Wallace", which he argues was not possible.[88] However, his rival claim that it is derived from "Belikin" is a "just so" story without any foundation at all (he cites no primary or secondary sources in support).[89] The idea is no longer fashionable, but at least the name lives on in Belize's most famous beer!

The first British settlers

Father Delgado's *entrada* in 1677 was not only important in terms of establishing the origin of the name "Belize". It was also the first direct evidence of a permanent British presence on the cayes. The men who held Delgado and his party captive included Bartholomew Sharp, a pirate who would go on to acquire fame in the southern seas after crossing the Isthmus

---

[83] See Squier (1858), p. 575.

[84] By coincidence, however, Frances Trollope in her *Domestic Manners of the Americans* (1832) wrote of the "muddy waters" where the Mississippi entered the Caribbean at the island of Belize. "Muddy waters", of course, is what Thompson claims to be the meaning of "Balis". See footnote 61 above.

[85] See *Belize Times*, 4 November, 1958. See also Grant (1976), p. 364, n.105.

[86] See García Bauer (1958).

[87] See Castañeda (1969).

[88] See Castañeda (1969), pp. 108-111.

[89] Castañeda's only "evidence" is that Delgado misunderstood when his Maya guides named the Haulover Creek "Balis" and that what he should have written was "Belikin". The reliability of Castañeda as a source can be gauged from this gem: "Wallace era escocés, pero debía ser galés. Debe haberlo sido porque su apellido deviene de *Wales*". See Castañeda (1969), p. 200.

of Darien in 1680.[90] However, there were others and they were not all pirates.[91] So when had these men (and a few women?) arrived and from where did they come?

We can be fairly certain that there was no permanent British presence in Belize before 1642 and the reasons for this are straightforward. The Bay of Honduras, including the Belize cayes, was guarded by two Spanish forts. The first was at Salamanca de Bacalar and had been constructed by the Pachecos in 1543-44 at the start of their brutal *entrada* into Belize. The second was at Trujillo on the northern coast of Honduras.[92]

The fortress at Salamanca de Bacalar was the most important from the point of view of deterring British settlers. In order to access the fort by boat, the Spanish had to pass through what are today Belizean waters by way of the channels that lead from the ocean through the barrier reef and the cayes. This gave the Spanish a good familiarity with the islands inside the reef and also explains why so many of them were given Spanish names early on.

While the fortress was in full operation, it would have been impossible for the British to gain a permanent foothold. However, Salamanca de Bacalar was sacked by Diego "El Mulato" in 1642. This man, who was an ally of the British and had visited Providence Island in 1631 (see below), was a renegade Spaniard from Cuba, whose nickname was "Lucifer".[93] His attack, in addition to the usual motive of plunder, may therefore have been a deliberate attempt to deprive the Spanish of a base from which the cayes could be monitored.

The fortress at Bacalar was not totally destroyed and the Spanish did their best to rebuild it. However, it was then sacked in 1648 and again in 1652 by Abraham (Albertus) Blauvelt, a Dutch sea captain whose brother William had already given his name to Bluefields in Nicaragua. From then onwards until 1729, the fortress at Salamanca de Bacalar was abandoned by the Spanish. Meanwhile, Captain William Jackson, of whom more later, had

---

[90] Sharp (or Sharpe in some sources) would become a pirate, but as late as 1679 he was still acting as a privateer. Following a successful raid on the Spanish settlements in the Gulf of Honduras, he was able to take his booty back to Jamaica without reprisal by the British Governor. See Haring (1910), pp. 223-24.

[91] Winzerling (1946), pp. 65-66, claims that the party that captured Delgado included Miskitos. See also Ximenez (1930).

[92] Puerto Caballos, west of Trujillo, had already been abandoned in 1604 in favour of Santo Tomás de Amatique, but this fort was never significant. There were also fortifications on the Rio Dulce leading to the Lago de Izabal, but these were away from the coast and designed to protect the overland route to the highlands of Guatemala.

[93] Diego el Mulato had to leave his wife in Santiago, Cuba. When his British comrades planned an attack on the city, he asked them to pass on his fond regards! See Kupperman (1993).

sacked Trujillo with exceptional ferocity in 1642 and rendered its fortifications unuseable for a number of years, so that the Spanish could no longer defend the Bay of Honduras from the south either.[94]

The necessary conditions for the permanent occupation of the Belizean cayes by the British were therefore in place by the end of 1642. Furthermore, by this time the Spanish had been forced to accept that their efforts to convert the Maya at Tipu and other settlements in Belize had been a complete failure. Father Fuensalida, who had visited Tipu some twenty years before, was lucky to escape with his life during his *entrada* of 1641 and the northern part of Belize was effectively abandoned by the Spanish until the final conquest of the Itzas in 1697.[95] Thus, the Spanish had temporarily lost the ability to patrol the cayes and at the same time had given up on attempts to "reduce" the Maya on the Belize mainland.

If the necessary conditions for a permanent British presence had been met by the end of 1642, this did not automatically mean that the British actually took advantage of the new situation. However, the British footprint in the Americas had also changed by 1642 in a way that favored an attempt at new settlements on the coast of Central America. It is to this that we now turn.

In the 17th century the British regarded their presence in the Americas as a single geographic space within which there were regular contacts and exchanges. Between the settlements in Newfoundland and the plantations in Suriname,[96] there was a series of British "toeholds" whose future was still very uncertain. These included the colonies in Massachusetts and Virginia as well as a few islands in the eastern and western Caribbean.

Before the 1640s the British Caribbean settlements included Tortuga (off the coast of Haiti), Providence Island (off the coast of Nicaragua) and Roatan (off the coast of Honduras). All three were covered by the Charter given to the Providence Island Company in 1630 by Charles I.[97] However, the French drove the British out of Tortuga in 1640, while the Spanish drove them out of Providence Island in 1641 and out of Roatan in 1642.

The English presence in the western Caribbean was therefore reduced to a small settlement at Cabo Gracias a Dios, which had been established in 1633 under the auspices of the Providence Island Company, and even smaller settlements further south along the Mosquito Coast towards Bluefields. Here the English established an alliance with the Sumus/Miskitos, which would endure for many decades and which was based on a mutual

---

[94] See Davidson (1974), p. 44.
[95] See Jones (1998) and Graham (2011). The southern part of Belize was still largely controlled by the Itzas and their allies at this time.
[96] Suriname was a British colony from 1630 to 1667, when it was exchanged with the Dutch for Manhattan.
[97] The Charter had actually been extended in 1631 to include Tortuga.

hostility towards the Spanish and on the principle "my enemy's enemy is my friend". There was also another attempt–this time by individuals rather than the defunct Providence Island Company–to settle on Roatan, but the Spanish drove them out again in 1650.

The refugees from Tortuga, Providence Island and Roatan might have been tempted in an earlier period to return to England. However, the Civil War had broken out in 1642 and would prove to be a long, bloody and costly affair. The attractions of the Central American mainland, despite the threat from the Spanish, must have been considerable if a suitable location could only be found.

These refugees were not the only ones to be interested in a new location. The settlers in North America had not prospered in the 1630s. Their attempts to build an export economy based on tobacco had been undermined by the fall in price and many had taken up an offer to relocate to Providence Island. Indeed, several hundred were on their way when the island was captured by the Spanish in 1641.[98]

Meanwhile, the English colonies in the eastern Caribbean were also undergoing a major transformation. The search for an export staple, including tobacco, had not gone well and many of the indentured laborers from Britain were in difficult economic circumstances. The successful introduction of sugar, paradoxically, would make their situation worse since the plantation owners preferred African slaves to British indentured labour. The English government, at least as far as the Caribbean was concerned, ceased to function after the Civil War broke out and these men with their families were left to their own devices.

It is no surprise, therefore, that when William Jackson arrived in the eastern Caribbean in 1642, he had no trouble recruiting the 1,500 sailors he needed for one of the most famous voyages ever undertaken.[99] The Providence Island Company had been authorized in 1635, following a failed Spanish attack on the island, to issue letters of marque to British sea captains. These "privateers" were then free to attack the Spanish in the knowledge that they were not breaking any English laws. They were therefore not pirates, although they could be loosely described as "buccaneers"–the term often used to cover both activities.[100]

Jackson was the last person to be authorized to engage in privateering activities by the Providence Island Company before its demise. His voyage lasted three years, from 1642 to 1645, and his sailors acquired an exceptional

---

[98] See Kupperman (1993).

[99] See Harlow (1923), p. xiii-xiv.

[100] The word "buccaneer" is derived from the indigenous word for curing meat in Hispaniola and was originally applied to the European settlers on Tortuga. See Haring (1910).

knowledge of the geography of the Caribbean and the Gulf of Mexico (we have already noted how he sacked Trujillo). Jackson would go on to capture Jamaica before leaving to attack other Spanish cities including Campeche. When the voyage ended in the middle of the English Civil War, there must have been many members of the crew who dreamt of returning to the Caribbean.

The republican forces would eventually triumph in England and Oliver Cromwell became Lord Protector in 1649. Persuaded by Thomas Gage and others that Spanish defences in the Caribbean were weak,[101] he launched the "western design" by which he hoped to capture Hispaniola. The expedition was an utter failure, so its leaders turned instead to the poorly defended Jamaica whose capture Jackson had already shown to be an easy undertaking. In 1655 Jamaica fell to the English, a seemingly poor prize at the time, but one which would prove to be very valuable for the British in the long-run.

British privateers now had a Jamaican base (Port Royal) where they could lay in stores, refit their ships and spend their profits. They took full advantage and Bartholomew Sharp, as well as others of his kind, was a frequent visitor. Captain Morgan, perhaps the most notorious, would even become Lieutenant Governor of Jamaica in 1674![102]

When the monarchy was restored in England in 1660, Charles II gave priority to improved relations with Spain. The result was the 1667 Treaty of Madrid followed three years later by a second Treaty of Madrid (often known as the American Treaty because it addressed the outstanding issues in the Americas between the two powers).

The two treaties were supposed to leave England in lawful possession of those parts of the Caribbean that had not been occupied by the Spanish (this obviously included Jamaica, but neither England nor Spain regarded any British settlers in the Bay of Honduras as falling under the terms of the treaty). Perhaps more important for the future of Belize was that England agreed to end privateering and to suppress piracy. Thus, 1670 is a watershed in the history of the British Caribbean because it meant that hereafter the former privateers would be regarded as pirates if they continued their activities. And this meant that, after a period of adjustment by all concerned, they could not expect a welcome in Jamaica.

For the settlement of Belize by the British, we should therefore distinguish between the period before 1670 and the period after. In the first

---

[101] Gage was an English Catholic who had spent many years in Spanish America. He eventually abandoned Catholicism for the Church of England and wrote a famous book on the "rottenness" of the Spanish Empire in the Americas that heavily influenced Cromwell. See Gage (1648).
[102] See Haring (1910), p. 205.

period, which starts from 1642, there may have been some scope for privateers to make Belize their home but it would not have been easy. The opportunities for laying in stores, refitting ships and spending profits were strictly limited on the Belizean cayes. From 1655, furthermore, Jamaica was a much more attractive base for such activities. Thus, any settlers before 1670 are likely to have been much less glamorous than the privateers (see below).

After 1670, when the former privateers were becoming pirates, Belize may have been more tempting and perhaps this explains the presence of Bartholomew Sharp in 1677. However, settlers in Belize were about to turn to a much more prosaic activity (the extraction of logwood), so this period in Belize's history was likely to have been very brief. Indeed, we know for sure that logwood was being cut and exported by 1680 (see next chapter).

Although we have shown there were many British subjects who might have had an interest in settling in Belize after 1642, we have very little solid evidence. Perhaps the most useful is place names. While the Spanish were content to take Mayan names for the rivers, they generally gave Spanish names to the cayes and atolls. Examples are Cayo Casina, Cayo Renegado and Cuatro Cayos. These names either mutated under the British or were later replaced by English ones.[103]

In a few cases, however, the English name appeared very early. Examples are Turneffe Island, Glover's Reef and Bluefields Range. "Turneffe" may be a corruption of "Terra Nova", the Spanish name for the atoll, but it is noteworthy that "Turneffe" is the name given to an island off the coast of Nicaragua during the time of the Providence Island Company.[104] "Glover", clearly an English name, may owe its origin to Roger Glover, who had first settled in the British Leeward Islands.[105] "Bluefields" may owe its origin to Abraham Blauvelt, who sacked Salamanca de Bacalar in 1648 and 1652.[106]

There is also Tobacco Caye, named by the Spanish Cayo Tabaco. Presumably, this is named after the tobacco plant, although it cannot be grown on the island. However, it was grown in Virginia, Providence Island and the eastern Caribbean, so it is not impossible that it was named by a British settler in memory of a previous incarnation. Cayo Renegado, or Ranguana Caye, is said to have been the base of the "renegade" Spaniard Diego el Mulato. And there are many islands, such as Gough's Caye, which probably

---

[103] Thus, Cayo Casina was renamed St. George's Caye, Cayo Renegado was corrupted to Ranguana Caye and Cuatro Cayos became Lighthouse Reef.
[104] See Newton (1914), opposite p. 144. The island is north of the Corn Islands.
[105] Winzerling, admittedly not the most reliable of sources, writes that Roger Glover had been trading on Nevis before moving to Tortuga. See Winzerling (1946), p. 54.
[106] On the Blauvelt brothers, see Kupperman (1993).

owe their names to these early settlers even if we cannot be sure who they were or when they arrived.

As for the activities in which these early settlers were engaged, we also have very little solid evidence. There may have been some privateering, although the Spanish would have been wary of sending their ships after 1642 through waters that could no longer be protected from Salamanca de Bacalar or Trujillo. One of the main targets of privateers was the logwood shipped by the Spanish from the area close to Campeche, but there was no reason for these ships to veer south after passing the Yucatan peninsula before heading for Cuba en route to Spain. The privateers, after 1655, generally set out from Jamaica–not Belize–to capture these ships laden with logwood.

More probable is that the activities of the early settlers were similar to those in the Bay Islands between 1638 and 1650, for which we do have historical records.[107] These included turtling for the shells and the extraction of pearls from oysters. Both these commodities could be exported in small quantities either to the British settlers on the Mosquito Shore or even as contraband to Spanish settlers along the Central American or Yucatan coast. There was also abundant opportunity for fishing–both for subsistence and also for export if salted. What is clear is that these early settlers stayed on the cayes and did not venture up the Belizean rivers where they would have encountered hostile Maya settlements not subject to Spanish rule.

After 1670 the attraction of the Belizean coastline for pirates would have been greater. However, governors at Jamaica were slow to crack down on piracy and did not do so consistently until the 1680s. A few pirates, such as Bartholomew Sharp, clearly did make use of the Belizean cayes. Edward Teach ("Blackbeard") may also have visited, but this was much later as he was only born around 1680.[108] The problem for the pirates was that the Belizean cayes could not provide them with their essential requirements. When Port Royal at Jamaica became less welcoming, many preferred to make New Providence in the Bahamas their base as the British governors there were much more accommodating.

Most of the privateers, in any case, opted for a more secure existence after 1670 and many found it in logwood extraction. Their first settlement was at Cabo Catoche at the north-eastern point of the Yucatan peninsula.[109]

---

[107] See Davidson (1974).

[108] The claim that the French corsair L'Ollonois spent time in Belize in 1665 is almost certainly false.

[109] Cabo Catoche may have been established as early as 1662–even before the end of privateering. See next chapter.

Later they would establish their camps at Trist and Beef Island in the Laguna de Terminos close to Campeche. Only when the logwood at Cabo de Catoche was exhausted did they turn their attention to the coast of Belize. When they started to arrive, probably in the 1670s, they would likely have found a small number of British settlers already scattered among the cayes.

2. The Logwood Economy: from First Settlement to the Treaty of Paris (1763)

The early economic history of the "British Settlement in the Bay of Honduras" is intimately associated with the trade in logwood. For a century after its formation in the 17th century, the settlement had virtually only one export (logwood), the revenue from which had to pay for all other expenses. This was extraction pure and simple–an even more extreme form of monoculture than was found in the small British islands of the eastern Caribbean. We may therefore speak of the British settlement, before it acquired formal status at the end of the Seven Years War (1756-63), as being a "logwood economy".

During these hundred years, the settlement had no legal basis. The Spanish regarded the British presence as being illegal and the British government rarely questioned–yet alone challenged–Spanish sovereignty. This position only started to change with the Treaty of Paris in 1763, when the right to cut logwood was first recognized by Spain. However, the settlers were then required to dismantle all fortifications, to limit their activities to logwood extraction and to accept Spanish sovereignty.

The key stages in the settlement's evolution involved the decision in 1662 to legalise the import of logwood into England; the suppression of privateering in the Anglo-Spanish treaties of 1667 and 1670; the exhaustion of logwood stands at Cabo Catoche in the Yucatan peninsula around 1670; the acceptance by the British judiciary that logwood from Belize did not fall within the Navigation Acts and could therefore be sold anywhere in the world; the eviction of the British settlers from their bases close to Campeche after the Treaty of Utrecht in 1713; and the failure of the Spanish, despite numerous attempts, to evict the British permanently from Belize.

The settlement's logwood economy evolved slowly and the population was always small. However, the volume of logwood exported was substantial as the settlers were able to extract the timber from a relatively large territorial area. In this they were aided coincidentally by the Spanish decision, following the defeat of the Itzas in 1697, to regroup the Maya villagers in the north and south of Belize across the "border" in what are today the Guatemalan provinces of Peten and Alta Verapaz. In some cases, however, this Maya migration appears to have been a response to British slaving raids as well.

The acknowledgement by the British authorities that Belizean logwood was not subject to the Navigation Acts meant that the settlers established an early connection with North America, especially Boston, where the import of their logwood was not subject to colonial duties. The Boston link proved to be of enormous importance in this early history of the settlement, although the logwood trade was also carried on through Jamaica and even directly with ports in continental Europe. As it was largely untaxed, Belize not yet being a British colony or even an official British settlement, the trade was also very profitable until over-supply led to a major fall in prices by the time of the Treaty of Paris in 1763.

The volume of logwood exports from Belize was considerable and the British settlers from an early stage employed African slave labour (see below). In this, they were following the practice of their forbears on Providence Island, Tortuga, Jamaica and in the eastern Caribbean. These African slaves were usually purchased through Jamaica. The British settlers did not try to enslave the Miskitos on the Mosquito Shore, with whom they retained a strategic alliance, but it seems that they did on occasions try to enslave the Maya and other indigenous peoples in Central America. Slave rebellions were always a risk for the settlers and, not surprisingly, the Spanish governors across the borders did their best to encourage the slaves to escape.

Foundations

Logwood (*Haematoxylum campechianum*) is a dyewood that is native to the Yucatan peninsula.[1] It was first imported into Europe in the 16th century for use in the textile industry. However, its importation into England was banned by Queen Elizabeth I when it was claimed that the dye obtained from the heart of the tree was not always fast.[2] The ban was not observed strictly by the first Stuart kings, but it may have been one of the reasons why the Providence Island Company abandoned a plan to export logwood from Tortuga in the 1630s.[3]

---

[1] See Wilson (1936), p. 1.
[2] See Joseph (1974), p. 16. The real reason for the ban, however, was probably the opposition to logwood imports from domestic producers of dyes made from native raw materials.
[3] See Kupperman (1993).

Most of the logwood entering the woolen industry in England at this time came from Spanish sources at a very high price (roughly 100 pounds per ton).[4]

This background is sufficient to demonstrate that the myth, first recorded by William Dampier in 1699, that British buccaneers only discovered the value of logwood after the capture of Jamaica in 1655 is false. Dampier, in a paragraph that has often been repeated or paraphrased, stated:[5]

> After the *English* had taken *Jamaica*, and began to cruise in this Bay [Campeche], they found many Barks laden with it [logwood], but not knowing its value then, they either set them adrift or burned them, saving only the Nails and Iron work; a thing now usual among the Privateers, taking no notice at all of the Cargo, till Capt. *James*, having taken a great ship laden with it and brought her home to *England*, to fit her for a Privateer, beyond his Expectation, sold his Wood at a great rate; tho' before he valued it so little that he burned of it all his Passage home.

Dampier was almost certainly wrong about buccaneers' ignorance of the value of logwood. However, he was right about the origins of the British logwood trade. British privateers either seized Spanish ships laden with logwood or raided Spanish locations close to Campeche where the timber had been stockpiled. To do this they needed a convenient base and Jamaica provided it after 1655. Some of this booty found its way to North America, rather than England where its importation was still restricted.

When Charles II legalised the import of logwood in 1662, it provided a strong incentive to promote the British trade. It is therefore no accident that the first British logwood settlement on the coast of the Americas, Cabo Catoche, is widely believed to have been established in that year.[6] At first this British settlement provided easily accessible supplies of logwood, no more than 300 paces from the logwood camps, but shortly before it was abandoned the settlers needed to travel up to 1,500 paces to reach the timber.[7] After cutting the logwood and loading it by the shore, the settlers would then wait for a ship to come from Jamaica.

At this point, according to Dampier, the settlers then moved both westwards towards Campeche and southwards towards the Bay of Honduras. In 1672, however, the principal logwood settlements–if we can trust Sir Thomas Modyford–still did not include Belize.[8] This did not mean that

---

[4] See Joseph (1974), p. 17.

[5] See Dampier (1931), p. 159.

[6] See Fancourt (1854), Calderón Quijano (1944) and Joseph (1974).

[7] See Dampier (1931), p. 134.

[8] In a letter to Lord Arlington, Sir Thomas Modyford (previously Governor of Jamaica) listed Cabo Catoche, Cozumel, Champatone, Port Royal (in Laguna de Términos) and St. Paulo as the main settlements. See Burdon (1931), p. 53.

Belize was not being used for logwood extraction, but it does mean that it was not yet important. Indeed, in 1670 when Sir Thomas Modyford had urged British recognition of "these new sucking colonies", he was certainly not thinking of Belize.[9]

This would soon change. The exhaustion of supplies at Cabo Catoche, long abandoned by the time Dampier visited in 1675, and the suppression of privateering after 1670 encouraged many more British subjects to try their hand at logwood extraction. Indeed, it is possible that this is what Bartholomew Sharp and his comrades were engaged in when they captured Father Delgado in 1677. In any case, by December 1680 we have historical evidence of a British trader being captured by the Spanish off the coast of Yucatan and dispatched in a canoe to Turneffe Island after his ship and its cargo (of logwood?) had been seized.[10]

In the 1670s governors of Jamaica had tried without success to win British government support for the logwood settlements. The Stuart kings, however, did not want to antagonize the Spanish monarch and steadfastly refused to acknowledge British claims on the mainland even though some settlements, such as Cabo Catoche, had been established before the 1667 Treaty of Madrid and might therefore have qualified as British possessions under Article VII of the treaty. For the Stuarts, the need for Spanish support to counter growing French dominance of Europe under Louis XIV far outweighed any small territorial gains that might be made at the expense of Spain.

By 1682, Governor Lynch of Jamaica had abandoned his previously sympathetic position and dispatched Captain Coxen to the Bay of Honduras to evict the settlers. This is the clearest evidence to date of a British logwood presence in Belize. However, Lynch would be sorely disappointed in his efforts to close down the settlement, as Coxen's crew mutinied before joining the settlers and–according to some reports–Coxen then did the same himself.[11]

Spurred on by high logwood prices, the settlement in the Bay of Honduras then expanded significantly. A report delivered to the Council of Trade in 1705 claimed that:[12] "Sixty leagues from Porto Cavallo lyeth the River of Bullys, where the English for the most part now load their logwood."

This may have been an exaggeration, as the British settlements near to Campeche were still very active in 1705 despite the fact that Trist had been

---

[9] See Burdon (1931), p. 49.
[10] See Burdon (1931), p. 56.
[11] See Burdon (1931), p. 57. According to Joseph (1974), however, Coxen returned to Jamaica and only joined the settlers in Belize on a subsequent trip.
[12] See Burdon (1931), p. 60.

captured by the Spanish in 1680[13] and that the Spanish were employing Dutch and Irish pirates to harass the British logwood trade in the Gulf of Mexico.[14] However, these Yucatan settlements would be subject to a much greater threat following the Treaty of Utrecht in 1713. Spain refused to make any concessions regarding the logwood trade and increased its attacks. The small settlements around Campeche were very vulnerable from the seaward side and were unable to put up much resistance.

Belize itself was attacked from the western side in 1718.[15] The Spanish were repulsed, however, and gradually the export of logwood shifted from Campeche to Belize. This did not mean that Belize was immune from attack–far from it. However, it was more difficult for the Spanish to harass the British settlers in Belize as the western or northern approach involved a long march over difficult terrain, while the eastern approach required navigation of the shallow waters inside the barrier reef.[16]

The Spanish attacks on the Belize settlement before 1763 are fairly well documented.[17] Occasionally they did succeed and the settlers would flee elsewhere. In 1730, for example, many settlers left for the Mosquito Shore following a Spanish attack from the sea.[18] It was perhaps this incident that persuaded the settlers that they needed to strengthen their system of administration, Henry Sharpe being chosen from among their number to act as their leader.[19] Perhaps as a result, the settlement was able to resist a major Spanish offensive in 1754 when 1,500 troops attacked from the west.[20]

The Spanish government also maintained strong diplomatic pressure against the logwood settlements in the first half of the 18th century. This time, however, the British government was less accommodating as relations with Spain were very strained before the Treaty of Paris. Great Britain could not persuade Spain to concede any rights to the logwood cutters, but the British government did appoint two commissioners in 1741 with a remit, among other things, to follow developments in Belize. Since the two

---

[13] As the Spanish did not occupy Trist, the settlers were able to return within a few years.

[14] This tactic was so successful that the Governor of Jamaica had to insist that ships bound for the logwood settlements close to Campeche sail in convoy.

[15] See McLeish (1926), p. 77.

[16] An attack from the south was never attempted because of the obstacle presented by the Maya mountains.

[17] See, for example, Shoman (2011), Dobson (1973), Burdon (1931) and McLeish (1926).

[18] See McLeish (1926), p. 81.

[19] See Gibbs (1883), p. 35.

[20] The Spanish force reached as far as Labouring Creek. See McLeish (1926), pp. 98-99. For a more "heroic", but probably less accurate account, see Gibbs (1883), pp. 36-37.

individuals concerned, Robert Hodgson and William Pitt, resided either at Roatan in the Bay Islands or on the Mosquito Shore, it is doubtful if this gesture had more than symbolic value.[21]

The British administration and the Jamaican governors never fought very hard in this period to put the Belize settlement on a legal footing. Their policy towards the Mosquito Shore, however, was much more pro-active. The Bay Islands were re-occupied in 1742 and a Superintendent for the Shore, based at Black River, was appointed in 1748.[22] The difference between the "Bay" (Belize) and the "Shore" was largely due to the presence of a relatively large Miskito population in the latter, which had a long standing alliance with the British crown and which could be relied on to harass the neighbouring Spanish in the case of hostilities. A new Miskito king would always head first to Jamaica to cement the alliance and the British governors there provided all the appropriate pomp and ceremony.[23] It was also the case that the Mosquito Shore was seen as a more secure place than Belize from which to conduct the profitable contraband trade with Spain.

The Seven Years War (1756-63) once again saw Britain and Spain on opposite sides in a European conflict. However, the Treaty of Paris at its conclusion brought the first concession from Spain towards the British logwood settlement at Belize. The settlers were now allowed to cut logwood provided all fortifications were dismantled and the British government duly complied.[24]

Unfortunately, as often happens in international treaties, the details of the Treaty of Paris with regard to Belize were left very vague. No boundaries were defined and the Governor of Yucatan took exception to the fact that the settlers had allegedly extended the area for timber extraction from the New River to the Hondo River after the end of hostilities. He therefore forced some 500-600 settlers to retreat south, while the commandant at Bacalar argued that the British should be withdrawn from the New River as well.[25] This time British diplomatic remonstrations were successful and the *de facto* boundaries of the settlement became the Hondo and the Belize Rivers with the New River lagoon as the western limit.

---

[21] Hodgson and Pitt were appointed commissioners primarily because the British government wanted to establish the feasibility of a military occupation of the Bay Islands. This duly took place in 1742, although they were abandoned again in 1749. See Davidson (1974).

[22] See McLeish (1926), pp. 236-37.

[23] See Floyd (1967), Naylor (1989) and Dozier (1985).

[24] See McLeish (1926), p. 113, who quotes in French the relevant provision (Article XVII) of the Treaty of Paris.

[25] See McLeish (1926), pp. 118-20. The fort at Bacalar had been rebuilt in the early 18th century.

Population

The European conquest of the Americas was achieved through military force, but it could only be sustained through access to labour. Voluntary labour was never sufficient and so the Europeans resorted to coercion. In the case of the British this at first took the form of indentured European labour (mainly from Great Britain and Ireland), but by the middle of the 17th century this was being replaced by slavery. The British settlers on Providence Island, for example, used African slave labour alongside European indentured labour during the colony's short life (1630-41), while the Providence Island Company's attempt to establish plantation agriculture on Association Island (Tortuga) also made use of African slave labour.[26]

From Dampier's detailed description of the settlements close to Campeche, we know that the British logwood cutters in 1675-76 were already using African slave labour.[27] However, it is clear from his account that they were using Native American ("Indian") slave labour as well.[28] Furthermore, the ships that came from the British settlements in North America to load the logwood also brought with them Native Americans as slaves.[29]

That slavery for the British in the Americas involved both African and indigenous slave labour should not be a matter of surprise. Unlike the Spanish, who–following the vigorous campaign of Bartolomé de las Casas–had ruled by the mid-16th century that enslavement of the indigenous people of the Americas was not permitted, the British never legislated against the practice.[30] If it eventually ended, this had more to do with the decline of the indigenous population than the judicial process. The British only made an exception in rare cases, such as the Miskitos on the Mosquito Shore, where the need for a strategic alliance ruled out enslavement.[31]

This is important because a myth has developed that the British settlers in the Bay of Honduras did not have slaves until the 1720s. This would imply that they had cut logwood for perhaps half a century by themselves without the use of coerced or slave labour. It is true that the first settlers were probably not rich men and certainly did not have access to the kind of capital available to the planters in the eastern Caribbean. On the other hand, logwood was at first an extremely valuable (and profitable) commodity, so it is highly unlikely that the early settlers would have failed to make

---

[26] See Newton (1914) and Kupperman (1993).

[27] See Dampier (1931), p. 188.

[28] See Dampier (1931), p. 163.

[29] See Dampier (1931), p. 214.

[30] See Elliott (2006), Washburn (1975) and (1995).

[31] The Miskitos themselves, however, did have slaves–both Africans and other Native Americans. See Conzemius (1932).

use of slave labour. They would have had no moral scruples about employing slaves and we know that it took place in the "sister" settlements close to Campeche (see above).

The myth has arisen because for a long time it was thought that the first documented evidence of African slaves in Belize referred to 1724. However, this does not mean there were no slaves in Belize before that. Indeed, we now know from the Spanish chroniclers that slaves were found in Belize much earlier, since on at least one occasion the Spanish took prisoner a group of British logwood cutters and their African slaves. One group, captured on the Upper Belize River, included 19 white men, one white woman and ten black slaves and the incident took place soon after 1700.[32]

Intriguingly, the Spanish source for this incident refers to six "indios" among the captured party. This could refer to Miskitos, in which case they would have been free, or they could have been Maya, in which case they would probably have been slaves. In any case, we now know that the British were in the habit of engaging in slave raids along the Belize rivers and may have taken with them Miskitos as guides.

Slave raiding expeditions by the British settlers only makes sense if there was a Maya population worth raiding. At the time of the first British settlers in Belize, the Maya population was still substantial even if it had been reduced significantly from its size before the European conquest. Tipu alone in the 17th century had a larger population than the British and their slaves put together and there were many other Maya villages in the north and south of Belize.[33]

The conquest of the Itzas in 1697 led to a decision by the Spanish authorities to relocate the Maya at Tipu to the Peten.[34] Tipu was formally abandoned in 1707, soon after the British settlers had carried out a final slaving raid.[35] Archaeological research shows that Tipu was not in fact completely abandoned, a small number of Mayas drifting back to the village as circumstances permitted. However, the Maya population of western and northern Belize–especially at Tipu and Lamanai–was substantially reduced by the end of the first decade of the 18th century.[36]

Much the same happened in the south of Belize. When Father Delgado carried out his famous *entrada* in 1677, he passed through numerous Maya villages on his way to the coast.[37] The British settlers, and their Miskito allies, are said to have carried out slave raids along the southern Belize rivers in

---

[32] See Jones (1998), pp. 411-12. See also Shoman (1994), p. 18.
[33] See Jones (1989), p. 116.
[34] See Shoman (2011), p. 12.
[35] See Graham (2011), p. 252.
[36] See Jones (1989), p. 116.
[37] See Thompson (1972), pp. 22-27.

subsequent years.[38] The Spanish authorities then relocated as many Maya as they could reach to the towns of Alta Verapaz. Although force was probably used, some Maya may have gone voluntarily as the dangers of enslavement by the British were very real. Some of the captured Maya were transported to Jamaica as slaves, so the purpose of the slave raids was not limited to the needs of logwood cutting in Belize.[39]

By the time we have the first estimates of the population of Belize, therefore, the Maya population had been dramatically reduced. That is one reason why British sources have so little to say about the Maya of Belize during the 18th century, although another reason was the desire to present an image of an "empty region" that was ripe for British settlement.

The British first settled on the cayes and their most important centre was Cayo Casina, which they would later rename St. George's Caye. It was already in use in 1677, since Father Delgado was taken to Cayo Casina during his capture and there met Bartholomew Sharp.[40] From here they would go to their camps along the rivers and coastal mangroves where they could cut logwood. They did not need to go far inland, except on slave raids, since logwood grows in abundance close to the coast and even–in some cases–on the cayes.

These British settlers have frequently been portrayed as a rough lot made up of pirates and other undesirables. The source for this claim is always the same as it is invariably based on Nathaniel Uring, a sea captain who visited Belize twice in 1719 and 1720 to purchase logwood.[41] Uring, however, is a very biased source. In addition to being a rather poor mariner (his ship was wrecked on Lighthouse Reef), Uring was constantly complaining about his crew and accusing them of planning a mutiny.[42] It is most unfortunate that Uring's description of the Baymen has so often been repeated as it gives a very misleading impression of the settlers.[43]

The first reasonably reliable population estimate dates from 1724,[44] when a Spanish missionary reported that there were:[45] "about three hundred English, besides Mosquito Indians and negro slaves, these latter having been introduced but a short time before from Jamaica and Bermuda."

Leaving aside the understandable error of "English", since the white

---

[38] See Jones (1998), p. 408.

[39] See Jones (1994) and Graham (2011), p. 255.

[40] See Ximenez (1930), p. 385.

[41] See Uring (1726).

[42] See Uring (1928), pp. 233-34.

[43] For quotations from Uring about the Baymen, see Bolland (1977), p. 28, and Shoman (2011), p. 21.

[44] There is a figure given in the *Honduras Almanack* (1829), p. 41, of 700 whites in 1670, but this is impossible.

[45] See Shoman (1994), p. 44.

population would have included at least Scots, Welsh and Irish, this testimony by the Spanish missionary has been interpreted to mean that there were no black slaves before the 1720s. This, as we have seen, is false. In any case, "a short time before" could mean either a generation or could possibly refer to the importation of these particular slaves.

By the 1720s, Belize was supplanting Trist and Beef Island as the leading British logwood settlement. Since the Campeche settlements in 1675 had a population of 265,[46] the Spanish missionary's figure might suggest a total population of around 500 consisting of 300 whites plus perhaps 200 black slaves and (free) Miskitos. The number of Miskitos, however, would have been small, probably not more than 50, so this would imply a black slave population of around 150.

A total population of 500 in 1724 is consistent with the estimate given by John Atkins during his visit a decade later.[47] By 1742 the population may have increased a little as the number of "white Baymen" only is given as 400[48] (it had been estimated at 300 in 1724–see above in this chapter). Yet in 1745, according to a letter from the inhabitants of the Bay of Honduras to Major Caulfield in Roatan, the population had been reduced to 50 whites and 120 slaves.[49]

The fall was a consequence of the Spanish attack in May 1745, when six ships sailed up the New River and destroyed the British encampments. Many of the settlers fled with their slaves to the Bay Islands and Mosquito Shore, waiting for a propitious moment to return. This was fairly typical of the fluid arrangements under which the British could move from one location to another, confident that the Spanish could not attack all at the same time. It was particularly easy in the 1740s, when Britain controlled Roatan in the Bay Islands.

There were no other population estimates before the Treaty of Paris in 1763.[50] However, the fact that the Governor of Yucatan was able to drive out 500-600 settlers and their slaves from the area between the Hondo and New Rivers shortly after the treaty was signed suggests that the population had not only recovered after 1745, but had expanded significantly. Indeed, the population in 1764 was estimated at 1,500.[51] This probably did not in-

---

[46] See Dampier (1931), p. 163.

[47] John Atkins, a much more sympathetic observer than Uring, put the total population at 500. See Atkins (1970), p. 227 (this is a facsimile reprint of the original 1735 edition).

[48] See Burdon (1931), p. 70.

[49] See Burdon (1931), p. 70.

[50] William Pitt, however, claimed that 500 had fled from the Bay of Honduras to the Mosquito Shore in 1754 following the Spanish attack of that year. See Burdon (1931), p. 80.

[51] See Burdon (1931), p. 93.

clude the 500-600 previously displaced, as it was not until 1765 that British diplomacy secured their right of return.[52]

No doubt part of the increase in population was due to the new status of the settlement under the Treaty of Paris. Yet it cannot explain most of the increase, since by 1764 there had been little time for new settlers to arrive. A more important reason would therefore have been the mahogany extraction that had already commenced. This activity was much more labour-intensive than logwood. We do not know in which year mahogany was first exported, but it is likely to have been before 1763. As early as 1750, for example, mahogany exports from the Mosquito Shore had reached 500,000 board feet and it is unlikely that the settlement in the Bay of Honduras was far behind.[53]

The population continued to increase and by 1779 is estimated to have reached 3,500, of which 3,000 were slaves.[54] In that year, however, the Spanish mounted a successful attack on St. George's Caye where they found nearly 400 people (white, free people of colour and slaves).[55] The Spanish removed as many of the settlers as they could find, marching them over land to Merida and eventually taking them to Havana in Cuba.[56]

Many of those not captured by the Spanish in 1779 fled to Black River–the main British settlement on the Mosquito Shore and still in British hands. They did not have to wait too long to return, however, as the British abandoned their superintendency of the Mosquito Shore in 1786 following a new Anglo-Spanish Treaty (see next chapter). At that time more than 3,000 people (excluding the Miskitos) lived at the British settlements on the Shore, of which 2,214 chose to move to Belize.[57] The population estimate for Belize in 1790 gave a figure of 2,656, suggesting that the number that had stayed after the Spanish attack of 1779 was less than 500.[58]

When the Spanish attacked in 1779, St. George's Caye was still the most important population centre in the settlement. A small number of people had built homes at the mouth of the Haulover Creek in what would come to be called the town of Belize. However, this location was very exposed to attack by the Spanish as well as being at risk from flooding. It was also not as salubrious as the cayes, where the trade winds provided respite from the flies and mosquitoes.

In an age of universal migration restrictions between countries, it is hard to imagine a time when the "free" population could move relatively easily

---

[52] See Burdon (1931), p. 99.
[53] See Offen (2000), p. 129.
[54] See Bolland (1977), p. 32.
[55] See Burdon (1931), p. 4 and p. 129. "Free people of colour" is the phrase used in British sources to refer to all those of African descent that were not slaves.
[56] See Bolland (1977), p. 30.
[57] See Dobson (1973), p. 85.
[58] See Bolland (1977), p. 42.

from one location to another across the Americas. Yet the British settlers in the Bay Islands, Belize, Campeche, Jamaica, the Mosquito Shore and even North America were part of a fluid trans-migration that could lead to sudden rises and falls in the population. It was only after the loss of the Campeche settlements, the abandonment of the Mosquito Shore and the US War of Independence (1775-83) that the population of Belize became more permanent and even then there were still many opportunities for the whites and free people of colour to move elsewhere.

For the slaves it was a different matter. The first African slaves were bought in Jamaica, but the small number of women among them meant that the slave population could only be expanded through additional purchases. The fact that the Belize settlement was on the mainland provided opportunities for flight not open to those on the islands in the Caribbean.[59] In addition, timber extraction in the forests of Belize gave the slaves more scope to flee than on the tightly controlled plantations of the islands. We will never know the exact number of escaped slaves, but it was not insignificant before 1763 and would become greater subsequently.

The market

Although logwood could be used to provide an ink for writing, its most important purpose commercially was as a dye for the textile and clothing industry. During much of the 17th and throughout the 18th centuries, the heart of the logwood was used to extract a dye that was an essential ingredient in many manufacturing activities. Furthermore, logwood was versatile as it could be used to create dyes of many different colors. A Memorial from the Baymen, written in 1783, put this very clearly:[60] "Logwood is chiefly used in dying Colours, Such as Blacks, Blues and Purples; Wherefore its Consumption is very great in all the Woollen, Linen, Cotton and Hatt Manufactories."

That logwood could produce so many different colors was perhaps surprising. However, the scientific reason is relatively simple:[61]

Logwood's dyestuff forms an orange-red solution in boiling water, becoming yellowish when cooled and turning violet and black when oxidized over time. With mordants, logwood can produce a range of colors and, in addition to dyes, was used in the manufacture of ink.

---

[59] The Spanish officials in the neighboring territories certainly encouraged it, offering freedom to those that succeeded.
[60] See Burdon (1931), pp. 134-35.
[61] See Offen (2000), p. 118, n.5. The quote is actually from Fairlie (1965).

Logwood was not the world's only dyewood nor was it the only dyewood from the Caribbean and Mesoamerica. Its regional competitors included indigo, brazilwood, Nicaragua wood and fustic, while there were different ones in other parts of the world. However, logwood was by far the most important and it was found in its natural state in only a small part of the world. This was the Yucatan peninsula from just south of Campeche to the Bay of Honduras. It was also imported for cultivation by the British and French in some of their Caribbean islands. Contrary to popular belief, it was not found on the Mosquito Shore.[62]

As the British settlements close to Campeche collapsed, Belize became increasingly important for the world's expanding textile and clothing industry. This activity was global, but in practice demand was concentrated in a small number of European countries. In addition to Great Britain and Ireland, these included France, Germany, Holland, Italy, Portugal, Russia and Spain. All but the last could be supplied from Belize.[63]

The British market represented about half of the European demand. However, it was Britain's ambition to secure a virtual monopoly of supply in order that it could then re-export to other countries. In this, Britain was following in the footsteps of Spain, Portugal and France whose trade policy was based on giving privileges to intra-imperial commerce. In the case of the Caribbean, this meant that tropical products were supposed to be sold only to the relevant imperial power, although they were still subject to import duties upon entry into the metropolis and in some cases export duties also when leaving the colonies.

In England the legal framework for this system was enshrined in the Navigation Acts introduced by Oliver Cromwell (1649-58) and that led indirectly to the three Anglo-Dutch Wars as Holland resisted the inevitable discrimination against its traders. As a new colony, for example, Jamaica was expected to ship all its exports to other colonies or to England, although the latter was then free to re-export them to other countries if domestic consumption was insufficient.

The first ships to carry away Belize logwood included some that came from Jamaica. When they returned to the island, the Governor expected the captains to register the logwood for onward shipment to England where the import duty had been set in 1662 by Charles II's administration at £5 per ton. When the price was high, this specific tax was not unduly burdensome.

---

[62] See Offen (2000).

[63] The Memorial from the Baymen referred to in Note 60 states: "From being possessed of this Commodity We not only Supplied all our home Manufactories, but exported large Quantities of it to Italy Portugal France Holland Germany and Russia."

However, as we shall see, logwood prices kept falling after 1650.

The traders therefore started to ship Belize logwood to other destinations. This was a direct threat to the English (later British) Navigation Acts and the practice was challenged on numerous occasions. However, on every occasion the traders were victorious and the reason was simple. Belize–the settlement in the Bay of Honduras–was not a British colony and the British government did not question Spanish sovereignty. Thus, much of the revenue from the logwood trade was lost to the British exchequer.

The first challenge occurred in 1686 in Jamaica, when Lieutenant Governor Molesworth seized a ship carrying logwood from Belize on the grounds that no bond had been given that it would be carried to England or its colonies. Following a trial, however, the ship was released. The second occasion took place in 1699 in Venice, where a vessel (the *Seaflower*) had arrived directly from Belize to sell logwood.[64] The English consul wrote to the Board of Trade asking for guidance and was told that there was no justification for asking the Venetian authorities to seize the logwood as Belize was not a colony.[65]

Some Belize logwood was therefore either shipped to Jamaica for onward sale to England or shipped directly to ports on the European continent. However, by far the most important destination was the British port of Boston in Massachusetts where the logwood was not subject to import duty and from where New England traders carried it either legally to England or as contraband direct to other countries. Indeed, Boston had already established itself as an important destination for logwood when Dampier visited the Campeche settlements in 1675-76, so it is not surprising that the logwood cutters in Belize carried on the tradition.[66]

The Boston connection would prove to be of great importance for Belize. Some Belize logwood did go to other ports in British North America, but the vast bulk of what was shipped to North America went to Boston. In 1730, for example, 17 vessels entered Boston from Belize compared with 19 from Barbados and 23 from Jamaica.[67] Curiously, however, no ships cleared Boston for Belize suggesting that the Baymen either secured their supplies for the homeward journey from other North American ports or that the ships went to Belize after calling at other destinations first.

---

[64] The *Seaflower* was also the name of the ship that had carried the first colonists to Providence Island, raising the intriguing possibility that it was the same ship. See Kupperman (1993).

[65] See McLeish (1926), pp. 32-33. There was a similar case two years later involving a shipment of logwood from Belize to Leghorn (Livorno in modern Italy).

[66] There was also a smaller trade with New York. See Rossano (1989).

[67] See Pares (1956), p. 49.

The Baymen clearly appreciated the Boston link and showed it in many ways. In the city's North Church,[68] for example, there is a pew reserved for them and it is dated 1727.[69] A few years later, in 1740, the church's steeple was hit by lightning and the Baymen donated the timber with which to build a new one.[70] When the Boston connection was temporarily severed during the US War of Independence, it must have been a big blow for the settlement.

Belize had a very strong position in the logwood trade–especially after the end of exports from the Campeche settlements. However, Belize never had a monopoly because the introduction of logwood to Jamaica by the British and to Haiti, Guadeloupe and Martinique by the French provided Europe with other sources of supply. Furthermore, indigo, brazilwood, Nicaragua wood and fustic provided some competition and were exported from many different parts of Central America and the Caribbean.

It was no surprise, therefore, that the market for logwood often became over-supplied. Demand may have been growing in line with the expansion of the textile and clothing industries, but supply could be increased very quickly since logwood is so easy to cut. Traders carrying logwood from Belize may have been able to evade the British import duty, but they could not avoid the impact of falling prices.

Before the entry of British logwood cutters into the market, English manufacturers–like their counterparts on the European continent–had purchased logwood from Spanish sources at around £100 per ton (see Figure 2.1). By 1670, soon after logwood cutting had begun at British settlements on the Yucatan peninsula, the price had fallen to £50 per ton. It would then carry on falling, with only occasional reversals, for another century (see Figure 2.1).

This almost continuous fall in price is perhaps surprising when one takes into account Spanish attempts to disrupt supplies of logwood from British settlements. For the Spanish, all logwood from the mainland was contraband before 1763 and they used their naval resources to capture logwood ships on numerous occasions. They also used foreign pirates for the same

---

68 This church became famous in the War of Independence, as Paul Revere began his horseback journey from it to warn the rebels of the British advance. The "midnight ride" was later immortalized in a poem by Henry Wadsworth Longfellow.
69 The inscription below "The Bay Pew" reads: "This Pew for the use of the Gentlemen of the Bay of Honduras."
70 An inscription about the steeple in the Church reads: "Gift of Honduras merchants 1740 as guide to mariners". All this, it should be remembered, was taking place at almost the same time as Captain Nathaniel Uring was writing his unflattering remarks about the Baymen. The episode of the North Church illustrates why his picture of the settlers is so distorted.

Figure 2.1: Logwood price (cif), pounds sterling per ton

Sources: Burdon (1931), McLeish (1926), Offen (2000), Joseph (1974), Bolland (1977) and Gibbs (1883).

purpose. These attacks are well documented, as are the equally numerous protestations by the British (and Dutch) authorities that the ships carrying logwood were engaged in lawful trade.[71] Yet the impact on supply of all these Spanish interventions appears to have been quite minor–at least as judged by the fall in price after 1650.

More significant were Spanish attempts to dislodge the logwood cutters themselves. Indeed, their persistent attacks on the Campeche settlements were ultimately successful. The Spanish never permanently dislodged the settlers from Belize, but they did drive them out a number of times. Perhaps it is no accident that the price of logwood rose between 1728 and 1749 (see Figure 2.1), as this coincided with the relatively successful attacks on the settlers in 1730 and 1745 when logwood cutting was seriously disrupted.[72]

Logwood was not the only tropical product subject to large-scale price declines and in any case the price had been artificially high when the only source was Spain. However, other prices, for example, sugar, showed more cyclical variation with low prices often followed by high ones. In the case of logwood, the decline was fairly relentless so it is not surprising that the early enthusiasm of the Belize settlers had evaporated by the time it became legal for them to cut and export logwood.

There were, however, some advantages to exporting logwood. First, the decline in the price in the British market was matched by a fall in the import duty. By the time the Treaty of Paris was signed in 1763, the duty had fallen

---

[71] See McLeish (1926), Wilson (1936) and Joseph (1976).
[72] On these attacks, see McLeish (1926).

to 20 shillings (£1) per ton. This compared with £5 per ton a century before. Secondly, logwood could be easily stored, allowing the cutters an opportunity to hoard it until, or in the hope that, prices recovered. Thirdly, virtually the only requirement for production was labour since the land was free and there was no need for much else.

These advantages should not be dismissed, but they were not sufficient to outweigh the disadvantage of a falling price. By the time the Treaty of Paris gave the settlers some security of tenure, the logwood economy had passed its peak. Mahogany was already being exported and, although illegal under the terms of the 1763 Anglo-Spanish Treaty, would soon overtake logwood in importance.[73]

Yet logwood did not disappear and would even make a comeback after 1860, when mahogany itself experienced a sharp fall in prices. And logwood would continue to be exported from Belize until 1932, when the last shipment was made. So Belize exported logwood in virtually every single year for 250 years–a substantial achievement. And we can be sure that a large proportion of the woolens, cottons, linens and hats sold in Europe and North America over that period owed their colour to logwood from the Bay of Honduras.

Production

The logwood tree was once so well known in Belize that it would have been unnecessary to describe it. That is no longer the case today, when logwood is not exported and so many Belizeans live in towns. The logwood tree is a small tree that grows to ten metres (33 feet) with a spreading crown that becomes gnarled with age producing an extremely hard wood. The trunk and branches are covered in sharp spines. The leaves are feather-like, each bearing from three to several pairs of leaves about one to three cm. long and are inversely heart-shaped. The small flowers are borne in "racemes" (from five to 12 cm. long) that originate from the leaf axil. Creamy yellow in colour, they are numerous, sweet smelling and very attractive to bees.[74]

Logwood is found in many parts of Belize, but it is concentrated in the northern part of the country between the Belize River and Hondo River. Not surprisingly, therefore, this is where the Baymen concentrated their efforts during the period of the logwood economy. They had no reason to go much further south, as there was plenty of logwood in the northern

---

[73] It would not become legal until 1786. See next chapter.
[74] See also Craig (1969), p. 53, which provides a rather imprecise quote from Standley and Record (1936) on the definition of logwood.

region that was relatively easy to access and ship to the coast by creeks and rivers. The distribution of logwood was therefore the main reason why the boundaries of the settlement did not move south towards the present frontier with Guatemala on the Sarstoon River.

This northern region had become largely depopulated by the beginning of the 18th century as a result of the policy of the Spanish towards the Maya. The inhabitants of Tipu were forcibly relocated in 1707 and the same was true of the other Maya villages along the Belize, New and Hondo Rivers. Only a small handful of Maya remained, hiding from Spanish control, and as the century advanced they were not in a strong position to resist the advance of the Baymen and their slaves along these rivers.

Not all the logwood tree was useful for commercial purposes. The most valuable bits were the lower part of the trunk and the roots. Digging out the roots might have led to an unsustainable economy, but logwood was so abundant in Belize that this was not a problem. In any case, the tree can grow from seedling to a commercially viable size in about seven years. Once the tree was felled:[75]

> In accordance with the custom of the trade, the loggers cut the wood into logs or "sticks" of about a yard in length and two or three inches in diameter. When the bundles of sticks arrived in the British Isles or in Europe they were dispatched to special mills which ground them into a fine powder used by dyers.

The equipment needed for felling logwood trees was relatively simple. Dampier, on resolving in 1675 to try his hand as a logwood cutter in the Campeche region, set sail to Jamaica to purchase hatchets, axes, machetes, saws, wedges, a gun with powder and shot as well as a "Pavillion" to sleep in.[76] It is safe to assume that the logwood cutters of Belize needed much the same equipment and that it was purchased either in Jamaica or in the ports of British North America.

Cutting logwood required long periods in camps along the creeks and rivers and we are fortunate to have several early descriptions of these settlements in Belize, while Dampier's account of logwood camps at Trist is also valid. John Atkins, for example, who visited Belize in the early 1730s, stated of the logwood cutters:[77]

> They are about 500 (merchants and slaves), and have taken up their residence at a place called Barcaderas, about 40 miles up a narrow river full of alligators; and what is a greater inconvenience against transporting their effects

---

[75] See Joseph (1974), p. 16.
[76] See Dampier (1931), p. 155.
[77] See Atkins (1970), p. 227.

is a strong current in it from the freshes up land, and the banks being covered with shrubs, that makes it difficult to walk and tow the boats; covered also with infinite numbers of sand-flies and muskitos. They live in pavilions; a servant at their time of lying down to rest, shaking them till cleared of these vermin, that are an unsufferable plague and impediment to sleep. At the season (once a year) they move their pavilions from the pleasurable spots, the better to attend the logwood cutting, which carries them sometimes many miles from this principal residence, to follow the wood, which runs in a line or vein …of some miles perhaps, and then as many, without a stick on it. They cut it into large pieces, and leave it on the ground till the land-flood favours their bringing it into the river and then canoes are laden away with it, to lay in store at Barcaderas, where the Chief are still left residing.

Nathaniel Uring, who first visited Belize in 1719, gave a similar account. In general, it is only Uring's disparaging remarks about the logwood cutters that are quoted. However, it is worth recording his statement about logwood cutting as he was in Belize for many months and purchased timber himself. Uring stated:[78]

In the dry time of the year the logwood cutters search for a work; that is, where there are a good number of logwood trees; and then build a hut near them, where they live during the time they are cutting. When they have cut down the tree, they log it and hip it, which is cutting off the bark and the sap, and then lay it in heaps, cutting away the underwood and making paths to each heap, that when the rains come in which overflows the ground, it serves as so many creeks and channels, where they go with small canows or dories and load 'em, which they bring to a creek-side and there lade their canows and carry it to the Barcadares, which they sometimes fetch thirty miles, from whence the people who buy it fetch it.

These two descriptions are valuable because, although they have many points in common, they each emphasize different features of the logwood economy. Both lay stress on the "Barcadare" as a settlement whose status lay somewhere between the temporary logging camp and the permanent community on Cayo Casina (there are 18th century maps of Belize showing these Barcadares on both the Belize River and New River).[79] Uring, however, emphasizes the Barcadare as the place where logwood can be purchased (as he did), while Atkins is more sensitive to the social distinctions that had already arisen between "chiefs" and "servants". This was not the same as the distinction between masters and slaves.

---

[78] See Uring (1928), p. 241.
[79] See, for example, the 1786 map of Belize by a Bayman reproduced in Burdon (1931).

This suggests that early on there were social and economic distinctions among the "free" population (white and non-white). In the island Caribbean, these distinctions arose primarily through ownership of land. In Belize, however, land was freely accessible. In theory, anyone who was not a slave could obtain access to land for cutting logwood according to a custom that was first written down in 1765. This involved three criteria:[80]

> FIRST, When a person finds a spot of logwood unoccupied and builds his hut, that spot shall be deemed his property and no person shall presume to cut or fall a tree or grub a stump within less than one thousand paces or yards of his hut to be continued on each side of said hut with the course of the river or creek on both sides...

> SECOND, That no inhabitant whatever shall occupy two works at any time in any one river.

> THIRD, That no inhabitant shall claim a double portion of logwood works under pretence of a partner, except that partner is and deemed to be an inhabitant of the Bay.

Superficially, these criteria would seem to rule out any great social distinctions among the free population. However, the mere fact that they had to be written down in this form suggests that abuse was common. In addition, the free people of colour would have faced all sorts of discrimination in seeking to exercise their rights. Finally, we know that some 20 years after these criteria had been agreed, the distribution of timber concessions among the free population was exceedingly unequal.[81] Much of this problem of inequality can be laid at the door of mahogany extraction, which only became significant after the Treaty of Paris and which is the subject of the next chapter.

We do not have figures on logwood exports from Belize in many years during the 18th century (there are none during the 17th century). Those that we do have are shown in Figure 2.2. The peak level of exports was 1756, when 18,000 tons were shipped. This would have been too great for the market to absorb. However, the subsequent decline in volume exported was also affected by the low world price, as we saw in the previous section.

Since the demand for logwood in Europe was steadily increasing, it is clear from Figure 2.2 that Belize must have supplied a smaller share of the total after the peak year of 1756. This is consistent with the increase in log-

---

[80] See Burdon (1931), p. 107.
[81] See Bolland (1977), Chapter 3.

**Figure 2.2: Logwood exports from Belize (tons)
in the 18th century**

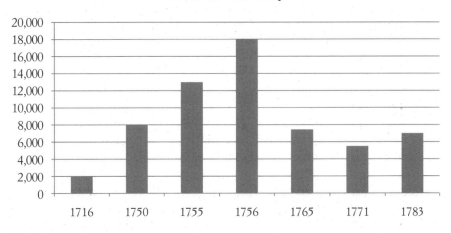

Sources: Gibbs (1883), McLeish (1926), Burdon (1931), Joseph (1974), Bolland (1977) and Offen (2000).

Note: The 1716 figure is derived from the figures for British imports of logwood from all sources between 1713 and 1716. These show a significant fall in 1716, when the Campeche settlements were attacked and therefore unable to ship logwood. Thus, Belize was virtually the only source of supply in that year. The 1765 figure is based on shipments between 25 March and 25 September only.

wood supply from other sources, such as Jamaica and the Bahamas, where it had been introduced by the British. Logwood was also being shipped in increasing quantities by the Spanish from Campeche and Cuba, while logwood was also being exported to France in greater volumes from Guadeloupe, Haiti and Martinique. These new sources of supply were less affected by the fall in price, as the logwood had in most cases been introduced for cultivation and was therefore easily accessible.

The "world" price in the previous section was the "cif" price, i.e., the price in Europe after paying transport and insurance. This was not the price received by the logwood cutters in Belize, who could expect to receive only the "fob" price, i.e., the price paid by the traders who came to the settlement to buy logwood. Nathaniel Uring was one of those and he tells us that, at the time of his visits, the fob price was approximately £5 per ton in Jamaica currency (this was roughly equivalent to £3.50 sterling).[82] Since the cif price at the time was around £16 per ton (see Figure 2.1), it is clear that the merchants who transported the logwood were well rewarded for the risks they carried.

---

[82] See Uring (1928), p. 241.

Some Baymen would have been both cutters and traders. However, most were not. Thus, what mattered for them–and for the Belizean economy–was the fob price. This fell in line with the cif price, so that it was only a little above one pound sterling at its lowest.[83] Taking the period before 1763 as a whole, and assuming average exports of 8,000 tons and an average fob price of £3, the average annual value of Belizean export earnings was £24,000. With population ranging from 500 to 1,500 during these years, this implies exports per head between £16 and £48.

This does not sound much in today's money, but it was substantial by the standards of the 18th century. In 1820, for example, the first year when we have figures for all the countries of the Caribbean, the average value of exports per head for all the British colonies was £9, for the French £6 and for the Spanish colonies £3.[84] Thus, Belize in the period of the logwood economy already had a value of exports per head that was far higher than that of the rest of the Caribbean. This was a consequence of concentration on a relatively high value product over which Belize had a quasi-monopoly for many years.

Belize may have received a substantial income from the sale of logwood, but this did not stimulate the domestic (non-export) economy. The small size of the population, the absence of secure property rights and the threat from Spain meant that the income was spent either on imports or transfers to the metropolis. Apart from the provision grounds used by the slaves for growing food, there was almost no domestic economy at all. Even the town of Belize was insignificant during the logwood economy and it is significant that neither Uring nor Atkins mentions it.

The most important import was slaves–purchased from Jamaica at a price that varied, but which averaged around £40. In addition, we know from Henderson that the cost of maintenance of a slave was £25 per year, of which around £15 represented imports.[85] Assuming steady growth of the slave population from 1745, when it was 120, to 1779, when it was 3,000, a Crude Birth Rate (CBR) of ten and a Crude Death Rate (CDR) of fifty, we can construct an estimate of the cost of imports associated with slavery that can be compared with income from logwood (see Table 2.1).[86] This shows

---

[83] See Burdon (1931), p. 131.

[84] Derived from Tables A.1a and A.11 in Bulmer-Thomas (2012) and converting US dollars to pounds sterling at 4.80.

[85] See Henderson (1811), pp. 66-67.

[86] The CBR and CDR measure the number of births and deaths per thousand of the population. Since the slave population was largely male, deaths would have exceeded births. Imputed slave imports are then the difference between the change in the slave population and net births.

that the logwood economy was highly profitable at first, but declined after 1755 and was running at a loss by 1771.

Table 2.1: The profitability of the logwood economy, 1745-1771

Year	Logwood exports (Tons)	Logwood exports (£) (fob)	Cost (£) of slave imports	Cost (£) of slave maintenance	Total imported costs (£)	Surplus (£)
1750	8,000	24,000	457	2,890	3,347	20,653
1755	13,000	39,000	734	4,639	5,373	33,627
1765	7,449	22,347	1,891	11,956	13,847	8,500
1771	5,500	16,500	3,337	21,100	24,437	-7,937

Note: Logwood exports in tons are from Figure 2.2, while the fob price is assumed to be £3. The cost of slave imports is the estimated number imported times the average price (£40). The cost of slave maintenance is from Henderson (1811), pp. 66-67, assuming that 60% of costs could only be met by imports. "Surplus" is then the difference between exports and imports.

By this time (1771), mahogany exports had started so the Belize economy was still profitable. However, logwood exports would rapidly decline from this point, averaging only 1,000-2,000 tons in the fifty years after 1780. Logwood therefore ceased to be a dynamic factor soon after the Treaty of Paris–precisely at the moment when its extraction became legal!

During the century when logwood was the driving force of the settlement, it had generated a good income for the small free population most of the time, a minimum subsistence for the growing slave population, declining customs duties for the British exchequer and strong demand for imports from Jamaica and British North America. It had not, however, generated a domestic or non-export economy. This would now change with the diversification of the economy after the Treaty of Paris.

3. The British Settlement in the Bay of Honduras

The Treaty of Paris in 1763 gave legal status to the "British Settlement in the Bay of Honduras"–as it would now be described in official documents. It would only cease to be a "settlement" when it became the colony of British Honduras in 1862. The British Settlement in the Bay of Honduras therefore survived one hundred years–almost exactly the same length of time as the illegal logwood economy that had endured from the 1660s to 1763.

During the century of the logwood economy, the key powers shaping the destiny of the illegal settlement were Spain and Great Britain. These European powers either took decisions directly or acted through proxies– the Governor of Yucatan and the President of Guatemala[1] in the case of Spain; the Governor of Jamaica and (from 1748) the Superintendent of the Mosquito Shore in the case of Great Britain.

During the century of the British settlement in the Bay of Honduras, the geopolitical forces shaping the country would change dramatically. Indeed, it is no exaggeration to say that this was the most crucial century in Belize's modern history. Spain would decline in importance, while the Superintendency of the Mosquito Shore would end in 1786 to be replaced by the Kingdom of Mosquitia recognized only by Great Britain. The new actors were the independent countries of Central America together with Mexico and the United States of America. Last, but not least, Great Britain (from 1802, the United Kingdom)[2] emerged triumphant from the Napoleonic Wars and would go on to become the most powerful country in Europe.

While the constitutional status of Belize was being determined by geopolitical struggles among these old and new powers, the logwood economy was giving way to the trade in mahogany, and in a much smaller way, cedar.

---

[1] This was the formal colonial title for the senior Spanish official responsible for the Audiencia de Guatemala, which covered all of modern Central America plus Chiapas.
[2] When the colony of Ireland was absorbed into Great Britain in 1802, the new entity was called the United Kingdom (UK).

Although a product of the forests, mahogany was as different from logwood as sugar from tobacco.[3] Its requirements of labour and capital were distinct, while the demand for mahogany was quite unlike the demand for logwood. Above all, mahogany was found in isolated locations on solid ground, forcing the Baymen to push south in search of profitable opportunities. Just as logwood shaped the northern boundaries of modern Belize, so mahogany would do the same for the southern frontiers.

Mahogany had replaced logwood as the most valuable domestic export long before it was legal for the Baymen to extract it. By the 1820s, however, a new and even more profitable economic activity had emerged. This was the entrepôt trade with Central America, by means of which the Belizean merchants supplied the neighbouring countries with most of their requirements for manufactured imports while shipping to Europe and North America their commodity exports such as indigo and cochineal. This re-export business would make the merchants in the town of Belize very prosperous–until in 1855 the opening of the US-built railroad across Panama and the upgrading of the ports on the Caribbean coast gave the neighbouring countries alternative outlets for their trade.

The century after the Treaty of Paris also saw the transformation of Belize society. The slave trade ended in 1808 and slavery itself in 1834, by which time the Garifuna were firmly established in the country. The small population was then swelled by immigration from Yucatan as refugees fled the upheavals associated with the *Guerra de Castas*. The Maya started returning to the south at about the same time, escaping from labour coercion and the alienation of communal land in Guatemala. As a result, the country's population increased ten-fold during the century of the British settlement–faster than any British colony in the Caribbean.

Geopolitics

When the Treaty of Paris was signed in 1763, the only foreign power of geopolitical interest to the British settlers was Spain. This remained the case for many years. When the US War of Independence broke out in 1775, Spain at first remained neutral. However, in 1779 she entered what had also become a European war on the side of France and against Great Britain. Belize was now very vulnerable, Britain being in no position to defend it, and St. George's Caye was captured in that year.

---

[3] See Ortiz (1940), which contrasts the very different impacts of sugar and tobacco on Cuba.

The 1783 Treaty of Versailles ended hostilities in Europe and the Americas, allowing the settlers and their slaves to return to Belize.[4] The treaty defined the boundaries, but restricted economic activity to cutting logwood.[5] Since mahogany was already more important, this was very irksome to the settlers who succeeded in pressuring Great Britain to agree a new arrangement with Spain.[6] This was the London Convention of 1786. It pushed the boundaries of the settlement south to the Sibun River, permitted the cutting of mahogany as well as logwood and allowed for bi-annual inspection by Spanish officers alongside a resident British Superintendent.[7] In return, however, Great Britain agreed to abandon its protectorate over the Mosquito Shore.[8]

Britain had therefore reversed its previous position, by which the "Shore" had been treated as more important than the "Bay". The decision may have had something to do with the (illegal) expansion of mahogany–a product of growing importance to the British economy. Whatever the reason, the settlers on the Shore were abandoned by the British authorities and offered the chance of relocating to the Bay. Many of these settlers had in fact fled the Bay of Honduras in 1779, at the time of the Spanish attack, but their return in 1787 proved to be difficult.[9] Indeed, the first British Superintendent, Colonel Marcus Despard, struggled to find an accommodation between the established settlers and the new arrivals.[10]

When in 1796 Spain joined France against Great Britain in the European war that erupted after the French Revolution, it was only a matter of time before Belize would come under attack. This duly occurred in 1798 at the Battle of St. George's Caye.[11] The Spanish failure on this occasion, however, did not change the position in international law since Great Britain did not claim sovereignty as a result of the Spanish defeat. The situation at the

---

[4] This time, however, St. George's Caye could not be occupied as the Treaty of Versailles excluded use of the cayes. In any case, in view of the successful Spanish attack in 1779, it was now thought to be unsafe as the main location and the town of Belize therefore became the principal centre. The first map of Belize town was made in 1787 showing it to be still very small. See Everitt (1986).

[5] The boundaries were set as the Hondo River to the north, the Belize River to the south and the New River to the west.

[6] In this they were aided by Robert White, who had become their agent in London in 1783. See Burdon (1931), p. 132.

[7] See Dobson (1973), p. 73.

[8] See Humphreys (1961), Floyd (1967), Dozier (1985) and Naylor (1989).

[9] They did not all go to Belize; a small number chose to remain at the Black River settlement. See Dawson (1983) and Dawson (1998).

[10] Convention Town was established on the Belize River to accommodate them, but it was not a success. See Bolland (1977), p. 34.

[11] This conflict has been examined in minute detail. See, for example, King (1991).

end of the Napoleonic Wars was therefore exactly the same as before, since the UK did not use the Amiens Treaty of 1802, the Treaty of Paris of 1814 or the Congress of Vienna in 1815 to force a change in the legal position of the settlement.[12]

This oversight, for that is what it turned out to be, was to be a source of endless difficulties for Belize. When Mexico and Central America declared their independence from Spain in 1821, the UK continued to regard Spain as the sovereign power for the British settlement. Perhaps this could be justified at first by the uncertainty over the status of the new countries, since Central America was annexed to Mexico until 1823.[13] However, the UK refused to discuss Belize with the United Provinces of Central America, the name of the new republic, even after a consul had been dispatched to the region.[14]

It was only when the United Provinces dissolved into the five Central American republics after 1838 that the UK began to accept that Spain had no authority in the region.[15] This meant, of course, that Britain had to enter into negotiations with Guatemala and Mexico to establish the boundaries of the British settlement. The negotiations with Guatemala proceeded relatively swiftly and resulted in the Anglo-Guatemalan Treaty of 1859–subsequently ratified by both parties. Negotiations with Mexico took much longer and the boundary was only settled in 1893.

The 1859 Treaty had included an ambiguous clause about the need for both parties to cooperate in the construction of a road. To iron out the ambiguities, in 1863 a Convention was signed committing the UK to contribute £50,000. Guatemala was unable to ratify in the time allotted and the UK refused to extend the deadline. The Convention therefore lapsed. Neither side, however, saw any reason at the time to abrogate the 1859 Anglo-Guatemalan Treaty that had established the boundaries. It was another 80 years before Guatemala would tear it up.[16]

---

[12] This was in stark contrast to Trinidad, captured by the British in 1797 and ceded by Spain to the UK in the 1802 Treaty of Amiens; or to Tobago, captured from France in the Napoleonic Wars and ceded to Britain in the 1814 Treaty of Paris.

[13] Central America declared independence from Spain and then immediately annexed itself to Mexico, at the time ruled by the Emperor Iturbide. When in 1823 Central America declared itself independent of Mexico, it was forced to lose Chiapas.

[14] The consul was sent to the United Provinces of Central America in 1825. See Naylor (1988). However, the Central American Federation collapsed before full diplomatic recognition could take place. See Rodríguez (1964).

[15] The five provinces–Costa Rica, El Salvador, Guatemala, Honduras and Nicaragua–declared themselves republics in the decade after the dissolution of the Central American Federation in 1838. See Parker (1964).

[16] See Lauterpacht et al. (2002).

In 1862 the British settlement then became the colony of British Hondu-ras. This ended a long struggle between the British Superintendent, resident since 1786, and the settlers over the constitutional status of the country. A British Parliamentary Act of 1817 had stated that Belize was:[17] "A settle-ment, for certain purposes, in the possession and under the protection of His Majesty, but not within the territory and dominion of his Majesty."

This ambiguous statement left open the extent to which British laws could be applied in the settlement. There was therefore much confusion and in-consistency, the settlers calling for the application of British laws only when it suited their purposes. The Superintendent was able to insist on the appli-cation of the British laws related to the abolition of the slave trade and the emancipation of the slaves.[18] However, he failed to secure the application of the Navigation Acts so that Belize–unlike the rest of the British Caribbean–faced very few restrictions on trade with the United States (US).[19]

This proved to be crucial for the welfare of the settlement since so much of Belize's trade during the logwood economy had passed through Boston. After the War of Independence trade ties were soon restored with the US, although they were temporarily disrupted by the US trade embargo against Great Britain starting in 1808 and by the outbreak of war in 1812 between the UK and US.[20] By 1820, however, nearly 20 per cent of Belize's exports were going to the US compared with less than three per cent for the British Caribbean as a whole.[21]

With the purchase of Louisiana from Napoleon in 1803 and of eastern Florida from Spain in 1819, the US had acquired a long coastline bordering the Caribbean and the Gulf of Mexico.[22] However, it was not yet a regional power and the Monroe Doctrine in 1823 was regarded with some contempt in European circles.[23] Instead, it was the incorporation of Texas (1845) as a state of the union and the US-Mexican War (1845-48) that transformed the US into a force to be reckoned with in Central America. The US was now a continental country with interests in both the Atlantic and the Pacific and a need to forge transport links between the two.

Before the construction of the trans-continental railway, the quickest and cheapest way for the US to link the Atlantic and the Pacific was through Central America. This had led to Commodore Vanderbilt's inter-oceanic

---

[17] See Dobson (1973), p. 79.
[18] See Bolland (1977), p. 80.
[19] See Burdon (1934), p. 3 and p. 63.
[20] See Bailey (1964), Chapters 9 and 10.
[21] See Bulmer-Thomas (2012), Table A.20.
[22] See Bailey (1964), Chapters 8 and 12.
[23] The Monroe Doctrine stated US opposition to any attempt by a European power to (re)establish colonies in the Americas. See Perkins (1941).

route through Nicaragua and to the tolerance shown at first by the US government to William Walker's pro-slavery filibusters in Central America.[24] It also led to US interest in a trans-isthmian transport route, for which a treaty was signed with Colombia. Construction of the railway across Panama was then completed in 1855.[25]

The commercial and strategic interests of the US, however, also extended to the possibility of an inter-oceanic canal. The UK, as the world's leading trading power, also had a strong interest in such a project. This led to a long period of Anglo-American rivalry that culminated in the signing of the Clayton-Bulwer Treaty of 1850, under which both countries agreed to protect the neutrality of any canal built across Central America and not to seek control of any territory in the vicinity.[26]

As is so often with these treaties, the wording was ambiguous. The US at times assumed this meant that Britain should abandon the Belize settlement, its protectorate over the Bay Islands and its recognition of an independent Kingdom of Mosquitia. The UK took the opposite view and even converted the Bay Islands into a British colony in 1852. A resolution of the differences was agreed in the Clarendon-Dallas Treaty of 1856.[27] In 1859 Britain accepted Honduran sovereignty over the Bay Islands and ended their colonization,[28] in 1860 signed the Treaty of Managua giving Nicaragua nominal sovereignty over Mosquitia[29] and in 1862 established the colony of British Honduras.

The UK itself also underwent many changes after the 1763 Treaty of Paris, which had major implications for the British Settlement in the Bay of Honduras. Industrialization created a conflict between the old landed elite that depended on tariff protection and the new manufacturing class that wanted free trade. The latter eventually won and the Corn Laws were repealed in 1846.[30] Imperial preference also came to an end and many tariffs were reduced or even abolished. Those parts of the British Empire, such as Jamaica, that had relied on discrimination by Britain against foreign products in favour of those from its colonies were in serious difficulties. For Belize, the major impact

---

[24] See Woodward (1985).

[25] Panama was a province of Colombia until 1903.

[26] See Williams (1916).

[27] The treaty was never ratified, but this was not due to a dispute over Belize. See Williams (1916).

[28] See Davidson (1974).

[29] The treaty included the right of Britain to intervene to protect the Miskitos. This became a major source of irritation for governments in Nicaragua, which only ended in 1894 when President Zelaya established direct rule over Mosquitia. See Williams (1916).

[30] The Corn Laws had protected British farmers from imports of basic grains by means of high tariffs.

was the elimination of all tariffs on mahogany leading to a huge increase in British imports.

After the Battle of Trafalgar in 1805, British naval supremacy went unchallenged for nearly a century. The navy was one of the cornerstones of British geo-strategy, so that as long as ships were built from timber, the UK had a strong interest in promoting mahogany exports from Belize. However, the switch from timber to iron took place soon after Belize became a colony, so that paradoxically Britain was always more interested in Belize during its time as a settlement.

At the Congress of Vienna in 1815, a number of British territorial gains were confirmed and the British Empire expanded significantly in size. The "golden age" of the British Empire still lay in the future, but by the time Belize became a colony it was well under way. Belize would therefore join the empire as a small part of a big whole. Its major interest to Britain was no longer as an exporter of forest products, but had much more to do with its location close to the route of a possible inter-oceanic canal. As it became clear that the US, not the UK, would control any canal that might be built, the British interest in Belize declined even further.

The mahogany trade

The mahogany tree was first used in Europe after the Spanish discovered it in the Americas, from where it would be exported to other parts of the world. The species in the Americas (*Swietenia*) was named after Baron Von Swieten, physician to Maria Theresa, Empress of Austria, and is native to the Caribbean and the tropical regions of the mainland. It is this tree that once was found in abundance in Belize.

Although both Walter Raleigh and Dampier (like the Spanish) used mahogany for ship repairs, it was not in common use in Great Britain until the middle of the 18th century. Indeed, there is a story (probably apocryphal) that it owes its widespread use to the importation in 1724 of a few planks by a Dr. Gibbons of London for which no use could be found on the grounds that the wood was too hard. However, the doctor's cabinet-maker used the wood to make a candle box that was widely admired and its popularity thereafter was assured.[31]

Whatever the truth of this story, and one must be fairly skeptical, it was certainly the case that the widespread importation of mahogany into Great Britain was due at first to the demands of furniture makers. Jamaica was an

[31] See Chaloner and Fleming (1851). The same story can be found in Bridges (1828).

Figure 3.1. UK mahogany imports (tons), 1820-1850

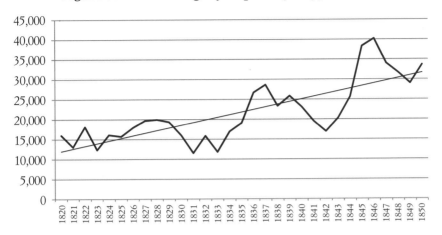

Sources: See *Statistical tables relating to the Colonial and other Possessions of the United Kingdom* (various years), *Statistical Abstract for the Principal and Other Foreign Countries* (various years) and Naylor (1988).

important supplier, but Jamaican mahogany was soon exhausted and the island had ceased to be an important source by the end of the 18th century creating opportunities for other countries.

One of those countries was Belize, which was already exporting over 400,000 board feet by 1765–at a time when the Treaty of Paris confined the settlers to cutting only logwood! This was just the beginning as British demand began to rise rapidly in response to the demands of other industries. These included shipbuilding, where many owners began to substitute mahogany for oak in their vessels. Not all were convinced, however, as mahogany cut in the wrong way could suffer from dry rot–no laughing matter for a ship–and the Lloyd's Register of British and Foreign Shipping placed certain restrictions on the naval use of mahogany (see p. 75).

Mahogany's popularity in furniture was not confined to households. Its uses included pulpits, altars and benches in churches; piano-fortes in concert halls; doors and tables for offices; scientific instruments; and dock gates. And from the 1830s onwards, there was a new demand for mahogany in the construction of railway carriages and coach panels. All this was reflected in British imports of mahogany after 1820 (see Figure 3.1), although some of these logs were then re-exported to other countries.

The settlers in Belize were quick to see the opportunity offered by the growing demand for mahogany. Robert White, appointed in 1773 by the Shoremen to represent their interests in London, was asked to do the same for the Baymen in 1783 (at a time when Belize was almost entirely abandoned) and his vigorous lobbying efforts helped to secure the concession from Spain in 1786 that mahogany could be cut as well as logwood with the boundaries of the settlement being extended to the River Sibun.

This was far from satisfying the needs of the Baymen, however, and the boundaries were pushed rapidly beyond the Sibun in search of new sources of mahogany. The Superintendent reported that by 1802 the settlers had reached Deep River. By 1806 they were said to have reached Rio Grande. By 1814 they were on the Moho River and by 1825 the Superintendent sent a map to London showing the Sarstoon River as the southern boundary.[32] There was even a claim by the London-based Honduras Merchants Committee that the settlers were nearly in sight of the Spanish fortifications at Omoa, although this is likely to have been an exaggeration.[33]

The Baymen had devised a method of awarding logwood concessions amongst themselves. When Admiral Burnaby was sent to the settlement in 1765, he included these practices in his famous Code that encapsulated the pragmatic decision-making methods used by the settlers to resolve issues of property rights, criminal charges and civil claims.[34]

These arrangements had served the Baymen well during the logwood economy and were relatively democratic–albeit they only applied to the few who were not slaves. However, they did not operate so successfully when the mahogany trade began to dominate the economic life of the settlement since mahogany in its wild form grows sparsely (roughly one tree per acre). This meant that the small concessions awarded for logwood cutting would no longer work and the settlers started to take larger tracts of land. Since the cutting of mahogany before 1786 was illegal, the methods by which this was done were highly dubious.

Suffice it to say that by the time Colonel Despard arrived in 1786 as the first resident Superintendent, and before the arrival of over 2,000 people from the Mosquito Shore, he found that twelve of the Baymen claimed 80 per cent of the land between the Rio Hondo and the Sibun River. Furthermore, in the short period since the boundary had been extended in 1786, a mere eleven Baymen (presumably a similar list to the twelve above) were in control of 75 per cent of the augmented area from the Belize River to the Sibun River.[35]

---

[32] See Lauterpacht, et al. (2002), pp. 36-37, based on Humphreys (1961).

[33] Omoa is well inside the territory of Honduras. As the claim was made in 1802, it is unlikely to have been true. See Lauterpacht, et al. (2002), p. 36.

[34] See Burdon (1931), pp. 101-106, for a complete record of Burnaby's Code. Burnaby was accompanied on this visit by Lieutenant James Cook, who has often been mistaken for the more famous navigator of the same name. See Cook and Haas (1935), which shows conclusively that they were different people.

[35] All this is very well described by Bolland (1977), Chapter 3, and Bolland and Shoman (1977), Chapter 1.

This was clearly sharp practice at its worst. Furthermore, the new arrivals from the Mosquito Shore (at least the free ones) found themselves very largely excluded from the mahogany works since they were not eligible to apply unless they had at least four slaves.[36] The correct response by the Superintendent should have been to regard all timber concessions as null and void and start again. This was not done, however, and the concessions north of the Sibun River were treated as *de facto* freeholds.

This was one of the gravest errors in the history of Belize, well documented by Nigel Bolland and Assad Shoman.[37] Although the Superintendent was careful to ensure that most of the land south of the Sibun remained in Crown hands, it could not disguise the fact that the Belize settlement was saddled at birth with a very unequal distribution of wealth. The "monied cutters", as they would come to be called, controlled the land, owned most of the slaves and received most of the income. Not surprisingly, as happens in all such unequal societies, they would exercise excessive influence on the political system.

By around 1820 the *de facto* boundaries of the settlement were those that would become the boundaries of the colony of British Honduras in 1862. These frontiers reflected the settlers' needs for locations that would provide sufficient mahogany, and to a lesser extent logwood, to meet the growing world demand–especially from the UK. This meant that in the north the boundary was pushed westwards beyond the New River Lagoon, while in the south–as we have seen–it meant the frontier was extended to the Sarstoon River. The western boundary corresponded roughly to a line drawn north and south of Garbutts Fall on the western branch of the Belize River.

This area was much larger than that permitted for timber extraction under the 1786 Anglo-Spanish Convention. Yet it still did not satisfy the ambitions of the Baymen, who cut mahogany at various points on the northern coast of Honduras in the Kingdom of Mosquitia as well.[38] Thus, the settlers were not constrained by geography in the first half of the 19th century and they therefore turned their attention to removing the remaining obstacles to the importation of Belize mahogany by the UK.

The most serious obstacle was the duty applied to mahogany imports. The Napoleonic Wars had disrupted British timber imports from the Baltic, previously the most important source, and led to a tariff structure that strongly encouraged colonial sources. Belize, not being a colony, should not have qualified for the lower tariff. However, strenuous lobbying by its supporters in the UK ensured not only that the foreign import tariff did not apply to Belize, but also that mahogany from the settlement would

---

[36] See Bolland (1977), p. 33.
[37] See Bolland and Shoman (1977), Chapter 3.
[38] See Bulmer-Thomas (2012), Chapter 11.

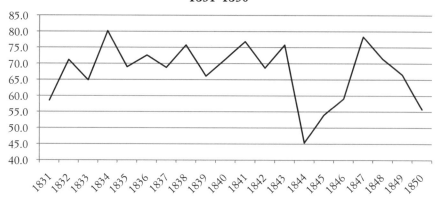

Figure 3.2: Belize share of British mahogany imports (%), 1831–1850

Source: Derived from Naylor (1988).

enter the UK at a lower tariff than imports from Jamaica. By 1821, therefore, Belize had secured a tariff of £3 16s 0d per ton compared with £5 for Jamaica and £11 17s 6d for other countries. When tariffs were revised downwards in 1826, Belize was again favored with a duty on mahogany in the UK market of £2 10s compared with £4 for Jamaica and £7 for foreign sources. This preference was further extended in 1832 when the Belize tariff was reduced to £1 10s.[39]

This still left unresolved the mahogany cut by the Baymen outside the *de facto* limits of the settlement and shipped to Belize before transportation to the UK. This was treated at first by the Superintendent as foreign mahogany and therefore subject to high duties on arrival in the UK. However, successful lobbying–this time by the Baymen in the settlement–ensured that from 1833 mahogany cut outside the limits would be treated the same as if it had been cut inside Belize.[40] Finally, the British government of Sir Robert Peel abolished all duties on imported mahogany in 1844-45.[41]

Peel's decision boosted British demand for mahogany (see Figure 3.1), but eliminated the discrimination against Belize's competitors since all countries were now subject to zero tariffs. By this time Belize had little to fear from other British colonies in the Caribbean, such as Bahamas and Jamaica, since their stocks of mahogany were largely exhausted. The main threat came from Cuba and Santo Domingo (independent from Haiti since 1844). However, as Figure 3.2 shows, Belize was the main source of imports with an average of 70 per cent from 1830-50, although it dropped briefly

---

[39] See Dobson (1973), p. 132.
[40] See Dobson (1973) p. 133.
[41] See Chaloner and Fleming (1851), p. 6.

below 50 per cent when the abolition of all tariffs led to a temporary surge in imports from Cuba and Santo Domingo.[42]

The second obstacle faced by Belize was the restrictions on the use of its mahogany in shipbuilding imposed by the Lloyd's Committee for the Registry of British and Foreign Shipping. Gradually, and thanks to tireless lobbying by the Honduras Merchants Committee and Robert White, these were lifted until the only remaining restriction concerned the use of mahogany in ships of the 12 year class. Finally, in October 1846 the Committee secured a major concession that deserves to be quoted in full as it illustrates the frustration of Lloyds at the extensive lobbying to which they had clearly been subject:[43]

> In regard to vessels of the 12 years grade, the Tables allow the unlimited use of Mahogany for the planking inside; and also for the outside plank, the only restriction being in the Wales and Blackstrakes, and Sheerstrakes and Plank-sheers. In the form of timber it is likewise allowed for the main Keelson and Beams, Hooks and Knees, and the Committee have now determined to allow it for Waterways and third futtocks and top timbers, but not for roughtree stations.The Committee greatly regret that it is not in their power fully to accede to the wishes of the Committee of Honduras Merchants; but a sense of duty compels them to decline giving their sanction to the unlimited use of Mahogany in vessels of the 12 years grade, notwithstanding the several applications which they have received. They believe that they have now done ample justice to the subject, and they trust they will be excused in frankly stating that they will not feel justified in the further agitation of this question, until at least sufficient time shall have elapsed for allowing a judgment to be formed on experience of the applicability of this material for all the purposes in Ship-building for which it is now admitted.[44]

The final obstacle to be overcome involved restrictions on shipbuilding. At first the Board of Trade ruled that ships built in the settlement could not be registered as British since Belize was not a colony. In 1820, however, successful lobbying secured an Act in the British parliament that extended the privilege of British-built ships to all vessels built in the Bay of Honduras provided they were owned by British subjects and used only in the direct trade between Belize and the UK.[45] Although this ruled out ships used in

---

[42] So important was Belize mahogany in the UK that several streets even today carry the name "Honduras".

[43] See Chaloner and Fleming (1851), p. 111.

[44] As the evidence indicates, the Honduras Merchants Committee ignored this request and had written back demanding further concessions within a few weeks! See Chaloner and Fleming (1851), pp. 112-14.

[45] See Dobson (1973), pp. 130-31.

Figure 3.3: Belize mahogany exports (000 bd ft), 1798-1851

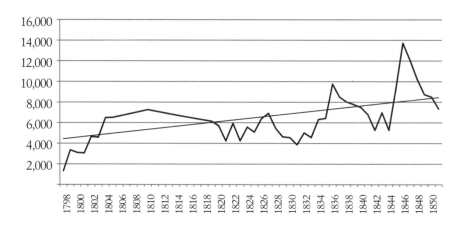

Sources: From 1798-1803, Bolland (1977), p. 159; 1804 is from Gibbs (1883), p. 74; 1805 and 1810 are from Dobson (1977), p. 129; 1819-51, from Bulmer-Thomas (2012), Appendix to Chapter 11; 1806-9 and 1811-18 have been filled by interpolation.

the coastal trade or on the Jamaica route, it did stimulate ship-building in Belize and many vessels were constructed.[46]

Belize even lobbied to reduce mahogany tariffs in France, where a Société Anglo-Française de Honduras was formed for this purpose. In the 1840s the duties on the importation of Belize mahogany were abolished if the wood was to be used in the construction of naval vessels. However, the lobbyists had less success in reducing the duty on mahogany for other purposes, which remained high.[47] As a result, the French market was never very important for Belize mahogany.

These changes helped Belize to shift from an economy that had relied entirely on logwood exports to one in which the main commodity export would be mahogany. Logwood did not disappear from the export list, but the volume fell from the high levels recorded before the Treaty of Paris. As late as 1771 logwood exports had been over 5,000 tons, but by 1800 they were below 2,000 tons. From this point onwards, they would slowly recover reaching nearly 5,000 tons again in 1850.

Mahogany, on the other hand, rose rapidly during this period (see Figure 3.3). By 1798, despite the Spanish attack, exports were already in excess of one million board feet (bd ft).[48] The following year they were above three million and had reached 6.5 million by 1805. Napoleon's blockade of the

---

[46] See Burdon (1934), *passim.*

[47] See Société Anglo-Française de Honduras (1857).

[48] Mahogany volume can be given in tons, cubic feet or board feet. The latter is used throughout this book unless otherwise specified.

European continent made it difficult to increase exports in the next decade, but by the 1830s exports had passed their previous peak and would reach the extraordinary (and unsustainable) level of 13.7 million board feet (bd. ft.) in 1846 after the abolition of all British duties on mahogany.

The expansion of mahogany exports from Belize was so rapid that it started to run ahead of the expansion of world demand. As a result, prices in the all important British market fell in the 1840s. This was partly as a result of the fall in duties, but by no means entirely. The merchants and cutters began to complain about "unfair" competition–especially from Cuba where mahogany was still cut by slaves.[49] These complaints fell on deaf ears in the UK and there was no more sympathy when the world mahogany industry entered into crisis in the 1860s–just as the settlement became a colony.

The entrepôt trade

Until the dying days of Spanish colonialism in Mesoamerica, the opportunities for Belize to trade with its neighbours were limited to contraband. This is hard to measure, but we know there was a lively exchange with the Yucatan peninsula through Bacalar where officials could be easily bribed. There was also a smaller trade with Guatemala through the Rio Dulce and the Lago de Izabal as well as ports on the northern coast of Honduras.

In 1819 the Captain-General of the Audiencia de Guatemala, which included all of modern Central America together with Chiapas, bowed to the inevitable and permitted free trade between the Spanish colony and Belize.[50] "Free trade" meant, of course, "freedom to trade" rather than the absence of any restrictions such as tariffs. However, Belize was now in a position to turn an illegal trade into something more legitimate and the incentives to do so became even greater two years later when Central America won its independence from Spain.

The United Provinces of Central America (UPCA), as the Confederation was called when it separated from Mexico in 1823,[51] recognized that for many years to come it would need to export raw materials and import manufactures. The UK, as the most advanced industrial country in the world, was in a strong position to satisfy the demand with goods at prices much lower than those Central America had previously paid. In the absence of direct trade routes between the UPCA's Caribbean ports and Great Britain,

---

[49] See Dobson (1973), p. 134.
[50] See Naylor (1995).
[51] See Woodward (1985).

Figure 3.4: Share of Central American imports from UK through Belize (%), 1825-1851

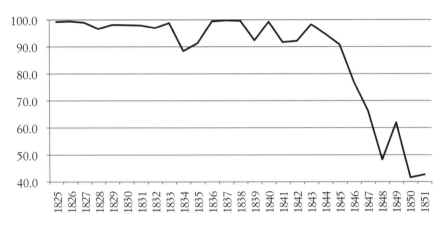

Source: Derived from Naylor (1988).

this gave merchants in Belize a huge opportunity of which they took full advantage.

The main UPCA imports from the UK were textiles–especially plain cottons, muslins and linens. As early as 1825 Belize was importing from the UK nearly five million yards of textiles. Since the Belize population was just over 4,000 at the time, we can be very confident that most of this was re-exported to Central America with a smaller amount going to Mexico.[52] And the amount imported by Belize kept rising, reaching a peak of nearly 17 million yards in 1840.[53]

The UPCA did import some goods directly from Great Britain, but the proportion at first was very small. Indeed, as Figure 3.4 shows, Belize controlled between 90 and 100 per cent of the value of Central American imports from the UK until the mid-1840s. As the trade was also increasing in value, always dominated by textiles but including many other products as well, it was a profitable business for the merchants located in Belize.

British control of Central America's imports via Belize was all the more impressive, given that the UK did not give diplomatic recognition to the UPCA (only consuls were sent) while the US did so, in 1825 signing a treaty of commerce, navigation and friendship and receiving trade preferences.[54]

---

[52] If each Belizean (man, woman and child) had needed ten yards in 1825 that would still only amount to 42,780 yards for domestic consumption–a drop in the ocean compared with the 4,753,625 yards actually imported.

[53] See Naylor (1988), p. 201.

[54] See Leonard (1995).

Yet the US was not yet in a position to challenge British commercial dominance, as its manufacturing sector was still small and uncompetitive.

To pay for its imports, about 75 per cent of which came from the UK, the UPCA exported a small number of raw materials. The most important were indigo, cochineal, sarsaparilla and–from Costa Rica after 1832–coffee. These were never enough to cover all the costs of imports, so there was also an outflow of *specie* (especially silver coins) to cover the difference. These exports, with one exception,[55] also passed through Belize from where they could be re-exported. If imported by the UK, as almost all the raw materials were, they paid only the preferential imperial tariff despite the fact that Belize was not a colony and that the goods originated in Central America.

The Belize re-export business, or entrepôt trade as it should be called, was enormously important for the settlement after 1820 and dwarfed the value of commodity exports (logwood and mahogany). The first beneficiaries were the small number of merchants already based in Belize, but they were soon joined by merchants from Great Britain. The companies established by these British merchants before 1830 included Campbell & Young, Woodburn & Noro and Angus, Andrew & Miller.[56]

The established Belize merchants included Marshall Bennett, John Waldron Wright, William Gentle, George Gibson, Charles Evans, James Hyde, George Hyde, William Hall, William Walsh, Thomas Pickstock and John Samuel August.[57] The most important of these was Marshall Bennett, who had moved to Belize in 1787 and would go on to become not only the richest man in the settlement, with interests in mahogany, shipping and trade, but would also build a fortune in Central America through trade and real estate.[58] He was so wealthy that a ship of 353 tons was even built in Liverpool in 1820 and named after him, although he did not own it.[59]

The Belize merchants then influenced decision-making through the Public Assembly and the magistracy. Indeed, in many cases they *were* the decision-makers. Marshall Bennett, for example, was elected annually to the magistracy in every year between 1816 and 1829 and was the chief magistrate for most of the 1820s. Their influence was used to ensure that the interests of the Belize merchants were given priority over all others. This

---

[55] The one exception was coffee, whose export was limited to Costa Rica in the first half of the 19th century. This coffee had to be shipped to Costa Rica's Pacific coast, from where it made its way to Europe via Cabo de Hornos at the tip of South America.

[56] See Naylor (1988), pp. 105-106.

[57] See Naylor (1988), p. 107.

[58] See Naylor (1995). For an unflattering portrait of Bennett and Wright, see Low (1824).

[59] See Naylor (1988), p. 267, n.40.

meant not only discriminating against foreign merchants, but also those that had recently arrived from the UK.

The discrimination against foreigners was done through manipulation of tariffs and had widespread support. The discrimination against British merchant houses was more tricky; one strategy was to impose a tax on goods imported into Belize if the consignee was resident in the UK. This led to a power struggle with the Superintendent, which was only resolved in the 1830s when Lieutenant-Colonel Cockburn was able to remove all restrictions against the British merchants.[60] This may have been one of the reasons why Marshall Bennett moved to Central America, from where he oversaw his operations in Belize and elsewhere.

The conflicts between the British authorities and the Baymen were well illustrated by Superintendent Colonel Arthur in 1822 when handing over to the Acting Superintendent Major General Pye. Arthur wrote:[61]

> You will observe my Proclamation dated 10th May, 1815, prohibited by orders from Home any Trade except such as admitted in the West India Islands. On a subsequent representation to the Earl of Bathurst this restriction was removed and a free trade granted. A few of the principal Merchants have since endeavoured to close this Trade, as they find it excludes the possibility of their demanding such exhorbitant prices as formerly for their goods; but in behalf of the poorer class of Cutters and Community at large, I have always felt it my duty to resist their scheme. The plausible plea which the Merchants set up is the benefit of the Mother Country but which I may venture to affirm they regard not one straw!

Although there was a small trade between Belize and Omoa on the north coast of Honduras, the main route for the re-export trade to Central America was from Belize through the Rio Dulce, leading to Gualan on the Lago de Izabal where the UPCA customs house was located. As this was some distance from the coast, there was plenty of scope for contraband in order to avoid paying customs duties. Import tariffs, the main source of revenue, were not at first very high, but they were raised steadily in the first decade of the UPCA's existence.[62] From the customs house, British manufactures were then taken by mule to the Guatemalan highlands from where they were distributed to other parts of Central America.[63]

---

[60] See Naylor (1988), pp. 61-62.

[61] See Burdon (1934), p. 260.

[62] The figures for the entrepôt trade come from British sources, so they are not affected by any subsequent contraband between Belize and Central America.

[63] Although this journey could take weeks, the cost of these imports was about one-tenth of what Central Americans had paid during the colonial period. In addition, the price of British textiles was steadily falling.

The re-export trade from Central America to Belize followed the same route in reverse. As there were various forms of discrimination against ships belonging to citizens of the UPCA by the Belize settlement, this coastal trade was largely controlled by British and Belizean merchants. Indeed, in this period there was a thriving ship-building business in Belize. These ships, however, had to be able to navigate the shallow coastal waters as well as rivers, so that the largest was no more than 160 tons and most were much smaller.[64]

The entrepôt trade affected almost all dimensions of the Belizean economy. In addition to strengthening the merchant class, making it dominant within the small elite, the entrepôt trade led to a concentration on trade with the UK. This was inevitable, given that Central American exports routed though Belize were destined to the British market, while the Belizean imports re-exported to Central America all came from the UK. However, it was also underpinned by the efforts–ultimately unsuccessful–of the Superintendent to try to apply British Navigation Acts to Belize.[65] The US share of Belizean trade had fallen to around five per cent by 1830, but it soon recovered and had reached 25 per cent of imports and 15 per cent of exports by 1850.[66]

Before the 1820s, Belize had used Jamaican currency. This stood at a 40 per cent discount to sterling, although confusingly both currencies often carried the same symbol (£).[67] The entrepôt trade brought a flood of silver coins to Belize to pay for the difference between Central American imports and exports. These coins were mainly from Mexico and Central America, but some came from as far away as Chile and Peru. The reason for this was that some goods destined for Europe were shipped down the Pacific coast by Central American merchants, who were then paid in the silver coins of the South American republics.[68] In any case, by 1838 Queen Victoria felt obliged to

---

[64] See *Honduras Almanack* (1830).

[65] These laws included a restatement of the exclusion of US shipping from British Caribbean ports in 1826. No US ships arrived in Belize between 1827 and 1829. See Martin (1834), pp. 488-89, and *Honduras Gazette*, May 26, 1827 (available as a Google book). However, the Baymen were then able to use their control of the magistracy and Public Assembly to ensure that British shipping laws once again did not apply to Belize.

[66] See Bulmer-Thomas (2012), Tables A.20 and A.27.

[67] The premium could go as high as 66%, as when £5 Jamaican currency was considered the same as £3 sterling, since the rates offered by merchants fluctuated considerably. See Naylor (1988), p. 69, and Bristowe and Wright (1890), p. 205.

[68] Two of these, the Peruvian and Chilean *sol*, would in due course lead all silver coins in Belize to be called *sol*.

issue a proclamation declaring all coins of the neighbouring republics to be legal tender.[69]

Before the mid-1840s there was no real threat to the Belizean domination of the entrepôt trade with Central America. However, at that point several things changed and the Belizean share of the trade started to fall. This can be seen very clearly in the case of British exports to Central America in Figure 3.4, but it applied also to the exports of Central America to the UK.

There were several reasons for this. First, the elimination by the UK in the 1840s of imperial preference and the reduction of tariffs, in many cases to zero, meant that Central America no longer had an incentive to route its exports through Belize. One of these exports was coffee, which had never gone through Belize. As other countries joined Costa Rica in exporting coffee, they also shipped their coffee directly to Europe and North America without the need to use Belize merchants.

Secondly, the dissolution after 1838 of the UPCA meant that five new republics would take its place in the next ten years. None of the smaller countries wanted to be as dependent on Guatemala as they had been before, especially now that tariffs on intra-regional imports were being imposed, so they looked for direct trade routes. When in 1848 Britain occupied San Juan (Greytown) on the Mosquito Shore, she established a regular shipping connection that did not pass through Belize and could be easily used by Costa Rica and Nicaragua. Meanwhile Guatemala, Honduras and El Salvador made use of their Pacific ports to establish more regular connections with Europe and North America.

The third reason was the opening of the Panama railroad in 1855. The US had negotiated a treaty with Colombia some years before that allowed for US investment in a trans-isthmian route. Although the railway fell short of the ambitions of those who hoped to see an inter-oceanic canal, it still provided a new opportunity for Central American countries to trade with the rest of the world without passing through Belize.

The Belize entrepôt trade did not end, but it declined in importance after 1840 (see Figure 3.5). At that point, re-exports were nearly three times more in value than domestic exports (almost entirely logwood and mahogany). After Belize became a colony in 1862, re-exports continued to fall in value and their composition would change. The new commodities would be forest products (logwood, mahogany and chicle) extracted from the forests of Mexico and Guatemala, shipped to Belize and re-exported to the rest of the world.

The three decades after 1820 were ones of exceptional prosperity for the settlement—at least for the free population. Merchandise exports (domestic

---

[69] See Bristowe and Wright (1890), p. 205.

Figure 3.5: Belize exports (US$000), 1820-1900

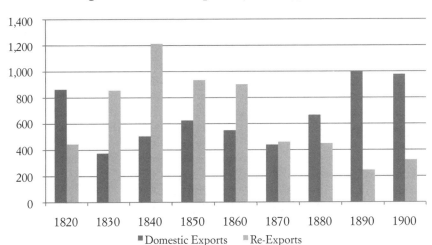

Domestic Exports   Re-Exports

Source: Bulmer-Thomas (2012), Tables A.11 and A.12.

plus re-exports) were very high for such a small country. Indeed, merchandise exports per head were the highest in all the Caribbean. Even if the comparison is limited to domestic exports per head, Belize still had by far the highest figure for most of these years. And the high value of domestic exports meant that retained imports (for domestic consumption) were also very large.[70]

This would turn out to be the boom before the bust. The profits made from timber exports and the entrepôt trade tended not to stay in the country. Marshall Bennett was not the only member of the elite to take his fortune and invest it elsewhere. The British authorities, mindful of the terms of the Anglo-Spanish treaties, refused for many years to permit the development of agriculture. As a result, there was no incentive to improve infrastructure. There was therefore no model of accumulation despite the capitalist nature of the system. The prosperity of the settlement in the first half of the 19th century would turn out to be largely an illusion.

Society

The census of 22nd October 1790, taken soon after the arrival of the evacuees from the Mosquito Shore, had revealed a population of 2,656 of which 76 per cent were slaves and 24 per cent free. The latter were then disaggregated into "whites" (10 per cent) and "free people of colour" (14 per cent).

---

[70] Derived from Bulmer-Thomas (2012), Tables A.1a, A.11, A.13, A.23 and A.25.

Table 3.1: Population in 1861

Ethnicity		Place of birth	
Whites	887	Belize	10,937
Spaniards (a)	1,713	UK	173
Indians	4,675	Jamaica	362
Crossbreeds	8,060	Barbados	179
Africans	2,528	Other British Colonies	443
Mulattos	4,032	East Indies	12
Sambos	841	USA	55
Caribs	1,825	Central America	2,346
Crossbreeds	560	Yucatan	9,817
Europeans	258	Western Europe	102
Chinese	7	Africa	894
Coolies	9	China	1
Not Stated (b)	240	Other places	314
Total	25,635	**Total**	25,635

Source: Bristowe and Wright (1890), p. 218.
(a) Source states "Not the pure Spaniard, but the Spaniard of Central America"; (b) source gives number as 215, but this has been rounded up so that the sum of the entries is the same as the total.

It was a class structure that was fairly typical of the Caribbean at the time, the main difference being that not all of the slaves were of African descent. These other slaves had come to Belize from the Mosquito Shore with their owners—despite the fact that by the end of the 18th century British practice, if not British law, ruled out the enslavement of the indigenous population of the Americas. This would lead to a long-running battle between the slave owners and the Superintendent that was only resolved in the 1820s when the British authorities gave an unequivocal ruling on the illegality of the practice.[71]

Estimates of the population were then made at various intervals up to 1861, when—in the last year before the settlement became a colony—a complete census was taken. This showed not only that the population had increased almost ten-fold since 1790, but also that the composition had changed out of all recognition. In place of the relatively simple class structure after the

---

[71] Even this was not an end of the matter as in 1830 the British government paid £7,890 as compensation to the owners for the indigenous slaves seized by Colonel Arthur some years before. See Burdon (1934), p. 322.

evacuation of the Mosquito Shore, there had emerged a complex mosaic that would become the template for the future.

The 1861 census, the first to include the Maya, used two categories. The first, relatively uncontroversial, was based on place of birth. The second was based on ethnicity and used a typology that is offensive to modern readers, but which is very revealing of colonial thinking. Both categories are shown here (see Table 3.1). In addition, the census disaggregated the population by three regions (Belize or Central District, Northern District and Southern District).

The largest group in 1861 was those born in Belize (10,937), although they were only 40 per cent of the total. The majority of this group consisted of ex-slaves or descendants of former slaves and they included the "Africans", "Mulattos" and "Sambos" in the first column of Table 3.1. The number of these "creoles", as they would later be called, had increased considerably since 1790 although they were now a much smaller share of the population.

The growth in their number was in some ways surprising, given what had happened since 1790. First, many slaves escaped across the borders.[72] Not only were they not returned, but the Spanish authorities strongly encouraged their flight from Belize. And the incentives to flee became stronger when slavery was abolished by the UPCA in 1824 and by Mexico in 1829. Nor is there much evidence that these escaped slaves returned to Belize after emancipation.

Secondly, the abolition in 1808 of the slave trade by the UK, which did apply to Belize despite the protests of some of the owners, meant that the change in the size of the slave population was largely determined by the difference between births and deaths.[73] In most of the Caribbean, slave deaths exceeded births–often by a large margin–so that the slave population in those countries fell after abolition. In Belize, however, slave births exceeded deaths in the three decades leading up to emancipation and net births in Belize remained positive thereafter.

Thirdly, following the emancipation of the slaves in 1834 and the end of the apprenticeship period in 1838, Belize did not receive large numbers of indentured labourers from India or China, as happened in other British colonies such as British Guiana, Jamaica and Trinidad. However, Belize did receive a number of *emancipados* in the 1830s. These were Africans who had been brought illegally as slaves to the Caribbean, but who had been inter-

---

[72] The treatment of slaves may not have been as harsh in Belize as in the sugar islands, but there were still several slave revolts and plenty of evidence of cruelty. See Bolland (1977), pp. 72-76.

[73] The other determinant of the size of the slave population was the rate of manumissions, which was similar in Belize to that in other countries.

cepted by the British navy. In addition, a number of workers came freely from other Caribbean islands–especially Barbados and Jamaica.

Despite the growth in the absolute size of the Creole population, the large employers still assumed that only coercion would ensure a regular supply of labour for timber extraction after emancipation. This led to the introduction of the "advance" and "truck" systems that would leave many workers in perpetual debt. Begun as informal labour practices by the employers, the system would be enshrined into law in 1846 with the blessing of the Superintendent and would not be abolished until the 20th century.[74]

The second largest group in 1861 consisted of the immigrants from Central America and the Yucatan peninsula, who together numbered 12,163. This group corresponded roughly to those listed in Table 3.1 as "Spaniards", "Indians" and "Crossbreeds". Most had come from Yucatan as refugees during the *Guerra de Castas* that had erupted in 1847 and would continue for more than 50 years. Others had come from Guatemala, where anti-vagrancy laws were very burdensome for those without property or unable to pay the fines to escape forced labour on public works.

The members of this group tended not to work in the timber extraction industry, but to concentrate instead on small-scale farming in the northern half of the country. Access to land was secured through squatting since purchase or lease was very difficult. They produced food for themselves and for sale, but the poor quality of the infrastructure in Belize meant that it was difficult to bring it to market. However, in the 1850s the first exports of coconuts took place from Belize. There was also one shipment of sugar (in 1857) as a result of efforts by Yucatecan immigrants to bring their knowledge of sugar cultivation to Belize, although sugar exports on a regular basis would not begin until 1862.

The third largest group in 1861 was the Garifuna ("Caribs" in Table 3.1), most of whom had been born in Belize. Their journey from St. Vincent to Roatan in 1797 and onwards to the mainland of Central America has been well documented.[75] The first Garifuna reached Belize early in the 19th century. As with the previous group, access to land could only be achieved through squatting, but as they settled in the south this was done on what would become Crown land. The whole of the Southern District in 1861 only had 2,687 people, so the Garifuna (1,825) formed a majority.[76] Their

---

[74] This system, much criticized later in the century, has been well described by Bolland (1977), pp. 121-22. See also Gibbs (1883) and Morris (1883).

[75] See González (1988), Chapter 2.

[76] The other inhabitants of the Southern District were mainly Creoles. The Maya would not return to Toledo in significant numbers until San Antonio was founded in 1883.

Figure 3.6: Public spending (US$), 1808-1862 (3-year average)

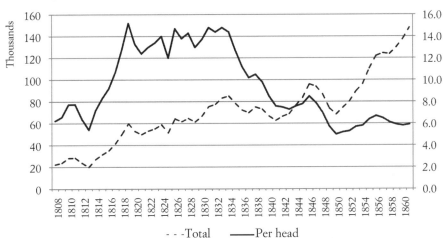

- - -Total   ——Per head

Source: Bulmer-Thomas (2012), Chapter 11.

villages were either on, or close to, the seashore where subsistence farming was combined with fishing and hunting.

The final group in 1861 was the small number who constituted the commercial elite of the settlement. This group included almost all the "whites" and "Europeans" in Table 3.1 as well as the descendants of the "free people of colour" enumerated in 1790. Most of this group had been born in Belize, although a few had come from outside. By this time, on the eve of colonisation, they had lost the dominant position they had once had in the decision-making process. However, they were still politically influential and exercised considerable economic power. Members of this group controlled–directly or indirectly–the private land of the settlement and constituted the elected membership of the Legislative Assembly that had replaced the Public Meeting in 1854.

Until then, the commercial elite had overseen public revenue through their control of taxation and had taken most decisions on public spending. The settlement's revenue was derived directly or indirectly from taxes on trade (customs duties, tonnage and port charges, etc.). As trade increased, so did public revenue. And, as revenue expanded, so did public expenditure. From the time that public spending figures were first published in 1807, until the settlement became the colony of British Honduras in 1862, the level of public expenditure increased six-fold (see Figure 3.6).

In *per capita* terms, public revenue and expenditure were also high–at least by comparison with the rest of the Caribbean.[77] However, they were

---

[77] Derived from Bulmer-Thomas (2012), Tables A.1a, A.33 and A.37.

not nearly as high as might have been expected from the level of exports per head. The reason for this was very simple. The Public Meeting controlled revenue and the Baymen–merchants and cutters–had no desire to tax themselves any more than was strictly necessary. Indeed, with very few exceptions, no holder of public office received a salary until the 1840s.[78] Public spending therefore did not keep pace with population growth and started to fall on a *per capita* basis after 1834 (see Figure 3.6).

The Baymen's responsibility for raising revenue meant that public spending was tightly controlled during the years before the Public Meeting was abolished. If we take the period 1824-35, when detailed figures on expenditure are available, we find that about 50 per cent of spending ("other") went on miscellaneous administrative costs and one-off items (see Figure 3.7).[79] The next most important item was public works, which consisted mainly of repair and maintenance in Belize town. This was followed by the salary of the Superintendent, which almost doubled after 1829, and the costs of the military.[80] The next item in importance consisted of payments to the London agent, whose activities on behalf of the settlers has been noted above.

These items constituted 92.5 per cent of total spending between 1824 and 1835–years of great prosperity in the settlement. That left little for public services such as religion, health and education (see Figure 3.7). The consecration of St. John's Cathedral in 1812, however, not only boosted the fortunes of the Anglican Church, but also paved the way for the foundation of the Honduras Free School in 1816 that was paid for at public expense.[81] Although limited at first to twelve children born of free parents, the Free School soon expanded and employed a schoolmistress as well as a schoolmaster in 1830.[82]

Schooling received a boost in the settlement with the arrival first of the English Baptist Church in 1822 and the Methodists in 1829. The Roman Catholic Church would arrive in 1851 in response to the immigration of many Catholics from Mexico and Central America. All these churches ran primary schools that competed with the Anglican Honduran Free School

---

[78] The main exception was the Superintendent.

[79] These included £194 in 1829 to Marshall Bennett, the richest man in the settlement, to cover the costs of his trip to England in 1825.

[80] At this time, there was a militia made up of Belizean volunteers (it was abolished in 1850). There was also a British West Indian Regiment whose costs were met by the metropolitan government. See Fairweather (1970). The military expenditure in Figure 3.7 therefore refers to the militia.

[81] See Bennett (2008), p. 10.

[82] Students of gender discrimination may wish to know that in that year (1830) the schoolmaster was paid £315 while the schoolmistress received £36!

Figure 3.7: Share of public spending (%), 1824-1835

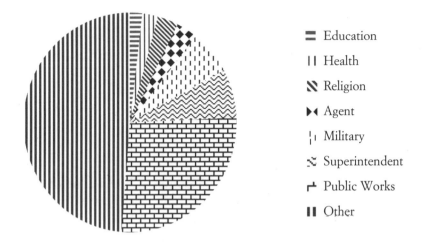

- ▬ Education
- || Health
- ◧ Religion
- ▶◀ Agent
- ¦¦ Military
- ≋ Superintendent
- ⌐ Public Works
- || Other

Source: Derived from Colonial Department (1836).

(known as the Honduras Grammar School in the 1840s).[83] As late as 1853, however, there were still only 631 pupils at all schools–equivalent to four per cent of the population.[84]

Public revenue and spending did rise sharply after the Public Meeting was replaced by the Legislative Assembly in 1854 (see Figure 3.6). However, it still barely kept pace with population growth, so the "British Settlement in the Bay of Honduras" came to an end without having addressed many of the structural weaknesses inherited from before the Anglo-Spanish treaties. There was still no internal market of any consequence, an infrastructure that was wholly inadequate and no incentive to accumulate capital inside the country other than through further timber extraction. As a result, mahogany cutting had proceeded at a rate that was not sustainable. Only logwood would remain in abundance and this traditional commodity would become the main economic pillar of the new colony of British Honduras in its first four decades.

---

[83] See Bennett (2008), Chapter 1.
[84] See Bulmer-Thomas (2012), Table A.7.

4. The Colony: 1862-1981

The British Settlement in the Bay of Honduras became the colony of British Honduras in 1862. The Superintendent was replaced by a Lieutenant-Governor who reported to the Governor of Jamaica. Although the Lieutenant-Governor was replaced by a Governor in 1884, no longer reporting to Jamaica, Belize had by then become a Crown Colony (in 1871) with no elected members of the legislature. In terms of representative democracy Belize, it would seem, had gone backwards since during its time as a settlement it had been to some extent self-governing.

The political economy of the colony was, however, much more complicated than this brief description of constitutional change implied. The local elites may have lost their ability to control the settlement's affairs through the Public Meeting, but they still dominated the Legislative Assembly that took its place in 1854 and neither the Lieutenant-Governor–nor later the Governor–could afford to ignore their wishes any more than the Superintendent. The first part of the chapter is therefore devoted to the political economy of the colony in the first decades after its establishment.

Far from ushering in a period of renewed prosperity, colonialism proved to be an uninspiring experience. The second part of this chapter therefore examines the decline of the economy up to 1900 as a result of the stagnation of mahogany exports, strict fiscal control and the reduction in the size of the entrepôt trade. Official efforts to shift the basis of the economy towards agriculture were thwarted by the structure of private landholdings, the dismal state of infrastructure and a lack of vision by the imperial government. Sugar and rum exports did begin in the 1860s, but they barely survived the collapse of sugar prices in 1883-84 and banana exports after 1880 could not fully compensate.

There was a brief revival in the fortunes of the colony in the first years of the 20th century, but this came to an abrupt end in 1914. The third part of the chapter then examines the fall of the economy during an extremely difficult period that culminated with devaluation at the end of 1949. These years included the end of logwood exports, the decline of the banana industry through disease and the emergence for the first time of surplus labour. There were riots in Belize on several occasions during this period and the authorities were forced to take steps that would eventually help the colony to shift away from forestry.

The final part of the chapter examines the diversification of the economy and the rise of non-traditional exports up to independence in 1981. The story begins with the devaluation of the Belize dollar on 31 December 1949 despite the repeated promises of the colonial authorities that it would remain pegged to the US dollar (as it had been since 1894). Devaluation, however, did help the country to promote exports other than forest products and Belize started to become a more diversified economy, although it was not until after independence that the infrastructure improved significantly and the Belizean economy acquired its modern character.

Appendix 2 is devoted to the Belize Estate & Produce Company (BEC). Formed out of the British Honduras Company in 1875, the BEC would play as dominant a role in the affairs of the colony as the United Fruit Company (UFCO) did in some of the neighbouring countries. Its influence on decision-making was unrivalled both because of its strong position in Belize, but also because of its powerful board of directors based in the UK with access to the British government.

The political economy of colonialism

When Superintendent Colonel Despard reached Belize in 1786, the British Empire–having lost the thirteen colonies that would become the USA a few years before–was reduced to the Canadian provinces, a few Caribbean islands and Gibraltar (New South Wales in Australia would not be colonised until the next year). There were no colonies in Africa and Asia (if the special case of India, which was ruled by the East India Co., is excluded). Although Belize was not yet a colony, it was a British settlement and received more metropolitan attention than might have been expected from its size alone. This was due both to its geopolitical importance and to the fact that there were still relatively few British possessions.

When Belize became a colony in 1862, the British Empire was very different. India, with some 250 million inhabitants, had become the jewel in the imperial crown in 1858, all of Australia had been colonised along with New Zealand, there was a wide variety of possessions in Asia and new colonies had been added in the Caribbean. Furthermore, many new colonies would soon be added in Africa to the South African provinces, Sierra Leone and Mauritius, which were already under British control. The chances of British Honduras receiving any serious attention were therefore minimal. Furthermore, British colonies were expected to be self-sufficient so metropolitan subsidies would only be available under exceptional circumstances.

Why therefore had the Belizean elites agreed–even pushed–to become a colony? The answers are complex, but have a great deal to do with the need for access to metropolitan capital, property rights and defence. Those cutters and merchants with no British commercial connections struggled to survive in the downward phases of the business cycle. Without colonisation, it would have been very difficult to convert "locations" into secure freeholds protected by laws recognized outside the country. And without imperial guarantees, the burden of defending the country–at a time when the boundary with Mexico was still undefined–would have fallen on the settlers. Indeed, in the year Belize became a colony, the *Guerra de Castas* was in full swing with the conflict threatening properties and lives in British Honduras.[1]

The Belizean elites must still have had some reservations about becoming a colony, but they would have taken heart from their skill in outmanoeuvring the Superintendent on numerous occasions through their control of the Public Meeting and later domination of the Legislative Assembly. They had suffered setbacks, as happened when "Indian" slavery had been outlawed in the 1820s, when election of magistrates was ended in 1832 and when the area south of the Sibun River was declared Crown land. However, they had secured very favourable trade treatment by Britain, their labour practices had been enshrined in law and they had received recognition of *de facto* title to their timber works north of the Sibun River.

No doubt most of them assumed that the new colonial representative would be equally subject to persuasion especially as they controlled the vast majority of the seats on the Legislative Assembly. However, they had not anticipated the full impact of the *Guerra de Castas* and the insistence by Britain that the colony contribute more to its own defence. Reluctantly, the elected members of the Legislative Assembly–all representatives of the elites–agreed in 1867 to a temporary land tax. When it became clear that the tax would need both to increase and to become permanent, in December 1870 they voted to abolish themselves. The result was the establishment of a Crown Colony government the following year with a Legislative Council that had no elected members–the *quid pro quo* being the imperial government taking more responsibility for defence.[2]

---

[1] The timber companies found themselves at the centre of the conflict because of their operations in the north and north-west of the colony. The boundary with Mexico was not finally settled until 1893.
[2] See Bolland (1977), pp. 191-92.

The elites were now reduced to five seats on the Council with all members nominated by the Crown's representative. These unofficial members were equal in number to the officials, so they still had some influence provided they spoke with one voice. This duly happened in 1890 when the "unofficials" walked out of the Council and no business could be conducted. The Colonial Office was obliged to establish a majority of unofficials on the Council in 1892 and business was resumed. From this point until 1932, when the Council was stripped of its fiscal powers, the unofficials exercised much more power than was normal in a British Crown Colony.[3]

The ability of the Governor to carry out imperial policies that ran counter to the interests of the elites therefore depended very largely on splits within the elites themselves. Divisions certainly existed, since some Baymen were mainly reliant on forestry extraction while others depended more on their role as merchants. The former were therefore opposed to a land tax, while the latter resisted high import tariffs. However, these divisions should not be exaggerated. The key members of the elites had interests in both–with the three largest landowners all being engaged in trade as well (see Table 4.1).

The most important interest for the colonial elites was establishing freeholds on the lands acquired through locations. Indeed, the first act of the Legislative Assembly established in 1854 was to recognize the previous usufruct rights as land titles. This, however, had no force in law outside Belize. Metropolitan connections were therefore mobilised and the Honduras Land Titles Act received the royal assent in 1859. This stimulated the interest of foreign capitalists with several British merchants establishing landowning firms in partnership with members of the Belizean elite.[4]

The landowners had other interests as well. They needed labour and this, they were convinced, could only be forthcoming if the imperial government agreed to three things: first, to maintain the draconian restrictions on workers enshrined in the settlement's labour laws; secondly, to ensure that Crown land was only made available in large parcels so that workers would not have the option of becoming small-scale farmers; and, thirdly, to encourage immigration schemes that increased the pool of labour.

With some qualifications, the imperial government met all these demands–to the huge detriment of the colony's long-run development. The labour laws were not seriously reformed until the 1920s, by which time Belize–in common with the most of the Caribbean–had a surplus rather than a shortage of labour. Crown land was not generally sold or leased in small

---

[3] The only major study on this is Ashdown (1979). This outstanding piece of research has not been readily available to Belizean scholars as it was previously unpublished. However, it is now available in digital form through the British Library.

[4] See Bolland and Shoman (1977), Chapter 3.

Table 4.1: Land ownership and merchant houses, 1896

Company	Status	Acres owned	% of Private land	Merchant house	Foundation year
BEC	Expatriate	1,109,540	36.1	Yes	1875
Bernard Cramer	Expatriate	179,840	5.8	Yes	1880
Mutrie, Arthur and Currie	Expatriate	152,650	5.0	Yes	?
R. Byass	Expatriate	135,400	4.4	No	NA
Burn Family	Creole	124,800	4.1	No	NA
Stevens Bros.	Expatriate	48,000	1.6	Yes	?
M.F. Wade	Creole	38,400	1.2	No	NA
E.A.H. Scholfield	Expatriate	32,000	1.0	No	NA
Rabon Bros	Expatriate	25,600	0.8	No	NA
Gabourel & Smith	Creole	21,120	0.7	No	NA
F. Escalante	Mestizo	20,480	0.7	No	NA
Wardlaw & Usher	Creole	17,280	0.6	No	NA
Mrs. Bowen	Creole	17,280	0.6	No	NA
Mrs. Usher	Creole	17,280	0.6	No	NA
P.H. Brinton	Expatriate	15,360	0.5	No	NA
M.J. Castillo	Creole	12,800	0.4	No	NA
W. Binney & Co.	Expatriate	9,600	0.3	Yes	?
John Harley	Expatriate	9,600	0.3	Yes	1864
C.T. Hunter	Expatriate	9,600	0.3	No	NA
James Brodie	Expatriate	NA	NA	Yes	1887
Beattic & Co.	Expatriate	NA	NA	Yes	?
John Gentle & Co	Expatriate	NA	NA	Yes	?
Cuthbert Bros.	Expatriate	NA	NA	Yes	1887
A. Williamson	Expatriate	NA	NA	Yes	?
Krug and Oswald	Expatriate	NA	NA	Yes	?
C. Pahmeyer	Expatriate	NA	NA	Yes	?
Hofius and Hildebrandt	Expatriate	NA	NA	Yes	1892
Henry Gansz	Expatriate	NA	NA	Yes	1853
W.G. Aikman	Expatriate	NA	NA	Yes	?
Morlans	Expatriate	NA	NA	Yes	1893

Source: Derived from Ashdown (1979), Tables 1-4, pp. 24-27.
Note: Acres owned, except for the four largest, are based on the northern districts only.

plots, while the infrastructure needed to stimulate agricultural development was not put in place. Finally, numerous immigration schemes were adopted that brought Chinese, Indian and Caribbean workers to Belize.

The cutters and the merchants also had a common interest in a more stable currency after the silver price of gold started to fall in the 1870s. The adoption of the Guatemalan peso as the colony's sole legal currency in 1887 had only exacerbated the problem as it was based on silver. The issue was finally resolved with the adoption of the British Honduran dollar in 1894, at par with the US dollar. This put Belize on the gold standard and, although it was clumsily done, it saved the colony from the massive currency devaluations and high inflation experienced by the neighbouring countries.

The one area where there was division between the cutters and merchants was on the issue of taxation. The landowners were viscerally opposed to a land tax, while the merchants had no objection. However, the more important merchants also owned large tracts of land so that the division between the two was not so deep. The elites could not completely block the introduction of a permanent land tax after the adoption of Crown Colony rule, but they were able to ensure that it was applied at a very low rate and never raised much revenue.

Indeed, the major elite division in Belize was not so much between merchants and cutters as between those members of the elites who were expatriates and those who were not. In this respect, the expatriates had a huge advantage. They had access to capital on much better terms than the locals; they could influence imperial policy in London; and they knew the foreign markets better than most of the locals. While the main export and import market was the UK, the British expatriates were in an exceptionally strong position. However, this began to change in the 1890s when trade shifted towards the USA–helped in part by the change in the currency in 1894. This brought US companies interested in new activities such as chicle and bananas to Belize, where they joined firms already operating logwood and mahogany works.

These US entrepreneurs, not being UK subjects, could not sit in the Legislative Assembly–unlike their British counterparts. They therefore needed allies. A subtle shift in power therefore took place among the expatriate interests that was perhaps best illustrated in 1935 when the representative of the BEC (by far the largest landowner–see Table 4.1) was defeated in his bid to retain his seat by Robert Sydney Turton, a Belizean businessman with strong connections to US companies.[5]

This shift of power did not unduly trouble the imperial government. Imperial preference had been reintroduced by Britain in 1919, thereby end-

---

[5] See Ashdown (1979), p. 220.

ing the experiment in free trade policies for which Britain had been famous in the 19th century and giving Belizean exporters to the UK an advantage. Belize had done the same and this had given British exporters to Belize an advantage over their US competitors. Furthermore, the colony was subject to Treasury control from 1932 until after the Second World War, giving the metropolitan government unprecedented control over the colony's affairs.

In 1950, however, nationalist politicians erupted onto the scene with the birth of the People's United Party (PUP). The political economy of the colony changed completely with the Colonial Office now pitted against representatives of the masses rather than the elites. With the introduction of universal franchise in 1954, the stage was set for the demise of British colonialism. This would have come in the 1960s–a century after the creation of the colony–if it had not been for the Guatemalan claim that delayed independence until 1981.

Colonialism and economic decline: 1860-1900

One of the first problems the new colony had to address was the wave of migration from the Yucatan peninsula after 1847. This was a consequence of the *Guerra de Castas*, which was to last half a century and involved not only a struggle between the Maya, the landowners and the Mexican state, but also major conflicts between the different Maya groups.[6] Without an officially recognized boundary between Belize and Mexico, the conflict spread across the border on many occasions while thousands of Yucatec chose to make their home in northern Belize as both economic and political refugees.

There was no official population figure after 1845 until 1861. However, contemporary estimates suggested the population had jumped to nearly 20,000 by 1857 and the 1861 census confirmed a figure in excess of 25,000. For a country that had recorded a population of less than 4,000 in 1816, this was a huge increase; yet it did not bring an end to the scarcity of labour as most of the new arrivals became squatters on private land and concentrated on subsistence agriculture. Indeed, within a few years of the census, the colony was importing indentured labour from China and India as well as workers from Barbados (with very disappointing results in all cases).[7]

A large part of the problem was the low natural rate of growth of the population. Although births had exceeded deaths among the slave popula-

---

[6] See Reed (1964) and Dumond (1997).

[7] Many of the Chinese were so badly treated that they fled across the border and joined the Santa Cruz Maya in Mexico. See Bolland (1977), p. 143.

tion just before emancipation, it was only by a small margin.[8] This low birth rate almost certainly continued for many decades so that the increase in population was mainly due to the inward migration from Mexico and Guatemala.[9] Furthermore, when reliable figures on births and deaths became available from 1886 onwards, it suggested that the natural rate of growth was still close to zero.[10] It was only after 1894 that the births finally exceeded deaths by a significant margin.

Under these circumstances British officials saw no reason to relax the policy of restricting access to land that the Colonial Office–and the private landholders–had exercised even before the establishment of the colony. Crown lands in the south were not at first made available in small parcels at low prices while private lands in the north were almost never sold to small farmers. Colonial policy was therefore in line with that preferred by the large landowners, who complained constantly of a shortage of labour despite the growth of population and who restricted access to their own land as vigorously as possible. Furthermore, when more enlightened Governors[11] explored the possibility of relaxing this land policy, the Colonial Office in London firmly overruled them.

Landholdings had been highly concentrated even before the last of the Anglo-Spanish treaties in 1786. It would continue to be concentrated after the establishment of the colony. By this time (c. 1860) it had become normal for exporters in Belize to have associations with merchants in the UK and in one case this had been formalised in a London-quoted company established under the provisions of the 1856 British legislation permitting limited liability. This enterprise, the British Honduras Company, was formed in 1859 and from the moment of its creation owned well in excess of one million acres of freehold land.[12] Its access to capital in London helped it not only to weather the mahogany crisis at the end of the 1860s, but also to buy

---

[8] As elsewhere in the Caribbean, male slaves in Belize outnumbered females before the abolition of the slave trade and slave deaths at first exceeded births. However, on the eve of emancipation net births had become positive.

[9] There was actually a small fall in the population between the 1861 and 1871 census.

[10] Before 1886, the number of deaths was based on recorded burials and gives an implausibly low figure. On the other hand the number of births, based on baptisms, was very high. It is only from 1886 onwards that the colony collected accurate figures and these suggested that annual births and deaths were at first roughly the same.

[11] When Belize became a colony in 1862, it was made a dependency of Jamaica so that the senior British official was called Lieutenant-Governor. It was only in 1884 that Belize ceased to be a dependency of Jamaica and the senior official became the Governor.

[12] This was about one-fifth of the whole colony. See Bolland (1977), pp. 186-87.

Figure 4.1: Belize, volume of logwood and mahogany exports, 1856-1900

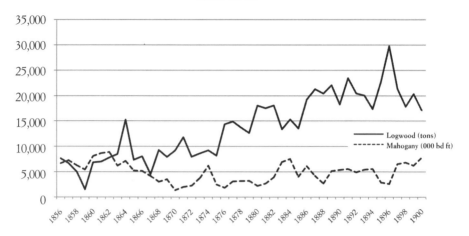

Sources: See Bulmer-Source: Thomas (2012), Appendix to Chapter 11.

out many of its competitors. When it became in 1875 the Belize Estate & Produce Company, the BEC would own more than one-third of all freehold land in the country (see Table 4.1).

The BEC, like General Motors in the US in the 20th century, considered its interests synonymous with that of the country as a whole and colonial officials saw no reason to disagree. Its influence on colonial policy included not only land and labour, but also taxation and the exchange rate. It was represented in all the colonial assemblies and could count on direct access to the Governor. Furthermore, it was influential in the UK through its shareholders and at least one of its directors sat in parliament for many years, so that the British government had to take heed of its interests as well. It is fair to say that BEC played just as crucial (and generally malign) a role in Belize during the first century of colonialism as did UFCO in Central America in the first decades after its formation in 1899.[13]

What BEC could not do was prevent the crisis in the mahogany industry that was brought about by the decline in demand and the fall in price after the mid-1860s. This was a consequence of the switch to iron in ships and the end of the boom in railway carriage construction in the UK. The company, therefore, switched back to logwood and other cutters followed suit (see Figure 4.1). By 1870 the value of logwood exports had overtaken that of mahogany, although both were below their levels at the beginning of the

---

[13] While there have been many excellent monographs on UFCO, there have sadly been none on BEC. Such a book needs to be written and Appendix 2 to this chapter should be seen as a first step.

century.[14] By 1890 logwood exports were worth twice as much as mahogany exports and the volume was ten times higher than in 1830. However, mahogany enjoyed a revival in the 1890s as a result of increased US demand.[15]

The mahogany crisis in the 1860s had been temporarily disguised in Belize by the boom in re-exports to the Confederacy during the US Civil War (1861-65).[16] Legal exports soared,[17] but illegal exports probably increased as well since part of the trade consisted of munitions. Britain–officially neutral in the Civil War–tried to stop the contraband, but the efforts of colonial officials were not very successful as Belizean merchants had been trading guns to the Maya insurgents in Yucatan for years and were very skilled at concealing the trade.[18]

As the re-export boom ended around 1850, officials finally concluded that the colony's long-term salvation depended on the development of agricultural exports alongside timber extraction.[19] It had been clear for years that the rate of extraction of mahogany was beyond what was sustainable in the long-run (unless conservation measures–unheard of that time–were undertaken). Belize, on the other hand, had an abundance of land suitable for agriculture. Yet the Colonial Office was unclear how to proceed and British officials missed many opportunities to promote the diversification of the economy.

The first missed opportunity had come with the arrival of migrants before the colony was even established. Neither the Garifuna nor the Yucatecans, let alone the *emancipados* or returning former slaves, were initially offered Crown lands on favourable terms so that a small-scale peasantry could not take root.[20] The minimal development in small-scale agriculture that did take place was mainly a result of squatting, but it never acquired

---

[14] See Bulmer-Thomas (2012), Table A.10.

[15] Because of the high US import duties on semi-processed products, the mahogany was shipped to the US as trees rather than as squared lumber (as happened in the case of exports to the UK).

[16] By this time, Belizean companies no longer had access to mahogany on the northern Mosquito Shore, as this area had been recognized by the UK as sovereign Honduran territory in 1860. See Naylor (1989).

[17] Merchandise exports, which include re-exports, went from US$1.4 million in 1861 to US$1.8 million in 1864 despite the fall in the value of mahogany exports during these years.

[18] See Clegern (1967), who makes use of the reports from the US Consul in Belize during these years.

[19] This was also the view of the manager of the British Honduras Company, who described in great detail the opportunities available. See *The Colony of British Honduras: its history, trade, and natural resources* (1867). A digital version of this article, largely based on a paper presented by Robert Temple to the Royal Society of Arts in 1857, can be found at http://www.jstor.org/.

[20] Crown lands were not offered to the Maya in the south either, but at least their traditional land use was not disrupted.

the same scale as in, for example, Guiana, Jamaica, Martinique or Suriname. Furthermore, these squatters were far from the town of Belize, the only significant urban centre, so that only a small marketable surplus was offered and the colony continued to depend mainly on imported foodstuffs.

The second missed opportunity came with the arrival of former Confederate soldiers after 1865, but they found the price of both private and Crown land exorbitant and most of them moved on to other countries or returned to the US.[21] At least one Governor asked permission from London to lower the price of Crown land or even make it available gratuitously, but these overtures were firmly resisted.[22] The notion of a scarcity of labour had taken such a firm hold that officials were not prepared to take any chances. A handful of Confederates did remain, however, and they helped to develop the sugar industry in the south (see next page).

The third missed opportunity was the (lack of) development of infrastructure. Private sector and colonial elites were convinced there could be no long-term development without a railway connecting Belize with Guatemala. When a US entrepreneur, Walter Regan, came with a serious offer in 1884 and surveyed a route that would have passed through the south-west corner of the colony, there was almost universal enthusiasm. However, the Colonial Office dithered as it wanted to ensure that any railway would meet the terms of the British obligation to Guatemala under the 1859 boundary treaty. The railway to Guatemala was therefore never built.[23]

Colonial officials were reluctant to use public resources to pursue developmental goals. Public revenue per head was higher than in most other British Caribbean colonies,[24] but the threat from the Yucatan meant that in many years much of this was absorbed by military expenditure. Indeed, the danger was so severe in the second half of the 1860s that the Legislative Assembly (responsible for raising taxes) abolished itself in 1870 and Crown Colony government was introduced in April 1871. This backward step had been taken to oblige the British government to absorb more of the cost of colonial defence, since the members of the Assembly had no wish for the land tax they had passed in 1867 to be anything other than temporary.[25]

---

[21] See Simmons (2001), pp. 48-53.

[22] The most famous case involved Lieutenant-Governor Austin, who had provisionally awarded a huge grant in the south to Confederate settlers, but was overruled and forced to return to London by the Colonial Office. See Simmons (2001), pp. 30-31.

[23] On railways, see Clegern (1967), pp. 72-75.

[24] Public revenue per head in Belize varied between US$6 and US$8 from 1860 to 1900. This was about 20% higher than the comparable figures for all British colonies (the numbers can be derived from Tables A.33 and A.1a in Bulmer-Thomas (2012).

[25] In this they were disappointed as the land tax was made permanent in 1871, albeit at a very low rate.

Public debt under colonialism was first issued in 1863, but it remained at very modest levels and was used primarily to make improvements to Belize town.[26] Frustration with the slow progress in infrastructure development finally persuaded the private sector to finance a tramway a few miles up the Stann Creek valley. This opened in 1892 and helped to promote banana exports (see below). When the shipping line carrying bananas was purchased by UFCO in 1900,[27] the colonial government was lobbied to build a full-scale railway down the whole length of the valley to the nearest sea port. This was built at public expense and opened in 1911, but the arrangement was far too generous to UFCO.[28]

Belize still had no all-weather roads and the 90-mile journey from Belize town to San Ignacio on the western border took many days by boat. The northern frontier was also inaccessible except by water and the south remained very isolated. Yet despite the dismal state of infrastructure, the first small steps towards export diversification had been taken by the end of the 19th century. This had little to do with colonial policy and initially had nothing to do with the landowners either, but it was very welcome and much needed all the same.

The first significant step was the establishment of a sugar industry by the Yucatecan refugees in the north of the country. While most refugees engaged in self-sufficient agriculture, a small number experimented with sugar and rum production around the town of Corozal. In 1857 the first small shipment of sugar was made, but this was not repeated until 1862. By then, the British Honduras Company had turned some of its idle lands into sugarcane plantations and the growth of sugar exports was rapid. The Confederate settlers, especially in the Toledo District, also contributed to the growth of the industry. However, Belize was not destined to become a sugar colony until after the Second World War. The sharp fall in the world price in 1883-84 undermined the industry and the value of exports declined rapidly (see Figure 4.2).

The next step was the development of a banana industry centred in the Stann Creek Valley. The first regular shipment was made in 1882 and within a few years exports had increased rapidly (see Figure 4.2). The trade was at

---

[26] In fairness, these improvements were much needed. They at first followed the recommendations made by Baron Siccama, but ended in scandal in the 1880s when Governor Goldsworthy mysteriously awarded the contract to a sworn enemy of his predecessor. See Clegern (1967), pp. 76-78.

[27] This was the Belize Royal Mail and Central America Steamship Company. See Moberg (2003).

[28] UFCO was able to buy Crown land very cheaply, transport its bananas at favourable rates on the public railway, pay no export taxes or import duties and was charged land tax at a lower rate than other growers. In addition, UFCO received a subsidy for carrying the mail to New Orleans. See Moberg (1997), pp. 23-27.

Figure 4.2: Belize non-traditional exports (US$000), 1871-1900

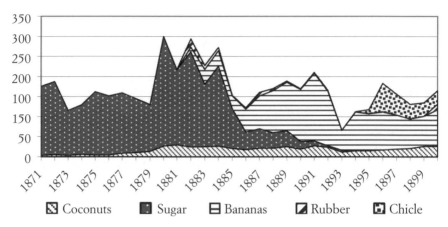

Source: Statistical tables relating to the Colonial and other Possessions of the United Kingdom (various years).

first in the hands of small-scale farmers, who were able to take advantage of the steamships that were now calling regularly from New Orleans following a decision of Governor Barlee in 1878 to transfer the mail subsidy away from the Jamaica route.[29] A British Honduras Syndicate was formed out of several smaller companies, UFCO entered the country after its formation in 1899 and soon afterwards Vaccaro Bros. (later Standard Fruit and Steamship Co.) started calling at Belize to buy bananas.[30] As the century ended, and even before the railway was planned, the prospects for banana exports looked bright.

Colonial officials could take some credit for the next two examples of non-traditional exports. Rubber (*Castilloa elastica*) had started to be exported in 1882, but it was at first harvested from the wild. A small botanic station had been established in the grounds of Government House in 1892 and rubber seedlings were distributed throughout the country.[31] Shortly afterwards, a small export trade in cacao and coffee was started. None of these products amounted to much in volume or value terms, but they did at least show that Belize could produce agricultural exports and cacao in particular would return to the export list a century later.

Ironically, it was a forest product (chicle) that was to prove the most enduring and successful non-traditional export as the 19th century ended.

---

[29] See Clegern (1967), p. 61.

[30] See Moberg (1997), p. 21.

[31] The Botanic Station is the subject of the next chapter. It had been recommended by Daniel Morris, who wrote a book about the colony's resources. See Morris (1883).

The bleeding of the sapodilla tree produces a latex, which is the basis of chewing gum and was much in demand in the US. It provided employment during the dead season for mahogany extraction. It served the needs of the big estates perfectly and they started to add chicle to their traditional exports from 1894 onwards (see Figure 4.2).

By no means all the chicle exported by Belize was produced in the country. By the late 19th century, the landowners had so exhausted their forest reserves that they were cutting logwood and mahogany across the borders in Guatemala and Mexico.[32] Chicle was soon added to the list and re-exports once again became of great importance to Belize. The traditional re-export trade to Central America and Yucatan had not entirely ended–indeed, merchants did a thriving trade supplying the forest workers across the borders–but it had changed character. It would remain important for many years.[33]

The rise of non-traditional exports took place as the currency question became especially awkward. The silver dollars (*sol*) circulating in the colony served their purpose well enough until the silver price of gold started to fall after 1873. By 1880 it was no longer possible to maintain the fiction of a fixed rate of exchange against sterling and the Treasury each year converted *sol* to sterling at a different rate. In 1887, by royal decree, the Guatemalan silver dollar was made the legal tender of the colony, although other silver dollars were still accepted up to small amounts.[34] However, this was only a temporary measure as the silver price continued to fall. Finally, bowing to pressure from different interest groups, the US gold dollar was made legal tender in 1894.

Belize was now effectively on the gold standard, but nominal wage rates had to be reduced in order that exports should remain competitive.[35] The average reduction was 30 per cent, which brought nominal wage rates back approximately to their level in 1892.[36] This caused much grumbling and some rioting (including by the police force in the Northern District).[37] From

---

[32] In the 1891 census, it was stated that nearly 1,500 Belizean workers and their families (four per cent of the population) were unenumerated as they were working in these camps outside the country.

[33] At the end of the 19th century, re-exports were equal to one-third of domestic exports. See Bulmer-Thomas (2012), Tables A.11 and A.12.

[34] See Bristowe and Wright (1890), pp. 205-10.

[35] When the gold dollar was adopted, it was worth roughly twice the value of the silver dollar.

[36] See *British Honduras Colonial Report* (1894), p. 6.

[37] One of the causes of the riots was the failure of the colonial authorities to adjust the specific import duties. These had been payable in silver, but now had to be paid in gold dollars. Importers therefore raised their prices and this caused great resentment. See Ashdown (1986a), p. 6.

this point onward, in common with the surrounding republics, Belize en joyed a period of economic recovery that lasted with only minor interruptions up to the First World War. Exports were becoming more diversified because of the growth not only of bananas and chicle, but also coconuts and cedar.

Yet the deep structural flaws remained in place. There was no forest management by either the public or private sector so that timber exports were unsustainable over the long-term. Mahogany trees were increasingly difficult to find and expensive to extract (hence the search for cheaper alternatives in Guatemala and Mexico). Chicle was also not being harvested in a sustainable fashion.[38] With the rise of the German chemical industry and the development of aniline dyes in the 1890s, logwood faced a synthetic competitor at the end of the century for the first time. Bananas, as elsewhere in Central America, were at the mercy of diseases for which there were no known cures. And there were still no roads, so that efforts to diversify the economy and encourage agricultural exports were seriously impeded. Finally, Belize was a small colony in a vast empire, which received neither the best officials nor much attention from London.

Under these circumstances, it is not surprising that the Belize economy by 1900 had lost its privileged position in the Caribbean (it had been ranked first in 1850 in terms of domestic exports per head and second–behind the Danish Virgin Islands–in terms of merchandise exports per head). By 1900 it had fallen to fourth position in terms of merchandise exports per head[39] and sixth position in terms of domestic exports per head.[40] These rankings were by no means disastrous, but more worrying was the absolute decline in the Belize position since domestic exports per head in 1900 were roughly half what they had been in 1850 while merchandise exports per head were only one-third of their earlier value.[41] The first four decades of colonialism, therefore, had proved to be a great disappointment.

---

[38] Chicle can be harvested in a sustainable fashion if the sapodilla tree is not bled too fiercely and if the tree is left untouched for seven years. There is plenty of evidence to suggest this was not the case in Belize. See Hummel (1921).

[39] Behind the Danish Virgin Islands, Trinidad and French Guiana. The figures are derived from Bulmer-Thomas (2012), Tables A.13 and A.1a.

[40] Behind French Guiana, Trinidad, Turks & Caicos Islands, British Guiana and Cuba. The figures are derived from Bulmer-Thomas (2012), Tables A.11 and A.1a.

[41] The precise figures are: domestic exports per head (US$45.7and US$26.4); merchandise exports per head (US$114.1 and US$35.2).

The fall of the Belize economy: 1900-1950

The Belizean economy made some progress in the first years of the 20th century. The first bank was established in 1903.[42] A new market had been found for mahogany in the US;[43] chicle had been added to the list of principal exports; bananas were expanding and the re-export trade was recovering.[44] Agricultural exports only contributed 20 per cent to domestic exports and Crown land leased to farmers (large and small) was less than one per cent of the colony's surface area,[45] but the authorities could convince themselves that a start had been made in diversifying the economy away from timber. Despite all that had gone wrong since the middle of the 19th century, Belize in the Caribbean was still in 1910 ranked tenth in terms of domestic exports per head and third in terms of merchandise exports per head. It was also ranked fifth in terms of public revenue per head, the bulk of income still coming from customs duties.[46]

In the next few decades, however, Belize's position would seriously deteriorate and by 1950 it would be ranked 14th in terms of domestic exports per head, placing it in the bottom half of all Caribbean countries. At that time, it was still ranked third in terms of public revenue per head, but this was due to the grants and loans received from the British Treasury after 1931 (see Table 4.3), not to the "true" revenue raised from local taxation. The four decades after 1910 were therefore critical ones for Belize and mark the years when the economy–still heavily based on forest products exploited in an unsustainable fashion–started to fail.

Although the period coincided with two world wars and the Great Depression, this was also true of all other countries. Thus, the relative decline of the Belize economy against other Caribbean countries needs to be explained as well as its absolute fall. Furthermore, the relative deterioration continued through the 1950s, although this will be examined in more detail in the next section.

---

[42] Its name was the Bank of British Honduras and its Directors included several members of the local elite. See Ashdown (1979), p. 139, n.108. It was purchased by the Royal Bank of Canada in 1912.

[43] The share of domestic exports going to the US jumped from less than 20% in 1900 to nearly 75% just before the First World War. See Bulmer-Thomas (2012), Table C.15.

[44] The re-export trade now consisted mainly of forest products imported from Guatemala and Mexico and then shipped to the US and Europe.

[45] Lease of Crown lands to smallholders had begun in the late 19th century, but it was on a very small scale.

[46] The land tax usually contributed less than five per cent to government income and an income tax would not be introduced until 1920. See Ashdown (1979), p. 37.

Table 4.2: Annual rate of change (%) of domestic exports per head (1930 prices), 1900-1960

	Belize	Hispaniola	Cuba	British	French	Dutch	US	Caribbean
					Dependencies:			
1900/20	-0.3	-0.3	1.3	0.5	1.5	0.3	6.8	2.0
1920/40	-0.6	-1.2	-3.7	0.3	0.0	10.2	0.4	-1.2
1940/60	-0.5	2.1	2.2	7.0	0.7	1.8	4.2	3.6
1900/60	-0.5	0.2	-0.1	2.6	0.7	4.0	3.8	1.5

Source: Derived from Bulmer-Thomas (2012), Tables C.9 and C.1a.
Note: Hispaniola is the sum of Haiti and the Dominican Republic.

As an illustration of both problems, the growth of domestic exports per head at constant prices is shown in Table 4.2 for three periods and it demonstrates clearly how poorly Belize performed not only in relation to the British colonies, but also relative to other sub-regions. Indeed, over the whole period from 1900 to 1960, domestic exports per head at constant prices fell and the Belizean performance was worse than all the other sub-regions shown.

The outbreak of World War I in August 1914 was, of course, a serious blow for Belize. The mahogany shipped to the US since the 1890s may have reduced the importance of the British market, but the UK was still a major customer and continental Europe (including Russia) was also important for logwood. Demand from Europe for timber fell immediately, but mahogany exports to the US also plummeted because contractors in Mexico, fearful of losing their concessions, had over-supplied the US market following the outbreak of revolution in December 1910. Furthermore, re exports (mahogany, logwood and chicle)–not just domestic exports–all suffered as a consequence of the Mexican Revolution. Imports, most of which came from the US,[47] could still be obtained, but the fall in export earnings reduced the Belizean demand.

The slump in demand for exports in the early years of the war reduced the need for labour. In the 1914-15 season forestry requirements were roughly half what they had been the previous year.[48] For the first time ever the colony experienced surplus labour, a situation made worse by the return of those workers who had migrated to Panama after 1903 to help in the

---

[47] The USA had been the main source of imports since the adoption of the B.H. dollar as the colony's currency in 1894.
[48] See *British Honduras Colonial Report* (1915), p. 14.

Figure 4.3: Belize, volume of logwood and mahogany exports, 1900-1950

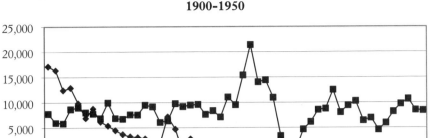

Source: Bulmer-Thomas (2012), Table C.5.

construction of the canal. Belize suffered net migration outwards in every decade after 1900, a complete reverse of what had happened in the 19th century.[49] The mahogany industry was rescued, however, by the decision of the British Admiralty to place a large order in 1916. This was used in part to make propellers for the Royal Air Force.[50]

When the war ended, traditional sources of demand for mahogany returned and exports rose to previously unheard of levels (see Figure 4.3).[51] Prices, as for other commodities in the Caribbean, fell sharply in 1921 but in Belize they soon recovered. And the colony now had a new and unexpected source of additional income as a result of US prohibition (1919-33). Re-exports, mainly of whisky imported from Canada, soared to destinations from which they could be smuggled into the US, while the contraband trade focused on the Mississippi delta.[52] The colonial authorities turned a blind eye until the bilateral treaty between Britain and the US in 1924 forced the UK to crack down on the trade.

---

[49] See Bulmer-Thomas (2012), Table A.6.

[50] Many Belizeans volunteered to fight, most being sent to Mesopotamia, but it is unlikely that this was the reason for the Admiralty decision.

[51] Before this happened, however, in 1919 there were serious riots when returning soldiers protested at the absence of employment opportunities and the poor social conditions. See Ashdown (1985) and Ashdown (1986).

[52] The alcohol trade worked in mysterious ways during the US Prohibition. While Belize imported alcoholic beverages from Canada for re-export to Mexico (and eventually the US), the Bahamas exported them to Miquelon (a French island in the mouth of the St. Lawrence River) from where they were presumably shipped to Canada before going to the US.

While Belize was benefiting from the boom in mahogany exports and the brief revival of the entrepôt trade, its other main commodity exports were facing ever more dismal prospects. The most serious case was logwood, which as late as 1900 was almost equal in value to mahogany. The First World War hit the trade hard (see Figure 4.3) and, despite a brief post-war boom, it never recovered. The textile industry now preferred the cheaper aniline dyes sold by chemical firms and Belizean logwood exports would fade away in the 1920s after 250 years of continuous exploitation. The trees were, and still are, available in abundance but the market had changed for ever. The last shipments were made during the Great Depression.

Chicle faced a similar problem, although it was nothing like as severe. Even before the First World War, manufacturers of chewing gum had been diluting chicle with cheaper substitutes–mainly from Asia where they could be obtained at one-third the cost. When peacetime conditions returned, manufacturers had grown accustomed to the cheaper substitutes. In Belize, this included Crown gum, an inferior product that had been mixed with chicle and had therefore damaged Belize's reputation for a high quality product. The 1920s were therefore a difficult time for the industry in Belize and exports fell.[53]

The banana industry faced no competition from cheaper substitutes and much had been expected from its development, especially after the opening of the Stann Creek Railway in 1911. However, Panama disease soon entered Belize and exports started to decline from 1917. This was no different from other parts of Central America, but the banana companies in the republics had dealt with the threat by opening new plantations. This option was more difficult in Belize–not because of a shortage of land, but because of the absence of transport and port facilities. As the multinational companies lost interest in Belize, ships called less frequently and exports became dependent on smallholders with no marketing expertise. The industry enjoyed a significant revival in the late 1930s,[54] but this was then undermined by the spread of Sigatoka disease.

Under these circumstances, the authorities could not postpone any longer the introduction of policies that should have been adopted much earlier. Following a very critical report on the state of the colony's forest resources, a Forestry Department was finally established in 1922, some Crown lands were turned into forest reserves and a public loan was taken out to establish timber on a sustainable basis through conservation on public and private lands (an income tax was finally introduced in 1920 to service this debt).

[53] See Bulmer-Thomas (2012), Table C.5.
[54] This occurred on lands to the south of the Stann Creek Valley that had not been tainted by Panama disease. The volume figures are given in Bulmer-Thomas (2012), Table C.5.

Mahogany was made a priority as the rate of extraction was far in excess of what the colony could sustain and the aim was to raise the density of mahogany trees from one to 40 per acre on conserved land. Finally, the land tax was also increased in the 1920s (first to 1.5 and then to 2.0 cents per acre).[55]

Even before the establishment of the Forestry Department, an Agricultural Commission had been set up in 1917. It emphasised the need for improved infrastructure, particularly roads, if there was to be any chance of export diversification. However, its recommendations were ignored on the grounds of cost and the first steps in road-building would not be taken until 1925. Progress was so slow, however, that the road from Belize town to Corozal near the Mexican border was not finished until 1938, while that to San Ignacio close to the western frontier would not be completed until after the Second World War. Not surprisingly, the main advances in agriculture were in coconut and copra exports,[56] where transportation was by sea not by road, and in citrus production along the Stann Creek Valley, where the industry filled the gap left by the banana industry and could make use of the railway.

By the end of the 1920s, Belize was therefore very vulnerable. Despite the efforts at diversification, the colony's prosperity still hinged on forest products and mahogany was once again the leading commodity–responsible for nearly 70 per cent of domestic exports. Mechanisation, using tractors instead of oxen and short-haul logging railways, began in the 1920s and this increased the rate of extraction. However, it reduced the need for labour. Furthermore, many firms started to hire labour for six months a year rather than 11 months as before. Employment peaked in 1924, but mahogany extraction carried on rising until 1927 (see Figure 4.3) at a rate that was not only far too high for Belize, but also saturated the world market.

Some pinned their hopes on marine products as a solution to the problem of export diversification. Belize, after all, has extensive rivers and coasts as well as offshore islands (cayes). Marine products began to be exported in the 1920s with a small sponge industry at Turneffe Island, lobster (canned and fresh) on Ambergris Caye and turtle throughout the coastal district, but the contribution of these products to domestic exports was still very small when world trade started to shrink at the end of the decade. Marine exports then disappeared to re-emerge after the Second World War.

With the start of the Great Depression in 1929, and shortly afterwards (in 1931) a devastating hurricane, the Belize economy went into a tailspin. The main problem for Belize was the global collapse in the demand for mahogany after 1929. Exports from Belize fell in one year from 14 to 11 million ft. before collapsing to 3.3 million ft. in 1931 (see Figure 4.3). Two

---

[55] The rate was much higher on land close to the Stann Creek Railway.
[56] Copra is the dried meat of the coconut, use to make products such as oils and soap.

Figure 4.4: Belize, exports per head (US$), 1850-1950

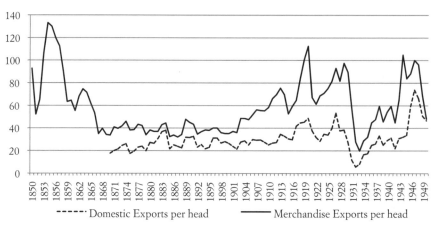

Domestic Exports per head   Merchandise Exports per head

Sources: 1900-50 from Bulmer-Thomas (2012), Tables C.1, C.6 and C.8. Earlier years derived from *Statistical tables relating to the Colonial and other Possessions of the United Kingdom* (various years) and Bulmer-Thomas (2012), Table A.1.

years later mahogany exports had fallen to 636,000 feet, their lowest level since the 18th century. The fall in demand for chicle was not so precipitate, but by now the logwood had gone, cedar collapsed in line with mahogany[57] and bananas were of negligible importance. Domestic exports per head fell to $5.8 in 1932 (the worst year) compared with $34.6 on the eve of the First World War and $48.8 in the boom year of 1920 (see Figure 4.4).[58]

Belize faced an additional problem in the Great Depression, which most other Caribbean countries were able to avoid. Imperial preference since 1919 had helped the UK to retain a significant share of the Belize market,[59] but the colony's currency was tied to the US dollar. When, therefore, Great Britain abandoned the gold standard in 1931 and devalued its currency, the Belize dollar was immediately revalued against the pound sterling. This helps to explain the astonishing collapse in the volume of Belizean exports after 1930. The decision by the United States to abandon the link with gold in 1933, thereby devaluing the US dollar against sterling and other European currencies, then helped Belize to recover from the depression.[60]

---

[57] Ever since the mahogany trade began, a small export of cedar had accompanied it as the cedar trees tended to be found in the wild alongside the mahogany.

[58] The fall in merchandise exports per head in the Great Depression was also very severe as the re-export trade collapsed as well (see Figure 4.4).

[59] The UK shares of exports and imports from 1900 are in Bulmer-Thomas (2012), Tables C.16 and C.23 respectively.

[60] It could not prevent serious riots in 1934, however, as a consequence of high levels of unemployment. See Bolland (1988), pp. 167-76.

The 1931 hurricane caused a significant loss of life and damage to property.[61] A loan was hastily agreed with the British Treasury to provide mortgages for those who had lost homes and businesses, but the impact of the depression on public revenue was so severe that the colonial government was forced to accept a loan-in-aid from the British Treasury in the fiscal year 1932-33.[62] Although modest in size, this was the first time the colony had been unable to balance its budget without Treasury assistance and it brought with it fiscal control from London.

Embarrassing though this was, this had a silver lining. The British officials now in charge of public finances were shocked by the poor state of infrastructure.[63] From 1932 onwards, therefore, Belize received a stream of Colonial Development Funds and loans-in-aid that continued after the Second World War. These were spent in large part to give the colony the rudiments of an all-weather road system, although the roads were barely passable in the wet season. As a result of control by the UK Treasury and the system of loans and grants, total revenue was much higher than "true" revenue (see Table 4.3) and public revenue per head performed better than expected after 1931.

Treasury control also helped to improve fiscal effort. Import duties had been steadily raised in the 1920s (to a maximum of 20 per cent) as a consequence of the introduction of imperial preference (yields would otherwise have fallen). They were raised again after the hurricane to a maximum of 25 per cent and customs duties then continued to provide the bulk of public revenue until 1946, when a new income tax law was forced through a reluctant assembly by the use of the Governor's reserve powers. Revenue from income tax then jumped by 50 per cent in one year (see Table 4.3). The land tax was increased in the 1930s, but the large landowners (including BEC) refused to pay the increase and the Colonial Office then lowered it to its previous rate. It continued to yield less than five per cent of government income (see Table 4.3).

Belize had entered the Second World War still heavily dependent on forest products, but without the benefit of logwood. When demand for mahogany fell sharply after 1941 (see Figure 4.3), the colony became increasingly dependent on chicle. This commodity, the raw material for chewing gum, was close to being a necessity for the US and demand fell less pre-

---

[61] It was the first hurricane to hit Belize town for 80 years; there was no early warning system and the public was completely unprepared.

[62] Most revenue came from customs duties, which fell in line with foreign trade after 1929.

[63] See Burns (1949), pp. 128-32. See also Pim (1934).

Table 4.3: Belize, public revenue (US$000), 1932-1948

Year (a)	Total revenue (b)	"True" revenue	Customs duties	Land tax	Income tax
1932	893.7	764.1	425.9	30.2	25.2
1933	1,056.2	685.1	376.2	27.4	10.5
1934	797.7	680.6	353.5	18.1	8.7
1935	1,192.7	825.2	405.0	30.8	26.5
1936	1,597.5	992.1	451.0	32.0	21.8
1937	1,550.8	1,188.5	528.7	38.9	24.4
1938	1,740.6	1,258.1	563.3	42.4	33.9
1941	1,577.0	1,230.0			
1942	1,645.0	1,269.0			
1943	1,878.0	1,428.0			
1944	2,510.6	1,675.0			132.8
1945	2,505.9	1,924.2	884.0	37.5	186.4
1946	2,634.8	2,203.8	920.4	40.2	260.5
1947	2,941.0	2,506.0	1,227.0	39.7	346.8
1948	3,209.0	2,580.0	999.6	39.4	414.1

Sources: British Honduras Colonial Report (various years) and Carey Jones (1953). (a) 1931-33 are fiscal years ending on March 31. 1935 onwards are calendar years. Colonial figures for 1934 are for nine months only (adjusted upwards here for 12 months). (b) Includes loans and grants from Imperial Treasury.

cipitately than for mahogany.[64] Banana and coconut exports, on the other hand, were reduced almost to nothing as shipping space was used for other purposes and citrus virtually disappeared from the export list. No new products emerged during the war, although in 1947 a small trade in pine lumber began with exports going mainly to Jamaica.[65]

Belize therefore found itself in a very difficult position when the war ended, a position not helped by increasing friction with Guatemala.[66] The

[64] See Bulmer-Thomas (2012), Table C.5.

[65] The colonial authorities had great expectations of pine exports when they signed in 1904 a contract giving a US citizen (Buckner Chipley) the right to extract as much pine as he could find on Crown land for 25 years. The contract, however, was sold and re-sold on numerous occasions with almost no pine being exported.

[66] Guatemala had unilaterally abrogated the 1859 treaty in 1939 and later closed the border. The situation became so tense in 1948 that Britain despatched a gunboat and war was considered a real possibility. The closure of the border had a very negative impact on the re-export trade.

infrastructure was slowly improving and the 1946 census showed that nearly 30 per cent of the labour force was now in agriculture, demonstrating the potential for diversification away from forestry.[67] However, private land was still tightly controlled by a tiny number of landowners, principally BEC, and the first national income estimates confirmed the modest position that Belize now held among even the British Caribbean colonies.[68] The colonial authorities seemed at a loss how to proceed and yet they were unwilling to encourage local participation in any shape or form. It was not until after devaluation (see below) that the political situation would start to change and the economic diversification of the Belizean economy could accelerate.

Devaluation, diversification and development

When sterling was devalued in September 1949, the Belize currency –alone in the British Empire–remained tied to the US dollar. It therefore appreciated against the British pound, making imports from the UK cheaper and exports more expensive.[69] Exports and imports to the US, the main trading partner, were unaffected–except, of course, for the substitution effects induced by the change in relative prices between the sterling and dollar areas.

Despite repeated assurances to the contrary, the British authorities changed their mind and the Belize dollar was devalued on the last day of the year (it was pegged to the pound at 4:1). This event is usually analysed through the prism of politics as it was the trigger for the birth of the nationalist movement and gave rise to the PUP, which would steer the country to independence in September 1981.[70] However, devaluation also had major economic consequences–in addition to the rise in the cost of living–that have not received the attention they deserve.

The British authorities justified devaluation in three ways, none of which stands up to serious analysis.[71] First was the slump in demand for forest products in the US in 1949, but this was due to over-stocking in previous months and would have soon been reversed. Second was the

---

[67] The census figures are reported in Carey Jones (1953).

[68] The first reliable estimate was made for 1946. See Carey Jones (1953). An unreliable (much lower) estimate had been made for 1945.

[69] Since sterling went from $4.03 to $2.80, the appreciation of the Belize dollar against the pound was roughly 30%.

[70] See Shoman (1973).

[71] The three justifications are explained in Carey Jones (1953), Appendix A, with quotes from the Financial Secretary's Report for 1949.

reduction in competitiveness of non-traditional products sold in the UK such as pine and citrus, but these were still a very small share of domestic exports. Third was the lack of confidence in the Belize dollar, which was "exhibited in many different ways". This was code for speculation by the private sector against the currency and therefore the worst possible argument for devaluation.

The real reason for devaluation was almost certainly the conclusions of the Evans Report published in September 1948.[72] This was an attempt by the colonial authorities to take a holistic approach to the British Caribbean as part of their efforts to build a Federation of the West Indies, which assumed that out-migration from the islands needed to accelerate and could be absorbed by land settlement schemes in Belize and British Guiana. This had been a common theme of colonial studies for some years, but the Evans Report went further by concluding that only large-scale settlement schemes would work and that these would require massive public sector investment in infrastructure.

These ideas were enthusiastically accepted by the post-war Labour government in the UK and the Colonial Office was ready to increase substantially grants-in-aid to Belize, drawing up projects that would meet the ambitions of the Evans Report.[73] Sterling devaluation, however, and the peg of the Belize currency to the US dollar effectively reduced the value of such grants by one-third. The only way, therefore, to avoid this was to devalue the Belize dollar.[74]

Ironically, the increase in grants-in-aid never fully materialised as the population of Belize was strongly opposed to large-scale immigration from the rest of the British Caribbean as well as to Federation itself.[75] However, devaluation made non-traditional exports to markets outside the sterling area much more competitive and maintained competitiveness inside the sterling area. By the end of the 1950s (see Figure 4.5), forestry was responsible for less than 50 per cent of domestic exports and this ratio continued to fall thereafter.

The shift away from forestry, a crucial moment in the history of Belize, was due above all to the rise of agricultural exports. Efforts were concentrated at first on citrus, bananas and cacao, but Belize also received a gener-

---

[72] The Evans Report had been published in September 1948 and presented to parliament by the Colonial Secretary. See *Report of the British Guiana and British Honduras Settlement Commission* (1948).

[73] The recommendations of the Evans Report were included in the 1949 Development Plan covering the years 1950-54. See Bennett (2008), Chapter 4.

[74] This is also suggested by Carey-Jones (1953), p. 141.

[75] When the Federation was finally established in 1958, Belize would remain outside it. See Mordecai (1968), p. 147.

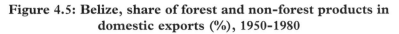

Figure 4.5: Belize, share of forest and non-forest products in domestic exports (%), 1950-1980

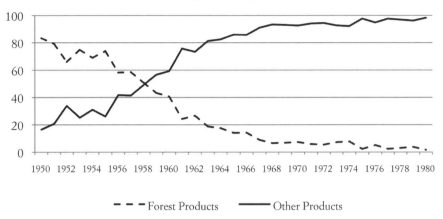

- - - Forest Products   ——— Other Products

Source: Derived by the authors from Bulmer-Thomas (2012), Table C.5; *British Honduras Colonial Report* (various years); and UNYITS.

ous quota from the UK in 1950 under the Commonwealth Sugar Agreement (CSA). This was finally filled in 1961 and the industry continued to expand as a result of increased quotas under the CSA, a small quota provided by the US following the suspension of US trade with Cuba and sales in the world market. By 1970 sugar had reached 50 per cent of domestic exports and this proportion would soar to 80 per cent a few years later when world sugar prices temporarily quadrupled.

The decline of forestry was at first only relative and the colonial administration continued to give the industry priority in its development efforts. However, it never recovered from Hurricane Hattie in October 1961 and exports thereafter steadily declined in both volume and value. The advent of internal self-government in 1964[76] also provided an opportunity to apply a tax and land policy that no longer favoured the large forestry companies, especially BEC, and by the time of independence Belize had finally emerged from the shadow of its origins as a timber exporting enclave in the 17th century.[77]

These structural changes in the Belizean economy, however long overdue, did not mean that the economy had resolved its outstanding problems.

---

[76] A universal adult franchise had been adopted in 1954 and internal self-government came on 1 January 1964. See Grant (1976).
[77] The BEC had never fully paid even those taxes for which it had been responsible and had therefore accumulated large arrears. In response to the new policies, it either sold land or gave it to the government in lieu of tax. As a result it had ceased to be a major force in Belize by the time of independence. See Bolland and Shoman (1977).

Figure 4.6: Net outward migration as percentage of population, 1950-1980

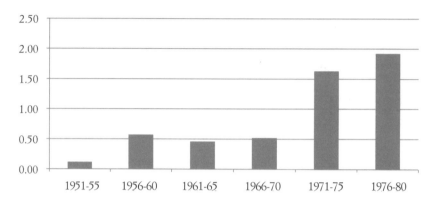

Source: Derived from Bulmer-Thomas (2012), Tables C.1, C.2, C.3, D.1, D.2 and D.3.

The rise of agricultural exports was not fast enough to compensate fully for the decline in forestry and unemployment remained a serious problem. Net migration had been outwards since 1900, but it accelerated after 1950 (see Figure 4.6). The 1970s witnessed exceptionally heavy outward migration with most of those leaving heading to the US.

Under internal self-government, nationalist politicians were responsible for economic policy. In 1973 Belize joined the newly formed Caribbean Community (CARICOM),[78] but this had very little impact as such a small part of the country's exports went to the other member states (trade links with Central America were even less important). Following the collapse of the Bretton Woods system of fixed currencies, the government took advantage of the fluctuation of the pound sterling in 1976 to peg the Belize currency once again to the US dollar (this time at 2:1).[79] This led to an increase in the share of trade with the US and a decline in the importance of the UK, so that in the year before independence the former colonial power was responsible for only 15 per cent of imports.

By the 1970s the Belizean economy had begun to resemble more closely other Caribbean countries. Domestic exports were mainly agricultural with

---

[78] This was also the year in which the name of the country was officially changed from British Honduras to Belize, although it remained a colony.

[79] Following devaluation at the end of 1949, the Belize dollar was valued at 1.43 to the US dollar and 4.0 to the British pound. Following the collapse in 1971 of the fixed exchange rate system, the pound drifted down against the US dollar leading to a decline in the value of the Belize dollar against the US dollar (see Bulmer-Thomas (2012), Table D.4). When the rate reached two for one in 1976, the Belize government re-established the peg with the US dollar.

Figure 4.7: Ratio of Belizean to Caribbean exports per head, 1951-1980

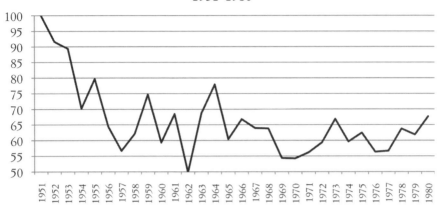

Source: Derived from Bulmer-Thomas (2012), Tables C.1, C.9, D.1 and D.10.
Note: 1951=100.

a small contribution from fishing and garment assembly. The agricultural exports depended heavily on preferential treatment in either the US or UK markets. However, British entry into the European Economic Community (EEC) in 1973 meant that Belize's preferences were now determined under the EEC's Lomé Convention applicable to all former and current European colonies rather than determined bilaterally between Belize and the UK.[80]

Belize's small population–it had still only reached 100,000 by the mid-1960s–meant that balancing the budget was a constant struggle. Resources for capital expenditure on infrastructure almost invariably had to come from official development assistance. In practice, given Belize's colonial status, this meant from the UK, whose own economic circumstances were far from favourable in the three decades before independence. The poor state of infrastructure before independence made it difficult to diversify the economy beyond the shift from forestry to agricultural exports and Belize failed to make any headway in developing exports of services.[81]

The result was an unimpressive macroeconomic performance in the last decades of colonialism. At the beginning of the 1950s domestic exports per head (at constant prices) were roughly the same as the average for the whole

[80] The first Lomé Convention was in 1975 and replaced the Yaoundé Convention that had applied only to former French colonies. The group of countries that benefited from the Lomé Convention were known as the ACP (African-Caribbean-Pacific) countries. See Hewitt and Stevens (1981).

[81] A modern tourist industry would not start until the 1980s. This was partly because of the reluctance of Premier George Price to promote the industry before Belize's independence. See Smith (2011), pp. 246-7.

Caribbean. From then onwards, the ratio would fall (see Figure 4.7) with only a brief respite when high sugar prices temporarily raised it.[82] The ratio of Belizean to Caribbean GDP per head, available from 1960, tells a similar story.[83] It was only in the last years before independence, when a serious effort was finally made by the colonial authorities to improve infrastructure, that the gap between Belize and the rest of the Caribbean in terms of GDP per head began to narrow.

Belize had enjoyed the highest exports per head in the Caribbean in the first half of the 19th century. Even when it became a British colony in 1862, it was still among the richest countries in the region. Thus, the decline of the economy in the subsequent century was a severe blow. The "forestocracy" (especially BEC), who resisted diversification and at the same time evaded the tax on land, must bear much of the blame. So should the imperial authorities who failed to confront the vested interests in the colony and refused before the 1930s to take a long-term approach to the development of infrastructure. Independence for Belize may not have been a panacea, but it was a huge advance on the mean-spirited and short-sighted approach to development that had characterised colonialism.

---

[82] The ratio in Figure 4.7 is a hybrid. From 1951, when the two were almost exactly the same, it measures the ratio of Belizean to Caribbean domestic exports per head at constant (1930) prices. From 1960 onwards it measures the ratio of total (merchandise and service) exports at constant (2000) prices.

[83] The comparison can be derived from Bulmer-Thomas (2012), Tables D.1 and D.19. In 1960 Belize GDP per head (at 2000 prices) was roughly 50% of the Caribbean average and it stayed at this level until just before independence.

5. The Belize Botanic Station: 1892-1933[1]

This chapter offers a case study of an institution, the Belize Botanic Station, which was of some importance in Belize for forty years during colonialism. It was founded in 1892 and the struggle to establish it tells us a great deal about the workings of the British Empire and the difficulties faced by small colonies such as Belize. In their efforts to diversify the Belize economy, the colonial authorities needed technical support from the Botanic Station, but this would prove to be insufficient to be an important driving force. The Station, like so much else in Belize during the period of colonialism, was crippled by lack of a clear aim and strategy, poor financial support and ideas shaped by colonial thinking.

It is possible to limit the story of the Belize Botanic Station just to the plants and the space they occupy, but plants in botanical gardens do not plant themselves. A garden must first exist as a thought. Especially in the case of the Belize Botanic Station, because of Belize's origin as an extractionist economy and later a British colony, there is a socio-historical and political context that is also part of the story: a complex of interested constituencies, each with different priorities as well as changing circumstances –both global and local–that became important at different times in its history. Understanding the context then is the key to understanding how the interplay of these interests affected the inception of the garden and shaped the way it changed over forty years.

The British West Indies was the most lucrative part of the British Empire during most of the 18th and into the 19th century. According to Richard Palmer, it supplied a quarter of the imports coming into the UK at its peak.[2] This wealth was derived from the single-crop plantation system based on sugarcane that was the innovation of the British settlers in the West Indies.

---

[1] For sources see Appendix 3. The Belize Botanic Garden was referred to by many names during its existence. In the early days especially the following are used: Depot Garden; Botanic Centre; Botanic Garden. As it became established, it was most consistently referred to as the Botanic Station.

[2] See Palmer (1950).

When this crop started to fail through disease in the 1870s, it became a serious matter for the British Government in London.[3]

One solution was the brainchild of Daniel Morris, Director of the Public Gardens and Plantations in Jamaica from 1879, and a product of Kew Gardens in London. His idea was a network of small botanic gardens or "depot" gardens as a step toward the diversification of agriculture in the West Indies. Detailed proposals were put forward to the Colonial Office in London in 1884 and by the end of the 1880s a network of ten such gardens was in existence in the West Indian islands.[4]

The kind of garden Morris had in mind was not purely a botanic garden in the usual sense. These gardens were to be gardens of one or two acres specializing in introducing plants of economic potential from around the globe, trying them out to see which survived best and which farmers wanted to plant. In function they were like agricultural experimental gardens. The Belize Botanic Station (BBS) was of this type and, interestingly, the first mention of Morris' idea was put forward in a handwritten note to the director of Kew two years earlier while on a visit to Belize.

The role of Kew Gardens and its relation to the Colonial Office

As we saw in the previous chapter, the status of Belize changed from that of British settlement to British colony in 1862 (Crown colony in 1871) and much of its government affairs, including whether or not to make a public botanical garden, were directed from the then Colonial Office (CO) in London. Understanding the context for the BBS therefore starts with:

The central role of plants to the functioning of the British 19th century economy.

The rise of Kew Gardens as repository and broker of botanical information.

Kew's relationship to the CO.

The importance of plants as a major impetus to exploration and imperial expansion has been well documented.[5] Perhaps it is too glib to say that the British Empire was built on plants. Certainly the conventional view held by economic historians is that the British Empire was built on trade. That trade, however, was largely in plant or plant derived materials. The connec-

---

[3] See Watts (1987).
[4] See McCracken (1997).
[5] See Hobhouse (1999); Musgrave (2000); Canny (1998); Brockway (1979); and Schiebinger (2004).

tion was not necessarily always simple, nor obvious, considering that crops had to be cultivated, harvested, shipped and processed–the chain of connections could be long. In the case of the West Indies, ships carrying British goods left Liverpool and Bristol, then traded the goods for African slaves on the Guinea coast and transported the slaves for sale in colonies such as Jamaica and Barbados. On the return journey the same ships brought sugar, grown by the slaves, for the London market.

The seven or eight plants (the spices, tobacco, sugarcane, cotton, tea, quinine, rubber and sisal) that are often said to have "changed the world" are the ones that have prominence in trade tables. In reality they are only the tip of the iceberg and many other plants were traded and shipped to European markets as foodstuffs, medicines, and raw materials for industrial processes. For example in the case of Belize, the incentive for settlement was the logwood, *Haematoxylum campechianum*, that, as we saw in the previous three chapters, fed the European dye market for some 250 years.

At the start of the Victorian period (1837-1901), British imperialism was about to enter its most dynamic phase dominating a world trade that was fuelled by plants. Expansion into new territories (See Chapter 4) held out the possibility of yet new plant riches. The West Indian sugar plantation model had been such a success that the aim was to replicate it using other crops. What those crops may be was the subject of exploration–indeed at that time rubber and quinine still lay in the future.

One institution in particular expressed the ethos of the day by developing a specialised interest and expertise (collections of specimens; of objects of plant manufacture and use in diverse cultures; information about plants and how to grow them) in the kind of plants with commercial potential. This institution, the Royal Botanic Gardens at Kew, eventually in an almost organic way came to define the topic of economic botany that made it an important part of the decision-making process of government.

By the 1880s, the period of relevance to the BBS, the Royal Botanic Gardens at Kew had become established as the centre of imperial botany. Kew, having been formerly the gardens of the Royal Family, in 1841 passed into the hands of the state. Interestingly, this transition from royal to state ownership was not smooth and the future of Kew was far from assured having suffered from decades of neglect and, at times, acrimonious debate about its future. Shortly afterwards William Hooker, often called the saviour of Kew, became its first director. He was followed by his son Joseph Hooker and William Thistleton-Dyer, at first Assistant to Joseph Hooker, and later director from 1885.

These three directors well understood the botanical needs of the imperialist government and were able to interpret them in such a way as to ensure the future of Kew by making themselves an important part of policy decisions on all matters botanical. They established an extensive botanical network throughout the growing empire and beyond. They were instrumental in establishing a chain of botanical gardens and supplying the personnel. From this base, plants, seeds and scientific information could be exchanged. The colonial gardens then became the means of introducing agricultural, horticultural and forestry plants and carrying out experiments to establish best cultural practices.[6]

Joseph Hooker wrote in a Report to the Office of Works in 1881:[7] "Kew has become the botanical centre of the work & literally carries on all economic and scientific botanical work of the Empire, under the direction of the various departments of State."

As Ray Desmond observes in the introduction to his History of Kew, a full account of Kew's relationship to the Colonial Office has yet to be written.[8] What is known is that the Colonial Office relied upon a network of unpaid advisors from many different institutions and that the Director of Kew was one of them.[9] This position was to be formalised in 1902 when the then director, William Thistleton-Dyer, was appointed botanical advisor to the Secretary of State for the Colonies.

Although without decision-making powers, the advisors were in a position to influence policy as the records abundantly show in the case of Kew. Its established network of garden connections around the empire and expertise in economic botany (agricultural crops) placed the Director of Kew in the position to become a powerful advocate for all botanical endeavours in the colonies and it is in this role that he becomes important to the BBS story.

As early as 1863 a Flora of Belize had been planned as part of William Hooker's Colonial Floras Project in which he aimed to cover all of the colonies. This Flora of Belize never materialised. The real trigger for Kew's interest in Belize was Goodman & Salvin's book *Biologia Centrali Americana* that was under preparation at Kew. When the work was brought to his attention, Thistleton-Dyer wrote to the CO:[10]

One result of Mr. Helmsley's studies has been to show that the botany of British Honduras is almost totally unknown. We possess scarcely any dried

---

[6] See Desmond (1995) and McCracken (1997).
[7] See Royal Botanic Gardens Kew (RBGK) Library and Archives Miscellaneous Reports (British Honduras, General Cultural Products) 1879-1913.
[8] See Desmond (1995).
[9] See Thurston and Pugh (1995).
[10] See letter 1880, 22nd March, from Thistleton-Dyer, RBGK, to R.H. Meade, Colonial Office, p. 83. Letters quoted in this chapter can be found in RBGK Library and Archives Miscellaneous Reports under either "British Honduras, General Cultural Products" or "Honduras Miscellaneous, 1892-1928".

plants from this colony other than a few kindly obtained for us and sent by Lieutenant Governor Barlee. It would be a very great aid to botanical science if anything could be done towards the exploration of its flora.

The real incentive was the possibility of locating *Castilloa elastica*, one of the commercial rubber plants. At that time Kew was in the process of establishing rubber, *Hevea brasiliensis*, plantations in India and Ceylon. The initial efforts were not going well as there was difficulty in germinating the seeds and Kew was very alive to the commercial possibilities of alternatives in other colonies.

As a result of promptings from Kew, Daniel Morris was commissioned by the CO to report on the "economic productions" of Belize. In 1882 Morris travelled to Belize accompanied by Alfred Hyde, a plant collector from the Jamaica Botanical Gardens, who made a collection of around sixty herbarium specimens that were incorporated into the collections at Kew.[11] This is arguably the first collection of Belize plants. Morris wrote:[12]

> I have just returned from a trip of 350 miles to the south of Belize and had a very successful time of it. *Castilloa elastica*[13] is abundant in the forest and I have carefully worked up its characteristics as well as seen the whole process of taking the rubber and its preparation for the market … here is an item which ought to make this colony several million pounds.

In the same letter quoted above, Morris continues:

> What they really want here is a small garden to act as a depot for plants which we might send them from Jamaica and possibly also a nursery to raise plants from seed. The colony generally is very poor in good fruit trees and in most of the tropical food plants which are so valuable in the West Indian gardens.

Morris' plan for a Botanic Station or Depot Garden was submitted to the CO in 1882.[14] It was at first approved, but later approval was withdrawn. There were a number of reasons for this:

The Station would have represented a move to an economy based on agriculture, but Belize was an extractionist economy totally dependent on

---

[11] See Morris (1883).

[12] See letter 1882, 23rd November, from D. Morris, Belize, to Thistleton-Dyer, p. 90.

[13] *Castilloa elastica* was eventually described in Hooker's 1900 *Icones Plantarium* Vol. VII and Vol. XXVII.

[14] See letter 1882, 14th December, from Thistleton-Dyer, RBGK, to the Hon. R.H. Meade, Colonial Office.

forestry products. The Belize Legislative Council (who had to approve and finance the garden) was largely comprised of logging interests who saw the introduction of agriculture as competing for an already scarce labour resource.

Within opinions favouring agriculture, one group (Kew), mindful from an early period of the possible environmental damage that monoculture may cause, preferred small owner-occupier style farming. Other opinions favoured West Indian style plantations that could be funded from outside capital.

At this time the CO decided to go along with the extractionists by constructing a railway to open up the Sibun area and transport logs to new markets in Central America via Guatemala. This project was to have been "a major financial undertaking" according to its main proponent, the Surveyor General. Kew responded by determined lobbying, but its ideas remained just that for the next ten years.

Establishing the Belize Botanic Station

Much had changed between 1882 and 1892. The proposed railway to Guatemala was still under discussion, but the Belize trade in logwood and mahogany were subject to strong competition from other sources and prices were falling.[15] The dangers of monoculture on tropical soils were made clear by the Report of the West India Royal Commission in 1897. Small scale agriculture that allowed diversification appeared to be the answer and so the idea of a Botanic Station once again looked like an attractive solution.

The chain of command appeared to be as follows: Kew proposed, the CO gave approval, but it was left to the Colonial Governor to implement and part of that was getting the agreement of the British Honduras Legislative Council, who met the costs. All that was needed now was someone who was willing and able to manage the project at the Belize end. Such a person was Alfred Maloney (Governor of Belize, 1891-1897).

By March 1892 Maloney had obtained the approval of the British Honduras Legislative Council. However, it now needed the approval of the imperial government in London. While the CO dithered, Maloney forced the issue by using the site of the Government House kitchen garden, which was already covered by his budget (for Government House), for the Botanic Station (see Figure 5.1). Further funds were then needed only for the salary

---

[15] See Chapter 4.

**Figure 5.1: The plan of the Botanic Station site at
Government House grounds**

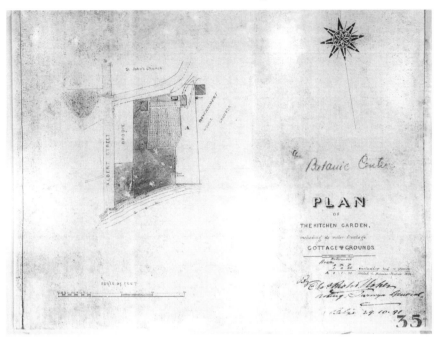

Source: Belize Archives and Records Service, Belmopan: Minute Paper 487/23.

of the Superintendent ($1,000).[16] Additionally, there was an existing cottage
in the grounds to provide accommodation. Having been presented with a
fait accompli, the CO gave its approval in April of the same year and the
garden could at last get underway.[17]

James McNair was appointed the first Superintendent of the Botanic
Station and arrived in Belize on 9th September, 1892, with one daughter.
His brief was to establish a distributing centre for economic plants for
small farmers. The garden became productive in 1893 and according to
the report for December 1894:

> 1,844 plants are in their permanent places, 9,422 in beds and pots avail-
> able for the public. The issues amounted to 25,024 of which 16,829 have
> been sold and 8,195 given away free. Amongst those were 19 nutmeg, 597
> coconut, 23,795 coffee, 49 cacoa, 68 casuarina, 136 roses.

---

[16] This was before the introduction of the British Honduran dollar in 1894, so the
figure of $1,000 must refer to Guatemalan silver dollars. See Chapter 4.
[17] Letter 1892, 27th April, from Edward Wingfield, Colonial Office, to Director
of Kew. p. 2.

Figure 5.2: The botanic station in Government House grounds

In The Botanical Station (Belize Br. Honduras.)   S. S. "Saba"
Compliments of the Season Dec 1st 1904

Source: Postcard collection belonging to Barbara & Victor Bulmer-Thomas.

Plants were supplied by Kew and the Botanical Department Jamaica. All this made for a very attractive garden (see Figure 5.2). Maloney's stated aims to the CO were that the garden should:

> serve not only as a nursery for the raising and distribution of seedlings both indigenous and exotic of economic and marketable value, but as a practical school for the agricultural education of youths…to serve as gardeners in plantation nurseries.

He worked tirelessly to lay the foundation for further developments. He toured the country and visited schools, giving lectures to explain why the Botanic Station was needed and repeatedly stressed the necessity for people to grow food.

To this end advertisements were placed in the Government Gazette for youths to be trained, but despite the offer of $7.50 (*sol*) per month the take up was less than enthusiastic. He set up a statutory Agricultural Society (Ordinance 23 and 24, 1894), consisting of a committee of twelve persons with himself as president. One of their first acts was to find a suitable site for a permanent home for the garden, as well as other sites to establish a network of satellite gardens–the site in Government House grounds was always seen as a temporary one. Four sites were acquired for extension:

Seventy-five acres at Hope Creek (Melinda) in Stann Creek donated by the British Honduras Syndicate. This site, established in 1902, was ear-marked to be the main garden, being in the centre of expected agricultural developments.

126

Ten acres at Fort Cairns in Orange Walk (originally in Corozal, but subsequent district boundary changes placed it in Orange Walk). This was established in 1899, but sadly the beautiful old wooden building dating from that year has now been demolished.

Twenty-five acres of Messrs. Price Estate at Kendal on the Sittee River. This was established in 1902 and was still in use in the 1950s as a centre for cacao trials.

Twenty-five acres on the Temash River in the Toledo District from the Arnold Brothers.

The management of the staff of the Botanic Station was put under the Surveyor General–forerunner of the Land and Survey Department.[18]

One example of just how crucial Maloney was to the whole scheme is shown by the following incident. While Maloney was away on leave in November 1895, the post of Superintendent of the Botanic Station was abolished by the Surveyor General, ostensibly due to lack of funds.[19] However, the Office of the Surveyor General had previously blocked the garden idea[20] by sending a report to the CO proposing the idea of a railway, suggesting a more fundamental disagreement.

Maloney, backed actively by Kew, started a new round of lobbying. By February 1896 the Garden was re-instated[21] with a budget increase to $3,000, but still met locally. Still sited at Government House, a bigger area obtained through land reclamation was set aside for it. McNair was kept in office, but in addition to having previously been made redundant he lost his daughter in a yellow fever epidemic in Belize, and he was now anxious to leave. He did so in August 1896.

McNair's replacement was Eugene Campbell, previously Acting Superintendent of Castleton Gardens, Jamaica. By August 1896 he had arrived in Belize, and his arrival marked the start of a very productive period in the history of the garden. Immediately the garden was open to the public complete with a bill of rules and regulations.[22]

The work of the Belize Botanic Station

In the early years the work of the BBS was recorded annually in the British Honduras Gazette and in the Governor's Report. From 1900-18 a stand alone

---

[18] See Maloney (1896).

[19] Letter 1895, 2nd November, from Surveyor General G. Allan, to Superintendent of Botanic Station, Mc Nair, p. 39.

[20] Letter 1883, 29th March, from Edward Wingfield, Colonial Office, to J.D. Hooker enclosing Report by Gustav von Ohlafsen, Colonial Engineer. p. 91.

[21] Letter 1896, 5th August, from A. Maloney to D. Morris. p. 90.

[22] See Appendix 4.

Report of the Botanic Station was published annually. From the report for 1900 (Covering years 1897-99) under the heading "Herbarium", [23] Campbell mentions that "want of space for drying and mounting specimens is a drawback to this work", but he had begun a plant collection and sent them to Kew for identification and mounting.[24] His collecting activity declined as other garden business took over, but he sent around 200 dried specimens to Kew that were incorporated into the collections there. He is commemorated in the plant *Bellotia campbelli.*

Part of Campbell's work was to establish the planned satellite gardens and this meant regular visits out of town to those sites as well as to various plantations in the colony. He also visited schools. A visitors' book was opened and the 1902 Report records a visit in 1901 from William Trelease, the first Director of the Missouri Botanical Gardens, while on a visit to Central America in search of yuccas.

When the garden started it was able to join an existing network, so there was an active and extensive exchange of botanical material–seeds, information, plants and journals–with other imperial gardens. These included the Royal Botanic Gardens, Calcutta; Victoria Gardens, Bombay; Botanic Gardens, Demerara; Botanic Station, Aburi, Gold Coast; Botanic Gardens, Singapore; Botanic Gardens, Queensland; and Royal Botanic Gardens, Kew. In addition, Ferdinand von Mueller, government botanist at the Victoria Botanical Garden in Australia, sent seeds of eucalyptus, melaleuccas and casuarinas–referred to as "hygienic plants" because they were thought to stave off epidemics–that were planted in public places and cemeteries. The main work was preparing plants for sale. Noteworthy in this list of plants is coca![25]

Originally, the intention was to make the Botanic Station at Stann Creek the headquarters and once that was established to close the Botanic Centre at Government House in Belize.[26] But the possibility of opening the Sibun River area by railway lingered on and as a result it was decided to keep the Belize garden, but to remove it to a different site as it had outgrown its present location. The new position was at Bolton Bank on the Belize River (see Figure 5.3). This garden came into production in 1906. In addition to the fifteen acres for the work of the garden, an additional six acres were laid out as a pleasure garden with ornamentals.[27]

Mr. and Mrs. Matthews, the auditors of the colony, took on a caretaker role during 1921-22 and have left a record that enables us to put together an

---

[23] See Appendix 7 .

[24] See Appendix 5.

[25] A list of plants grown at the Botanic Station for 1909 is given in Appendix 6.

[26] At the time, "Belize" was the name of the town that is today called "Belize City".

[27] See the Botanic Station Report for 1907.

Figure 5.3: Plan of site of the Botanic Station at Bolton Bank

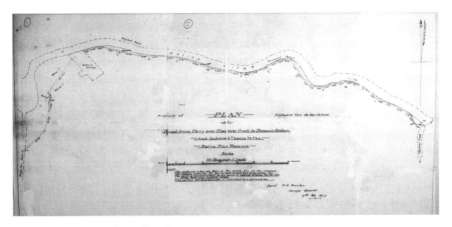

Source: Johnny Searle, Belize City.

idea of what the garden looked like.[28] Arrival at the Botanic Station was by boat from Belize (price $2.00) along the Haulover Creek. A lawn area swept down to the river. There was a house for the Superintendent and "links" for the labourers (presumably barrack-style housing). The garden was divided into sections. One of these was the Forest Section, the Matthews' commenting: "Although the Forest Section appears to be nothing but neglected bush, a valuable silvicultural experiment in natural re-generation is under way". A silk grass trial was also in progress in this section.

The Economic Section consisted of mature plants of commercial value, e.g., coconuts and sugarcane. The fruit was sold to supplement the budget of the garden. Vegetable gardens were also maintained to establish best cultural techniques. There were orchards of oranges (various cultivars including Seville that supplied the root stock for budding and grafting), tangerines, lemons, citrons, grapefruit, etc. In the Horticultural Section, as well as an ornamental garden, there were nurseries offering plants for sale. A formal garden had been started, next to the nurseries–to extend "eastwards as far as the Boardwalk". There was also a collection of around 25 "indigenous" ferns.[29]

The Matthews also co-opted numerous sources of voluntary help in a clean-up programme: "various ladies and gentlemen to lay stone paths". This help included the use of a boat, this being the only means of reaching the gardens from Belize, donations of tubs, supply of horse manure from the police horses, as well as gifts and loans from various business people in the town.

---

[28] See Belize Archives, Minute Paper 641-22.
[29] See Sutton, Hughes and Bulmer-Thomas (2000).

They concluded their report: "It has been a great pleasure ... to see from the visitors book that quite a large number of people from Belize visit the Station on Saturday and Sunday and that many of them repeat their visit".

Despite this optimistic account, the Botanic Station had been in crisis for a number of years by the time of the Matthews' report. Campbell was transferred to the Botanic Station in Stann Creek in 1917 to establish rice experiments and thereafter, until its closure, the Bolton Bank Station had a number of caretakers only.

This was undoubtedly precipitated by the United Fruit Company fiasco. Morris, in his book on the colony, mentions four banana producers growing and shipping bananas in the Stann Creek District.[30] These and other growers in the region were amalgamated to form the United Fruit Company (UFCO) in 1899.[31] The UFCO was able to extract many concessions from the British Government in various forms eventually coming to control the shipping business. The British were also made to bear the cost of the construction of the railway running from Commerce Bight to Middlesex in the Stann Creek District and to subsidise the running costs against their wishes.

All this diverted funds and personnel from the Botanic Station. However, the real disaster was the advent of Panama disease in the Stann Creek Valley.[32] The UFCO then withdrew to carry on operations in Guatemala and Honduras and the colonial government discovered that, in working out the terms of the agreement, they had been no match for the masters of the fine print. Instead of leasing the land, they had inadvertently sold it and were forced to buy it back at market value.

This was a salutary lesson for the CO, amounting to something of a crisis, especially coming as it did during the war years (1914-18). The old debate about the direction toward "development" of agriculture the country should take was thrown wide open and on this occasion treated more seriously. As a result an Agricultural Commission was set up in 1917 led by Sir Francis Watts, Imperial Commissioner of Agriculture for the West Indies, into the future of agriculture in the Stann Creek Valley. The big question was what could replace bananas? There were two possibilities: large scale industries such as sugar and cacao or what was seen as a natural line of development food for local consumption grown on small farms. For this latter a Department of Agriculture was essential.[33]

Times were changing, however. Great Britain was fast losing its dominance in world trade and agricultural plant products were beginning to move

---

[30] See Morris (1883).

[31] See Chapter 4.

[32] See Despatch 1920, 11th February, from Governor Hutson to Colonial Office, PRO CO 123 300, Public Record Office, Kew, London.

[33] See Dunlop (1921).

to the periphery of emerging trade patterns. Moreover, the First World War drew attention in the United Kingdom to the importance of forests. Fortunately the CO, in recognition of new thinking in this direction, commissioned a survey of the Belize forests. Cornelius Hummel, formerly Deputy Conservator of Forests to the Federated Malay States, with the approval of David Prain at Kew, was appointed to undertake this work in 1920.[34] It was no accident that a German was the person of choice for the post. Even at this early date the Germans were the leaders in forest conservation.

In its implementation of the recommendations resulting from the various reports, the CO hedged its bets and chose a mix of all options. The conservation of forests became an important objective and Hummel was appointed as the first Conservator of Forests. The Forest Trust, the statutory body set up to enable this to occur, was the forerunner of the Forestry Department and the first Conservation of Forests Legislation was passed in 1923. Incidentally, this is one of the earliest forest conservation laws anywhere to be passed. Its main aim was the sustainable use of forests. This law applied only to Crown lands and some of the early work concentrated on maintaining and augmenting existing stands of *Pinus caribea*, locating, protecting and encouraging regeneration of mahogany trees, and cataloguing and identifying secondary timber trees with commercial potential.

Hummel's successor put it this way: "agriculture in this country must always play second fiddle to forestry", mindful of the fact that at this time forest products were still a major export for Belize. Nevertheless, a Department of Agriculture was initiated to encourage small farmers. Although the lesson of monoculture was well learnt–both sugarcane in the Caribbean and bananas in Belize had failed catastrophically due to intensive use of the soil in the case of the former and disease in the case of the latter–the lure of monoculture never truly died and an experimental project in the Stann Creek Valley was started to grow rice, sugar and sisal–considered the best option for replacing bananas.

Once these decisions were taken, the Bolton Bank Botanic Station and satellite gardens in the rest of the country were placed in the care of the Department of Agriculture. The new Agricultural Officer was Hugh Sampson, Kew's first economic botanist. Sampson's comment[35] "I have no further use for the Bolton Bank Station" meant that it was doomed.

Many suggestions were put forward for its continuation: use as a Preventative Home for Girls, use as a Public Garden, use as a Botanic Garden under the control of the Agricultural Society. Hummel championed this last possibility and appealed to Sir David Prain, then the Director at Kew. Prain's response was sympathetic:

[34] Hummel would later go on to work for the Belize Estate & Produce Co.
[35] See Belize Archives, Minute Paper 1976-29.

The difficulty to which you refer always does arise when the question of placing a Botanical Station under the control of a Department of Agriculture has to be considered. Agricultural Officers are naturally fully cognisant of the nature of the work undertaken at an Experimental Station but they are unfamiliar with the functions of a Botanical one and are therefore apt at times to regard the two types of station as identical in purpose and to expect a botanical station to be able to do the work proper to an Experimental Station. When as usually happens, they find that this is not really possible they either advise their government to convert a Botanical Station into an Experimental one or advise that a Botanical Station be abandoned as a source of expense useless from an Agricultural point of view.[36]

However, although sympathetic, Prain could do little to help. Along with the marginalisation of plant products in commerce the influence of Kew in government had also waned. The Belize government decided to close the gardens and return it to the owners.

In preparation for handing back, the station was stripped of building and plants. Most of the plants were transported to the Stann Creek Station at Melinda. Aerial photos from the 1990s show only the boundary drainage system. However, at last the intention to make Melinda in Stann Creek the headquarters of operations was realised and it became the centre for the new Agricultural Department. The name was changed from Botanic Station to Agricultural Station and at the time of writing this station can still be seen at its old site, although much in decline.

In reality the transition from Botanic to Agricultural Station was purely semantic and organisational. After a cursory start, the early expectation that it should carry out scientific botanical work was never met. It is difficult for the public to understand that all work underpinning any activity involving plants depends on taxonomic study. The collection of the plants of a country, the naming and classification of their relationship need other scientific tools and specialists to undertake the work. No taxonomic botanists were ever appointed to the BBS (Kew carried out this work) nor were efforts made to engage the local population in this endeavour (unlike in Costa Rica). Later, when plant collections were made, this was always the result of international projects. Most exploration and taxonomic work has to be undertaken purely for scientific gain. Where there have been economic gains, only small benefits have accrued to Belize.[37]

---

[36] Kew Archives, British Honduras: Miscellaneous.
[37] See Bridgewater (2011), p. 197.

Impact of the Belize Botanic Station

Since the Botanic Station concept had such a strong economic objective it begs the question: what was its impact on the Belize economy? In arriving at an answer, several factors need to be considered. The trade figures for years up to the 1950s show overwhelmingly that agricultural exports had never been a strong factor.[38] Belize for most of its existence since the 17th century had depended on the export of forestry products that were harvested from the wild. Nor had it been self-sufficient in food. The efforts to encourage small farming were hampered by the structure of land ownership as shown in Chapter 4. Moreover, the high hopes for *Castilloa elastica*, that it would be as lucrative or even better than sugar in the West Indies, were never fulfilled.

When Morris wrote his letter (see p. 123), it was not known whether one of eight possible rubber producing plants with commercial potential would be best or indeed if all would be suitable. Belize was just one of the colonies where experimental plantings were tried in order to answer this question.[39] Eventually, after more than two decades of development–taxonomic work, technical innovations and distance planting trials–it became clear that *Hevea brasiliensis* would be the plant of choice and South-East Asia the place for rubber plantations. By 1912, if not before, it was clear that Central America could never rival South-East Asia in rubber production.[40]

Belize is now competitive in the world market in three exportable agricultural crops: bananas, citrus and sugar. This trio expanded very slowly over a long period and they have been kept afloat, in part, through preferential trade agreements and subsidies. In the case of bananas, the industry collapsed soon after the First World War due to disease. It began again in the 1930s and was further boosted when Green & Atkins, a small company based in Alabama, began to plant and ship bananas in the Sittee area (Waha Leaf), South Stann Creek, in the 1950s. The Belize Botanic Station played no part in the rise of the banana industry–it was already established when the station was first opened. Monitoring its fall consumed much of the time and effort of Campbell, the Superintendent of the Botanic Station. And its recovery was supported by the successor of the Botanic Station, the Agricultural Department.

In the case of sugar, that industry had its beginnings when Mexican refugees, fleeing the *Guerra de Castas* in the Yucatan, settled in the Corozal and

---

[38] See Chapter 4.
[39] Plantations of *Hevea* and *Castilloa* were made by private individuals at Melinda in Stann Creek and in the Toledo District and some rubber was shipped. See Figure 4.2.
[40] See Wright (1912), p. 44.

Orange Walk Districts starting in the late 1840s. They brought sugarcane plants and techniques that they put to good use. The industry only really took off in the 1930s, however, when a processing factory was set up. This time, the Agricultural Station at Corozal did play a supportive role through the introduction of better cane cultivars and cultural techniques.

In the case of citrus the Botanic Station played a more significant role. With the collapse of the banana industry in the 1920s, there was an urgent need for agricultural crops to take its place. Citrus succeeded admirably. Indeed, the list of citrus cultivars in Appendix 6 reads like an economic history of the citrus industry of the Stann Creek Valley. Citrus was one of the agricultural products from which much was expected by the founders of the Belize Botanic Station and they were not disappointed.

Perhaps one unexpected outcome was the stimulus to decorative gardening. Early lists from the station reports show many ornamental and horticultural plants–in particular: Crotons, *Codiaeum* varigatum; Roses, *Rosa sps.*; Oleander, *Nerium oleander*; Plumbago, *Plumbago sps.*; Crape Myrtle, *Lagerstroemia indica*; Hibiscus, *Hibiscus rosa-sinensis*; Ixora, *Ixora coccinea*. These were the flowers that dominated garden planting in the 1960s and still form the backbone of many private plantings, although the choice of garden plants has been considerably expanded through a new wave in the 1990s from private sources. Street plantings too benefited and trees such as Barbados Pride, *Caesalpina pulcherrima,* and Eucalyptus date from early introductions. The same is true for fruit trees. Most of the seasonal fruit going to local markets in Belize were part of the early Botanic Station experiments.

Although the Botanic Station never had the kind of impact its originators expected, nevertheless its contribution has been a lasting one. It experimented to find suitable crops and acted as a reservoir of both plants and skill that could be drawn upon as the opportunity arose. Further, it laid the foundation for the Agricultural and Forestry Departments that continued and expanded its work.

6. The Belize Economy since Independence

Belize became independent on 21st September 1981 after 120 years as a British colony. During that time its economy had performed relatively poorly–especially when comparisons are made with the rest of the Caribbean. Indeed, Belize began life as an independent country ranked 22nd in terms of Gross Domestic Product (GDP) per head among the 28 countries of the Caribbean.[1] This placed her in the bottom quartile and indicated the long distance Belize needed to travel in order to regain the status she enjoyed after the Napoleonic Wars when she had been ranked first in terms of exports per head.

The period since independence has been marked by an explosion of statistics that allow researchers to measure characteristics of the economy that were not available for the earlier periods. The most important of these relate to production, distribution and employment. Collectively, they capture the structure and performance of the Belizean economy and they are examined in the first three parts of the chapter. The final part looks at macroeconomic policy since independence, as this has an important bearing on structure and performance.

The first part of the chapter is devoted to production and is concerned with the change in the output of the economy as measured by GDP and GDP per head. Since GDP is equal to both the sum of final expenditures[2] and the sum of value added in each sector, the emphasis on production allows us to reveal the changing structure of the economy in different ways. At the same time, we can observe in more detail the marked cycles in the evolution of the Belizean economy since independence. These cycles are a feature of all small economies that are strongly dependent on events in the outside world over which they have little or no control, but the cycles have been exacerbated in Belize by large fluctuations in investment.

---

[1] Defined as all the islands plus the three Guianas and Belize.

[2] Defined as the sum of consumption and investment (both private and public) and net exports, i.e., exports less imports.

The second part is devoted to distribution. This refers to the way in which the fruits of production are divided among the population. There are many ways in which this can be done. One is the division of income between residents and non-residents, which can be approximated by the difference between GDP (all incomes) and Gross National Income (resident income only). There is also the division between the poorest and the richest, which is known as the "size" distribution of income and is captured by the percentage of income received by each decile or quintile of the population.[3]

The third part explores employment. This is one of the largest problems throughout the Caribbean and Central America, since these economies have struggled to find jobs for all their citizens of working age. We need therefore to examine the Belize economy in terms of its ability to generate jobs in each sector—by gender, age, region and educational attainment. We can also see to what extent the economy has failed to generate jobs at a sufficient rate by examining statistics both on unemployment and on outward migration.

The final part analyses the macroeconomic framework since independence, looking in particular at exchange rate, monetary and fiscal policies. The first, based on the peg to the US dollar, has been relatively uncontroversial although it may become so in the future. The second has seen huge changes within a highly concentrated banking system that has helped to keep the spread between lending and borrowing rates among the highest in the world. The third has been fraught with difficulties as a result of the numerous exemptions applied within the tax system.

Production

As a result of internal self-government, Belizeans had been in control of most aspects of economic policy for nearly two decades before the end of colonization. However, independence still brought some immediate changes.[4] Belize was now free to join those international institutions in which membership was limited to independent countries and these included the United Nations (UN), the World Bank (WB), the International Monetary Fund (IMF), the Inter-American Development Bank (IDB) and the UN Economic Commission for Latin America and the Caribbean (ECLAC). In due course, Belize would also join the Organization of American States (OAS) and the Sistema de Integración Centroamericana (SICA).[5]

---

[3] "Deciles" divide the population into tenths; "quintiles" into fifths.
[4] Belize was already a member of the Caribbean Community (CARICOM).
[5] OAS membership was not possible immediately after independence because of Guatemalan objections.

Membership of these organizations gave Belize either access to funding that would otherwise have not been available or influence on the world and regional stage. At the same time independence meant that Belize was eligible for the Preferential Trade Agreements (PTAs) that could only be signed by sovereign countries. The first was the Caribbean Basin Initiative (CBI), launched in 1984, that gave Belize duty-free entry to the US on a range of exports.[6] The second was the Lomé Convention that defined the terms under which exports from the African-Caribbean-Pacific (ACP) countries could enter the European Community (EC).[7]

For a country that depended on exports for its development, these trading arrangements were important. However, they excluded many goods and all services, so that Belize–together with other countries in the Caribbean–became frustrated at times with the arrangements. This sense of disappointment was then aggravated when the US and EU signed PTAs with other countries and regions that eroded the preferences given to Caribbean states.[8]

Belize had specialized in forestry for much of its life. However, the timber industry had gone into sharp decline after 1950. By the time Belize became independent, the structure of the economy had become similar to other countries in the Caribbean and Central America. Primary activities (mainly agriculture, but also forestry, fishing and mining) accounted for just over one quarter of GDP (see Table 6.1). This was roughly the same as secondary activities (mainly manufacturing, but also construction, electricity and water), but less than services which accounted for some 40 per cent of GDP. Thirty years later, however, primary activities were little more than ten per cent, while two-thirds of GDP was accounted for by services. Secondary activities, including petroleum, had fallen to just over 20 per cent.[9]

Belize had therefore become specialized in services–in common with almost all other countries in the Caribbean. Since one of the most important services is tourism, it is no surprise to find that the pattern of final

---

6 The CBI would be expanded in later years to include more goods. See Bulmer-Thomas (2012), Chapter 12.
7 The EC would become the European Union (EU) in 1993, while the Lomé Convention would be replaced by the Cotonou Convention in 2000. Finally, in 2008 the preferential trade arrangements were replaced by an Economic Partnership Agreement (EPA) between the EU on the one hand and CARIFORUM on the other with the latter consisting of all CARICOM states together with the Dominican Republic.
8 The North American Free Trade Agreement (NAFTA) was especially problematic, as it gave Mexico unrestricted access to the US across a whole range of goods in which the Caribbean could only compete with preferences.
9 When this book was completed, the latest figures on shares of GDP at current prices from the Central Bank of Belize were for 2008. That is why Table 6.1 stops in that year.

Table 6.1: Sectoral and final expenditure shares of GDP (%), 1980-2008

	Primary	Secondary	Services	Exports of goods & services	Household consumption	Public Expenditure	Investment	Imports of goods & services
1980	27.4	30.9	41.7	55.4	71.9	17.2	24.1	68.6
1990	20.0	22.2	57.8	62.2	64.6	12.9	20.4	60.1
2000	16.7	21.2	62.1	53.0	74.1	12.9	33.7	73.7
2008	12.2	22.8	65.1	62.1	64.7	15.8	27.4	70.0

Sources: World Bank, *World Development Indicators* (WDI) and Central Bank of Belize (2011a).
Note: Shares are based on GDP at current prices.

expenditure had also changed. Although household consumption is still the largest item of expenditure, exports of goods and services (see Table 6.1) are now almost as important. However, imports of goods and services are usually an even higher share of GDP than exports with the difference explained by current transfers (mainly remittances) and net capital inflows. Public current spending, on the other hand, accounts for only a small share of final expenditure, while investment has averaged around one-quarter of GDP.[10]

The long-run performance of the Belizean economy is usually measured by GDP at constant prices.[11] However, this takes no account of population growth so a better measure is GDP per head at constant prices. The statistics on the Belizean population have, unfortunately, become controversial following the 2010 census. Before publication, estimates based on sample data and forecasts based on demographic models had suggested that the population had reached 344,000 by mid-2010. Yet the census recorded only 312,000. The difference, 32,000, represents around ten per cent of the population–a not inconsiderable figure.

It is normal for population figures to be revised after census publication, but the revisions required for Belize have been very large. Nevertheless, they must be done since one has to assume that the census figure is accurate what

---

[10] Investment is mainly gross fixed capital formation by the public and private sectors, but it also includes changes in inventories.
[11] The World Bank, *World Development Indicators* (WDI) convert the GDP of all countries to US dollars at 2000 prices using official exchange rates. This source, available digitally, is used here in order to facilitate international comparisons. The data are, of course, derived from official Belize sources.

ever reservations have been expressed. In fairness to the census, the implied annual population growth after 2000 (the last census) is 2.6 per cent–perhaps a more realistic figure than the 3.4 per cent suggested by the previous estimate.

If we take first the whole post-independence period (1980-2010), the Belizean economy, measured by GDP at constant prices, has grown at nearly five per cent per year (see Table 6.2). Most of this growth, however, is explained by the increase in population so that the growth of GDP per head has been a more modest 2.2 per cent. This equates to a doubling of GDP per head roughly every thirty years–a respectable performance and one that compares favorably over the same period (1980-2010) both with Central America (0.8 per cent) and the Caribbean as a whole (1.7 per cent).

Table 6.2: GDP and GDP per head growth (% per year at 2000 prices), 1980-2010

	GDP	Population	GDP per head	Central America	Caribbean
1980-1985	0.4	2.6	-2.1	-3.1	1.6
1985-1990	9.7	2.7	6.9	0.4	1.5
1990-1995	5.8	2.9	2.8	2.4	-0.3
1995-2000	6.0	2.7	3.2	2.0	3.0
2000-2005	5.4	2.4	2.9	1.5	2.3
2005-2010	2.3	2.6	-0.3	1.5	2.7
1980-2010	4.9	2.6	2.2	0.8	1.7

Source: WDI and Bulmer-Thomas (2012); Population plus GDP per head may not equal GDP due to rounding.
Notes: Central America is an aggregate of the five members of Central American Common Market CACM; the Caribbean is an aggregate of the 28 countries in the Statistical Appendix to Bulmer-Thomas (2012); the population figures for Belize from 2000 onwards have been adjusted in view of the 2010 census results.

There is no room for complacency, however, as Belize was still ranked only 22 out of the 28 countries of the Caribbean in 2010 in terms of GDP per head at constant prices–exactly the same ranking as in 1980. Given the above average growth rate of Belize, this might seem surprising. However, the Caribbean growth rate is dragged down by the poor performance of Haiti–one of the largest countries in terms of population. And the ranking of Belize in terms of GDP per head in current (not constant) dollars is even worse, having fallen to 25 out of 28.[12]

---

[12] These rankings refer to 2008 and can be obtained from Bulmer-Thomas (2012), Tables A.1a, A.18 and A.19.

Figure 6.1: GDP per head, 1981-2010, annual rate of change (%)

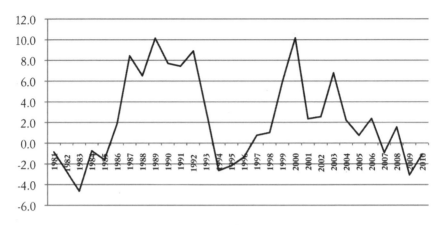

Sources: GDP (at 2000 US dollars) from WDI; population figures from Bulmer-Thomas (2012), Table A.1, updated from 2000 onwards based on 2010 Census.

Table 6.2 also suggests a worrying characteristic of the Belizean economy. This is the high volatility of the GDP per head growth rate from one five-year period to the next. The first few years of independence coincided with the onset of the Latin American debt crisis that had major implications for commodity prices and contributed to Belize's negative growth in GDP per head between 1980 and 1985. This was followed by an unsustainable boom, when the growth rate of GDP per head reached nearly seven per cent per year (see Table 6.2). GDP per head growth then turned negative again after 2005.

It is easier to observe the fluctuations in the Belizean economy when annual data are used. This is shown in Figure 6.1, where the alternation of periods of "boom" and "slump" are very clear. The first thirty years of independence include three short slumps, when GDP per head declined, and two longer booms. In this 30-year period, the PUP was in power for 15 years, the United Democratic Party (UDP) for ten years and the two parties were both in office in five election years when power changed hands. The average growth rate was 3.2 per cent when the PUP was in power compared with only 0.57 per cent for the UDP and 3.04 per cent for the shared years.

The fluctuations in the growth of the Belize economy since independence have several causes.[13] If we look at the Coefficient of Variation (CV) of the different components of GDP growth (see Table 6.3), we can see

---

[13] This approach is different to that taken by Martin and Manzano (2010), Chapter 1, where the authors seek to identify the binding constraints on growth and find the main one to be low domestic savings.

that the most volatile has been investment.[14] This is true whether constant or current prices are used. Since the annual growth in investment is highly correlated with the annual growth of GDP (see Table 6.3), it is easy to see why the Belize economy is so volatile.[15]

Investment is undertaken by both the private and public sectors. In Belize the government has been responsible on average for a high share of this investment since independence (around 40 per cent), although it has fluctuated between 20 and 60 per cent.[16] Gross fixed capital formation by the public sector has been by far the most volatile component of GDP. In a boom, public investment has occasionally doubled in value over the previous year–only to fall by as much as 40 per cent in a slump. Since public investment in boom years is normally financed by borrowing from abroad, it can lead to a problem of external indebtedness with the central government struggling to service the debt in slump years. This has certainly been the case in Belize and will be revisited in Chapter 6.

Table 6.3: Sources of volatility in the Belize economy, 1981-2008

| | Growth Rate Correlations | | Coefficient of Variation (CV) | |
| | Constant prices | Current prices | Constant prices | Current prices |
	GDP	GDP	CV	CV
GDP	1	1	0.84	0.79
Exports of Goods and Services	0.33	0.68	1.73	1.56
Imports of Goods and Services	0.46	0.52	1.98	1.46
Private Consumption	0.57	0.65	3.50	1.05
Public Consumption	0.01	0.10	1.76	0.87
Investment	0.50	0.64	3.09	2.04

Source: Derived by authors from WDI.
Note: The coefficient in the first two columns has a maximum value of 1.0 in the case of a perfect correlation; the CV in the next two columns has no maximum value.

---

[14] The CV is the standard deviation divided by the mean (average). It is therefore a good measure of volatility in any series.

[15] This result is robust since it makes little difference again whether the correlation coefficient between GDP and investment growth is calculated using constant (0.50) or current (0.64) prices. See Table 6.3.

[16] These figures are derived by taking total investment at current prices as given by WDI and capital spending by the government as reported in Belize Central Bank (2011a), Table 26.

Figure 6.2: Oil and tourism as percentage of total exports, 1980-2010

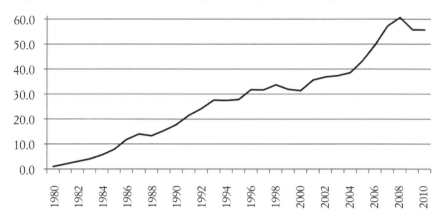

Source: Derived from WDI.

The second source of volatility has been foreign trade.[17] Exports of goods and services have fluctuated in volume and value as a result of world market conditions and supply constraints. This has then led to fluctuations in imports of goods and services. Not surprisingly, therefore, both exports and imports have had high CVs since independence (see Table 6.3), although not as high as in the case of investment. The annual growth of exports and imports is then closely correlated with the annual growth of GDP, although the correlation is much higher when current rather than constant prices are used (see Table 6.3).[18]

By 1981 Belize had shaken off its dependence on forestry exports. Instead, exports came mainly from a small number of agricultural and marine exports such as sugar, bananas, citrus and shrimp. Indeed, in the year of independence these four products accounted for almost all domestic exports and about two-thirds of merchandise exports.[19] Since their prices were determined in world markets over which Belize had no control, there were bound to be fluctuations in the value of export earnings and this could easily be compounded by changes on the supply side due to the weather. Service exports were still small, accounting for a little over ten per cent of total exports.[20]

---

[17] Readers may have noted that the CV for private consumption at constant prices is even higher than for foreign trade. However, it is much lower at current prices. Careful examination of the data suggest that the constant price data for private consumption in the 1980s (see Central Bank of Belize (2011a), Table 36) are not entirely reliable, so too much should not be read into the high CV.

[18] This is because a large part of the volatility in exports has to do with prices.

[19] Merchandise exports are the sum of domestic exports and re-exports.

[20] Total exports are the sum of merchandise exports and service exports.

Thirty years later the situation had changed completely. The "traditional" commodity exports now represented barely 20 per cent of merchandise exports. Instead, the main commodity export had become oil. This started to be exported in 2006 and by the following year was more important than all the "traditional" commodity exports put together. Even this, however, was dwarfed by the rise in the importance of service exports. These included business and government services, but by far the most important was tourism (overnight and cruise ship visitors). Indeed, oil and tourism went from one per cent of total exports at the time of independence to approximately 60 per cent thirty years later (see Figure 6.2).

Belize, as so often before, has therefore re-invented its export sector.[21] However, it has not eliminated the problem of volatility. World commodity prices, especially for oil, are still very important, but they have been joined by income fluctuations and exchange rate variations in the countries from which the tourists come. And tourism is just as susceptible to weather conditions in Belize as agricultural and fisheries exports.

Distribution

We can think of "production" as the cake and "distribution" as the way in which the cake is divided. It can be in equal portions or done very unequally. One distribution may also be economically efficient, but socially very unfair. This in broad terms is what happened in the US in the 30 years after the mid-1970s when the share of income received by the richest one per cent jumped from 10 to 20 per cent. On the other hand, it is possible to give priority to distribution even at the expense of production. This is what happened in Cuba in the 1960s when output rose very slowly, but income inequality declined dramatically.

What has been the situation in Belize? We are limited in what we can say, because until recently there were no reliable studies on distribution. At the time of independence, however, all contemporary observers were struck by the lack of extremes in the Belizean distribution of income. There were many poor people, but the rich did not flaunt their wealth and the Prime Minister, George Price, was famous for the austere example that he set.[22]

---

[21] Belize has also re-invented its re-exports through the launch of the Corozal Free Zone (CFZ). The Belize Central Bank and the Statistical Institute of Belize include sales through the CFZ in merchandise exports, but the World Bank (WB) excludes them. As CFZ sales are so different to other types of exports, we have chosen to follow the WB methodology.

[22] See Smith (2011).

The contrast with the neighbouring countries, where the rich engaged in conspicuous consumption while living in communities with high security, could not have been more marked.

Nor, at first, did Belize experience the problem found in many parts of the Caribbean where a large part of production accrued to foreigners, making GNI[23]–the income received by residents–much smaller than GDP. The extreme case was Puerto Rico, where foreign-owned companies were so dominant that GNI had fallen to two-thirds of GDP by the 1980s. However, many Caribbean countries had a similar experience as a result of the presence of key foreign companies in the crucial export sector.

In the year before independence, the ratio of GNI to GDP was 99 per cent (see Figure 6.3). The Belize Estate & Produce Co. was a shadow of its former self and the foreign companies such as Tate & Lyle were not making large profits that could be transferred out of the country. However, Direct Foreign Investment (DFI) increased in the 1980s and 1990s, so that the ratio of GNI to GDP had fallen to 90 per cent by the start of the new millennium (see Figure 6.3). The new investment was certainly needed in Belize, but the outflow of profits was substantial. Indeed, investment income payments abroad–adjusted by the Central Bank of Belize to include an estimate for profit remittances from the tourism industry[24]–rose from around US$15 million in the mid-1980s to US$150 million in 2010.[25]

The position in Belize is now much more typical of that found in the rest of the Caribbean and the neighbouring countries. In that narrow sense there is no special cause for alarm. However, Belize has a relatively large number of expatriates from rich countries whose payments of income received in Belize and deposited in their own foreign bank accounts are almost certainly not fully captured in the Central Bank figures. Indeed, large parts of the real estate and other businesses are "under the radar" as far as the authorities are concerned and there is anecdotal evidence that transfer pricing is widespread in the import trade as a way of transferring profits abroad.[26] Thus, 85 per cent is probably a more realistic figure for the ratio of GNI to GDP in Belize today.

---

[23] GNI is Gross National Income; it adjusts GDP by adding income from abroad and subtracting income paid abroad.

[24] See Central Bank of Belize (2011), p. 92.

[25] This increase has coincided with the period when Michael Ashcroft, a British billionaire, has made major investments in Belize that often have been very profitable. It is not unreasonable, therefore, to refer to the rise in investment income payments abroad and the fall in the ratio of GNI to GDP as the "Ashcroft effect".

[26] Transfer pricing occurs if a merchant pays a higher price for imports than necessary, the excess being then paid into a foreign bank account owned by the merchant. It is also a way of reducing tax liability.

Figure 6.3: Ratio of GNI to GDP, 1980-2010

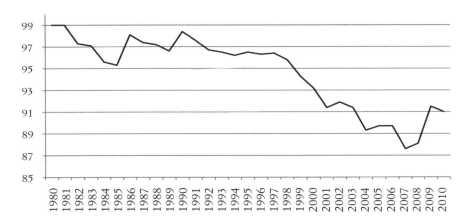

Source: United Nations National Accounts (http://unstats.un.org/unsd/snaama/Introduction.asp).

If true, this means that 15 per cent of GDP does not accrue to citizens of Belize. What, however, happens to the remaining 85 per cent? The first attempt to measure the distribution of income took place in 1995 and the statistics suggested that Belize had a degree of income inequality that rivaled Brazil (at that time the most unequal country in the world).[27] While it may well have been true that income inequality had increased since independence, such an extreme distribution did not seem plausible. Fortunately, we now know that there were serious flaws in the 1995 study and it is therefore safest to disregard its results.[28]

The first reliable study of poverty and inequality in Belize was not carried out until 2002 and a second one, using the same methodology, was done in 2009. The first year, however, was one of moderate growth while the second coincided with a recession. This needs to be remembered when evaluating the published statistics. Nonetheless, these two studies are of excellent quality and are the first opportunity to address in detail the question of distribution in Belize.

---

[27] The Belize Gini coefficient (the most widely used measure of income inequality with a maximum of 1.0) was given as 0.596. The top 10 per cent of income recipients were said to receive 45.8 per cent of national income and the bottom 10 per cent were said to receive 0.6 per cent (the results can be found in WDI). All these statistics were much more extreme than those for Guatemala–a country notorious for its inequality.

[28] There is an excellent discussion of the methodological problems in Government of Belize (2004).

Table 6.4: Poverty and distribution as percentage of population, 2002 and 2009

	Indigence	*All poor*	*Gini*	*Expenditure by quintile*	
				Top	*Bottom*
2002	10.8	33.8	0.40	na	na
2009	15.8	41.3	0.42	48.8	5.8

Sources: Government of Belize (2004) and Government of Belize (2011).
Note: Numbers refer to individuals–not households.

The 2002 Poverty Assessment Report revealed the extent of extreme poverty (indigence), which happens when an individual's income is insufficient even to purchase the minimum food requirements for their gender and age. The level of indigence was estimated at just over ten per cent (see Table 6.4).[29] The Report then estimated the minimum non-food expenditure needed to avoid poverty and found that a further 23 per cent did not have sufficient income for this. Thus, one-third of all Belizeans were defined as poor in 2002–despite the fact that the economy had been growing in the previous few years (see Figure 6.1). Income inequality, however, was not severe with a Gini coefficient estimated at 0.4.[30]

The results of the 2002 study suggested that poverty in Belize was comparable to the levels found in other countries with similar incomes per head, while income inequality was a little lower. However, any complacency that might have been suggested by these findings was swept away with the publication of the 2009 Poverty Assessment Report. Although the survey was carried out in a recession year, the results were nonetheless very shocking.

The most striking result was the increase in indigence. This had jumped to 15.8 per cent by 2009 (see Table 6.4), meaning that Belize now had the same level of extreme poverty as Guatemala in 2000. Poverty as a whole had climbed to 41.3 per cent, so that "moderate" poverty had also increased. The survey also estimated that the top quintile was responsible for nearly half of all expenditure while the bottom quintile accounted for only 5.8 per cent (see Table 6.4). The Gini coefficient had increased, but not greatly–a

---

[29] The numbers reported in Table 6.5 refer to individuals. The Report also records poverty by households. This is lower as poor households tend to have larger than average families.

[30] The income reported in the survey should include remittances from abroad. It is likely that these favour the poorer groups in Belize society and this may help to explain the relatively low Gini.

result that some might find surprising in view of the rise in conspicuous consumption since 2002.[31]

The 2009 Poverty Assessment Report, made widely available in 2011, suggested that something had gone seriously wrong in Belize as the country prepared to celebrate 30 years of independence. Indeed, in the Caribbean only Haiti and the Dominican Republic had higher levels of poverty.[32] The Report was also exceptionally useful in identifying the characteristics of indigent and poor households.[33]

The first characteristic identified was the extent to which indigence in particular was associated with rural areas. No less than 80 per cent of indigent households were found in the rural economy. This helps to explain why Belize is different from the rest of the Caribbean, since in Belize the proportion of the population in rural areas is both high (c.50 per cent) and has been rising. This, in turn, reflects the increase in immigration from Central America–especially Guatemala–since so many of the migrants come from an agricultural background. In the long-run this may prove to be beneficial for Belize, but in the short-run it is a major factor behind the increase in indigence.

A second characteristic has to do with education levels. Among indigent households, only 12 per cent of heads of family had a secondary or post-secondary education compared with 35 per cent for heads of households nationally. In other words, nearly 90 per cent of heads of indigent households left school with only a primary school education–and in a few cases not even that. Secondary school attendance rates in Belize are low by international standards, so it is not surprising that so few heads of indigent households have had access. This is clearly an area where Belize is falling badly behind in comparison with other countries in Central America and the Caribbean.

The biggest surprise, however, in the 2009 study was the regional dimension of poverty. It had been known for many decades that Toledo contained a disproportionate number of poor households among the six Belizean districts. This had been confirmed as recently as 2002, when it was shown that 45 per cent of households in Toledo were indigent compared with 7.5 per

---

[31] The Gini coefficient shown in Table 6.5 is based on income as reported by those sampled. All groups tend to under-report their income, but the degree of under-reporting is often greatest among the rich.

[32] See Bulmer-Thomas (2012), Table 15.3. The reader should be aware, however, that international comparisons of poverty are sensitive to the extent to which non-food consumption is included in the definition.

[33] The Poverty Assessment Reports have much less to say about the characteristics of the rich. In general, however, the top decile–in Belize and elsewhere–receives less of its income from wages and salaries and more from rents, distributed profits and bank interest. These non-labor sources of income are not heavily taxed in Belize so that fiscal policy contributes very little to the distribution of income.

cent nationally.[34] By contrast, household indigence rates in other districts in 2002 were five per cent or less.

The Report found that in 2009 the proportion of households in Toledo living in extreme poverty had fallen to 37.5 per cent–a welcome and surprising development.[35] This was attributed to the fact that Toledo was:[36] "less affected by economic downturn due to remoteness, increase in cocoa production, government programmes [that] reduce social isolation increasing search for employment in towns."

However, the proportion in Corozal had jumped to 15.7 per cent, while in Orange Walk and Stann Creek it had risen above ten per cent. In all three cases, the increase was attributed to declines in traditional exports (especially sugar and bananas) coupled with floods and hurricanes in the previous two years.

Poverty and indigence in Belize are clearly influenced by many factors, some of which are structural and some cyclical. If the next Poverty Assessment Report were to coincide with a "boom" year, when prices for export commodities were high and when the economies from which tourists and remittances come were growing strongly, then it is highly likely that the rates of indigence and poverty would be much lower than in 2009. On the other hand, the opposite could easily be true and the poor quantity and quality of education in Belize will be a structural cause of poverty for many years.

What the 2009 Poverty Assessment Report also showed is that the rate of unemployment is much higher among poor households than in the population as a whole. This is hardly surprising and is true across the Caribbean and Central America as well. However, it demonstrates the importance of job creation in efforts to improve distribution and it is to this that we now turn.

Employment

Employment has been the Achilles heel of the Caribbean development model in the last half century. The rate of unemployment is high in almost all countries.[37] This is the case of relatively rich countries like Martinique as well as poor countries such as Suriname. Only Cuba has had a very low rate, but this has been due to the existence of high rates of disguised unemploy-

---

[34] Because this figure refers to households, it is different from Table 6.4, which refers to individuals. See also footnote 28.
[35] See Government of Belize (2011), Table 3.7.
[36] See Government of Belize (2011), Table ES6.
[37] See Bulmer-Thomas (2012), Figure 15.7.

ment in the public sector rather than being a true reflection of the state of the labour market. The highest rates of unemployment (in excess of 20 per cent) are found in a number of ex-British colonies such as Dominica and Grenada.

The labour market in Belize is far from satisfactory and that has been true for almost all the period since independence (and, indeed, for many years before it). New entrants to the labour force struggle to find work, while employers complain about the quality of those they hire. Unemployment is high, although just how high depends on how it is measured (the decennial census, for example, uses a definition that is very different from that used in the annual labor market survey).[38] Whatever measure is used, however, cannot disguise the fact that the employment situation in Belize leaves a lot to be desired.

The Belizean labour market has many features in common with other countries in the Caribbean and Central America. However, there are also important differences. This is perhaps not surprising in view of the fact that Belize is the only country that belongs to both regions. We will explore the similarities below, but here we start with the differences.

Most countries of the Caribbean and Central America, including Belize, have experienced net outward migration in the last 30 years. Yet Belize has also experienced high levels of gross inward migration since independence. Belizeans may have emigrated, in other words, but at the same time many others have come to Belize to take their place. The 2010 census estimated the foreign-born at 14.8 per cent of the population with over 80 per cent of these migrants having come from Guatemala, El Salvador, Honduras and Mexico.[39]

Most of these immigrants to Belize have come from an agricultural background. Not surprisingly, therefore, they have chosen to work in the agricultural sector. Thus, the proportion of the labor force employed in agriculture has remained high, fluctuating between 20 and 25 per cent.[40] While in most countries there has been a marked shift in employment from agriculture to industry and services, Belize has experienced only a small decline in the agricultural share. At the same time there has been a fall in the industrial share (from around 20 per cent in 1993 to 15 per cent in 2009).

---

[38] In 2000, for example, the census suggested a rate of unemployment of 20.3 per cent while the annual survey estimated it at 11.1 per cent.

[39] See Statistical Institute of Belize (2011).

[40] Agriculture is defined here to include forestry and fishing, although forestry today is unimportant. If we compare the figure for agriculture alone (i.e., excluding forestry), it was 29 per cent in 1946 (see Carey-Jones (1953), p. 97). Thus, Belize has experienced a much smaller decline in the share of agricultural employment in the last 70 years than almost any other country.

Because of the importance of agriculture, Belize has therefore remained a relatively rural country. Indeed, the rural share of the population has remained around 50 per cent throughout the period since independence.[41] This is very different from other countries in the Caribbean and Central America, where rising levels of income per head have been associated with an increase in urbanization. And Belize has not experienced the extreme concentrations in a single city found in many of the countries in these two regions.

These are the main differences and they help to explain the workings of the Belizean labour market. Agriculture is still important and its growth has enabled Belize to become self-sufficient in a number of important foodstuffs such as rice. Industry, especially manufacturing, has suffered from the combination of a small domestic market, declining tariff rates and PTAs (this is unlikely to change with the recent emergence of the oil industry as it creates so few jobs).

There are also many similarities with neighbouring countries. The service sectors have been growing in importance and now account for around two-thirds of all jobs compared with perhaps 50 per cent at the time of independence. This trend seems set to continue with its share increasing in the future at the expense of agriculture rather than industry. This is a result of industry being reduced to a core of activities that have learnt to survive in the face of import competition while many agricultural sectors will struggle to move from self-sufficiency to exports. And existing agricultural export activities, such as sugar and bananas, face very uncertain prospects.

Belize has also experienced the same rise in female participation[42] as other regional countries. While the male participation in Belize has remained fairly constant at around 75 per cent, the female rate has jumped from around one-quarter at the time of independence to around 50 per cent thirty years later.[43] As a result, the total participation rate has steadily increased. More Belizeans of working age are therefore in the labour force, although this does not mean they are necessarily employed as they may be seeking work rather than in a job.

Another similarity is the gendered nature of sectoral jobs. Nearly 90 per cent of female jobs are in services with less than five per cent in agriculture. Female jobs in industry are also relatively unimportant today, although they were much more important before the collapse of garment exports.[44]

---

[41] See Government of Belize (2011), Table 2.7.

[42] The participation rate is defined as the ratio of those aged 15 and above in work to the total population of that age.

[43] See Government of Belize (2011), Table 2.20.

[44] In the 1990s industrial jobs accounted for between 10 and 13 per cent of all female employment.

By contrast, only half of all male jobs are in services compared with 30 per cent in agriculture and 20 per cent in industry. If the service sectors continue to be the main drivers of the Belizean economy with a decline in the relative importance of agriculture, this can therefore be expected to favour female over male employment unless jobs become less "gendered" than in the past.

In 1984, shortly after independence, the Central Statistical Office conducted a labour force survey.[45] Although not strictly comparable with the results of the annual surveys carried out from the 1990s onwards, this was the most thorough attempt to date to understand the workings of the Belizean labour market. One of the most striking features of the survey was what it revealed about unemployment. It estimated the rate at 14 per cent with female unemployment at 24.1 per cent and male at 9.1 per cent. Furthermore, the survey also showed a wide disparity among the six districts with the highest rate (male and female combined) in Stann Creek (23.7 per cent) and the lowest in Corozal (8.4 per cent).[46]

Some of the gap between labour supply and demand could be attributed to the recession that Belize experienced at the time of independence (see Figure 6.1). However, when surveys started to provide annual data in the 1990s, the rate of unemployment was still very high. In 1993, for example, when the economy was growing rapidly, the rate was nearly ten per cent (see Figure 6.4) with a female rate of 14.5 per cent and a male rate of 7.5 per cent. The unemployment rate then rose as the economy entered a period of stagnation, reaching a peak of 14.3 per cent in 1998.

The unemployment rate in Belize is very sensitive to the business cycle, falling when the economy is booming and rising when it is stagnant. This explains the sharp rise in 2009 when the economy once again entered a recession. However, the trend rate is flat with the total unemployment rate averaging around 11 per cent (higher for women and lower for men). It has proved very difficult to lower this trend rate despite recognition by policymakers that unemployment carries huge economic, social and political costs.

The definition of unemployment used in the decennial census gives much higher figures with the 2010 unemployment rate estimated at 23.1 per cent–nearly one-quarter of the labour force.[47] This can be compared with a figure of 20.3 per cent in 2000 and 14 per cent in 1984, when a similar definition of unemployment was used. As before, female rates of unemployment are much higher than male rates when the census definitions of unemployment are used (see Table 6.5). Furthermore, there is a

---

[45] The results are reported in Central Statistical Office (1987).
[46] In every district, the female unemployment rate was much larger than the male rate.
[47] See Statistical Institute of Belize (2011).

Figure 6.4: Rates of unemployment (%), 1993-2009

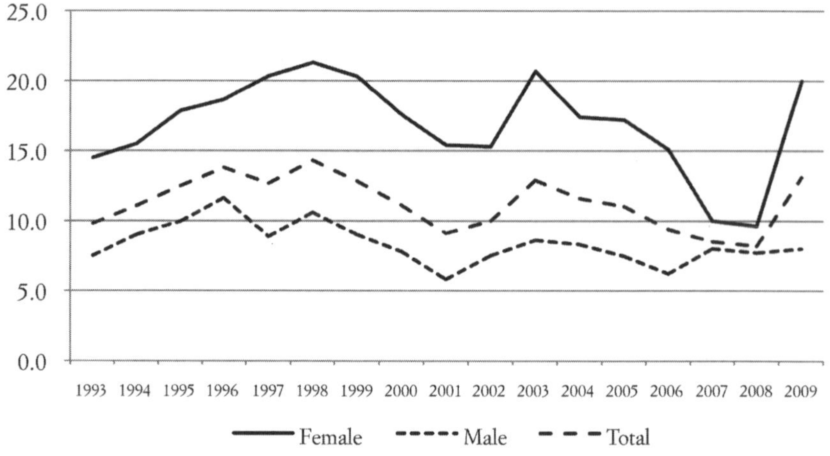

Legend: Female ——— Male ····· Total — — —

Source: For 1993-2008, WDI; for 2009, Government of Belize (2011), Table 2.21.
Note: WDI does not give male and female rates of unemployment in 2000 and 2008; these have therefore been estimated assuming they moved in line with the total rate.

regional dimension to these rates of unemployment, although the differences had narrowed in 2010 compared with 1984 and the highest rate was now found in Cayo. The most worrying development, however, was the sharp rise in the unemployment rate in Corozal where the sugar sector was so badly affected.

Table 6.5: Unemployment rates by district (%), 1984 and 2010

District	1984			2010		
	Male	Female	Total	Male	Female	Total
Corozal	3.1	23.9	8.4	15.1	41.0	24.5
Orange Walk	6.6	23.0	9.8	12.8	35.7	20.4
Belize	13.0	21.0	16.1	18.8	27.3	22.6
Cayo	5.4	20.4	10.3	19.5	36.7	26.2
Stann Creek	13.6	38.8	23.7	15.5	30.7	21.1
Toledo	12.4	32.1	17.9	12.9	38.7	21.1
Total	9.1	24.1	14.0	16.7	33.0	23.1

Source: Central Statistical Office (1987) and Statistical Institute of Belize (2011).

The persistence of such high rates of unemployment demands explanations. One possibility, favored by employers, is the minimum wage rate. As

Table 6.6 shows, the Belizean rate in 2007–even before minimum wages were raised in 2010[48]–was much higher than for all the neighbouring countries. Although only 16 per cent of Belize workers are estimated to be paid the minimum, the wages and salaries of many other workers are set in relation to it so that there is a cascading effect.[49] That is why employers so often complain about the level of the minimum wage rate, citing it as a reason why many firms are unable to compete internationally.

Table 6.6: Minimum wage rates, US dollars per day 2007

Belize	10 to 12	Honduras	2.88 to 6.29
El Salvador	2.27 to 5.81	Mexico	4.35 to 4.63
Guatemala	5.81 to 5.97	Nicaragua	1.85 to 2.81

Source: International Labour Organisation (ILO), Minimum Wages Database (http://www.ilo.org/travaildatabase/servlet/minimumwages/).
Note: The Belizean rate is established per hour; this has been multiplied by eight to give a daily rate; national currencies have been converted to US dollars at the average official exchange rate for the relevant year. The rates for El Salvador are for 2006.

Even if there is some truth in this, the notion that the Belizean minimum wage rate could be reduced to the level of the neighbouring countries is absurd. Any reduction would push many more Belizeans into poverty.[50] The rate is high because the cost of living is high and this is a consequence of Belize being a small country that imports a much larger proportion of what it consumes than its neighbours. Even for those goods produced locally, the costs of distribution tend to be higher than in other countries because of the small size of the internal market.

Minimum wage rates higher than in neighbouring countries can always be justified if the labour force is more productive. This depends on skills, which in turn are highly correlated with the level of education of the em-

---

[48] An increase to BZ$3.0 per hour for all workers had been promised in 2007, but was not implemented until 2010 when it was set at BZ$3.10.

[49] According to the 2010 census, the median monthly wage was around BZ$900 (for males BZ$922 and for females BZ$882). This is equivalent to a daily rate of US$22.5, assuming 20 days of work per calendar month, compared with a minimum wage of $12.40 in the same year.

[50] The 2009 Poverty Assessment Report set the indigence line at US$1,000 and the poverty line at $US1,700 (adult male per year). This is equivalent to a daily rate of US$7.55 to avoid poverty, assuming 20 days worked each month and three weeks holiday. Although the minimum wage is higher than this (see Table 6.7), not everyone on the minimum wage is able to work full-time throughout the year.

ployed population. Unfortunately, despite recognition by all political parties that education should be a priority, the Belizean workforce is not highly skilled. According to the 2009 Poverty Assessment Report only one in three heads of household had a secondary or tertiary qualification while the gross enrolment ratio for secondary schools has remained around 55 per cent for the whole period since independence.[51] Last, but not least, functional literacy is estimated at only 75 per cent compared with a Latin American and Caribbean average of 90 per cent.[52]

Public policy has given priority to education, so these results make depressing reading. However, they are not entirely surprising. The Belizean population is still very rural and access to secondary schools for pupils outside the main towns is often difficult. Thus, nearly 30 years after independence around 50 per cent of primary school pupils live in rural areas (the same as the share of the population), but only 23 per cent of secondary school students were from rural areas. In time, with increasing urbanization, this problem will resolve itself. However, Belize does not have the luxury of waiting and the skill levels of the future labour force need to be addressed as a matter of urgency.

There is, however, a significant difference between males and females with respect to education. While the 2010 census revealed that there were slightly more boys than girls in pre-school and primary, there were more girls than boys in secondary and tertiary institutions. Indeed, at university level the number of women outnumbered men by two to one. Coupled with the strong presence of women in the service sectors, the prospects for female employment are clearly a lot brighter than for men. This is not, however, peculiar to Belize as similar trends are found in other parts of Central America and the Caribbean.

Faced with high rates of unemployment and poor job prospects, it is not surprising that so many Belizeans have emigrated. This outflow started in the first decade of the 20th century when many Belizeans left for Panama to find work in the Canal Zone. It accelerated after Hurricane Hattie in 1961.[53] It did not stop with independence, some 40,000 leaving in the 1980s. Tighter entry requirements, especially in the US, reduced the outflow in the 1990s when an estimated 25,000 left with an additional 20,000 in the first decade of the 21st century.

Outward migration in the first two decades after independence was so high that it exceeded the large number of immigrants coming to Belize. The rate of gross outward migration (see Table 6.7) can be estimated at two per

---

[51] The gross enrolment ratio refers to the proportion of the total age cohort in secondary schools.
[52] See United Nations Development Programme (2010).
[53] See Bulmer-Thomas (2012), Figure 11.9.

cent of the population in each year in the 1980s and a little over one per cent in the 1990s. In these two decades, net births exceeded the change in the population so there was net outward migration despite the large numbers coming to Belize as immigrants.

Table 6.7: Belize migration rates since Independence

Period	Net migration as %age of change in population	Rate of net outward migration (% per year)	Rate of gross outward migration (% per year)	Rate of gross inward migration (% per year)
1981-1990	-30.2	0.76	2.03	1.26
1991-2000	-4.9	0.13	1.15	1.02
2001-2010	8.5	-0.21	0.72	0.92

Sources: Derived by authors from data on population, births and deaths in WDI (with population data after 2000 adjusted in the light of 2010 census) and from data on gross outward migration in Straughan (n.d.).
Note: Net migration estimated as the difference between population change and net births; gross inward migration estimated as the difference between net migration and gross outward migration.

It was only in the first decade of the 21st century that the numbers entering exceeded the numbers leaving Belize (see Table 6.7). In both cases the rate was lower than before. Emigration became more difficult, while the rate of immigration slowed down as a result of improved economic conditions in Central America. And there was an improvement in the average education of the foreign-born population. In the 2000 census 60 per cent had no education at all, while this had fallen to less than one-third by 2010.[54]

The biggest impact of these changes has been on Belizean ethnicity. The Creole population by 2010 had fallen to 21 per cent compared with 50 per cent for the Mestizos.[55] The Garifuna population even declined in absolute terms, its share of the total population falling by nearly half to 4.6 per cent compared with 1980.[56] Yet, despite the change in the balance of ethnicities, there was no real prospect of Belize becoming "just another" Central

---

[54] It might be assumed that the high figure among the foreign-born in 2000 was due to a large number of small children being included in the 2000 census. However, this is not correct as only 4,459 out of 34,279 were under the age of 14 in the year 2000 (it was 4,928 out of 45,994 in the year 2010).
[55] In 1980 the Creole share had been 39% and the Mestizo share 33.1% (the Maya share remained the same in 1980 and 2010 at nearly 10%). See Bolland and Moberg (1995).
[56] This was not much bigger than the Mennonite population in 2010 (3.6 per cent).

American country. The children of the foreign-born population were being rapidly assimilated into Belizean culture and these changes–including a largely bilingual population–increased Belize's claim to be a "bridge" between Central America and the Caribbean.

Macroeconomic policy

After independence, Belize was, in theory, free to determine its own policies. However, Belize soon discovered that its freedom of action could still be restricted in various ways. The balance of payments crisis at the beginning of the 1980s forced the PUP government to seek a loan from the IMF and the loan came with numerous strings attached. The Fund would later apply pressure to Belize through its regular Article IV consultation process and the same would happen through other international agencies when they wanted a change in policy.[57]

These pressures could come not only from multilateral institutions, but also from foreign governments. The British government in the mid-1990s, for example, used the bilateral tax treaty between the two countries to ensure that the UDP government did not end the fiscal privileges extended to Michael Ashcroft's companies by the 1990 International Business Companies (IBC) Act.[58] The US government, for its part, used its unilateral drugs certification process to pressure Belize into signing other bilateral treaties that may in some cases have had nothing to do with the trade in narcotics.[59]

Governments in Belize have also faced external challenges to their economic policies from the judicial system, since the court of appeal is composed mainly of non-Belizean judges while the final court of appeal until recently was the judicial committee of the Privy Council in London (it is

---

[57] One example was the sustained campaign by the Organization of Economic Cooperation and Development (OECD) at the end of the 1990s against Belize's offshore financial industry.

[58] The 1990 IBC Act, drafted by Michael Ashcroft's lawyers, authorized the establishment of Public Investment Companies (PICs) with major fiscal concessions. Only two PICs were established before the Act was amended in 1995, the most important being Ashcroft's holding company that has changed names several times since it was created. The 1995 amendment preserved the tax privileges of the two PICs already established.

[59] In a presentation to a US/CARICOM summit in May 1997, Dean Barrow–at the time Deputy Prime Minister–stated: "The suspicion, too, can never be far from our minds that certification is a form of pressure to force us to sign certain treaties … that …, in individual clauses, require modification to bring them into conformity with our Constitution."

now the Caribbean Court of Justice in Trinidad & Tobago). The nationalization in 2009 of Belize Telemedia Ltd (BTL) was challenged in this way, as was the ninth amendment to the Constitution in 2011 mandating that public utilities should have a majority government stake.[60]

Economic policy in Belize, therefore, has had to be shaped taking into account external realities. However, the domestic constraints have been even more important and at the centre of the macroeconomic framework since independence has been exchange rate policy. Indeed, the mandate of the Central Bank of Belize, established in 1982, could not make this more clear since Clause 6 of the Bank Act states:[61]

> Within the context of the economic policy of the Government, the Bank shall be guided in all its actions by the objectives of fostering monetary stability especially as regards stability of the exchange rate and promoting credit conditions conducive to the growth of the economy of Belize.

"Stability of the exchange rate" in the above quote refers to the peg of the Belize dollar against the US dollar. As we saw in Chapter 4, this had been set in 1976 when the newly established Belize Monetary Authority broke the link with sterling set on 31 December 1949. Belize therefore once again linked its currency to the US dollar, as it had first done in 1894, but this time at 2:1 rather than at parity.

The main economic argument for linking the Belize to the US dollar rather than the pound sterling was the overwhelming importance of the US in the country's external trade. The US was already the most important partner before 1976 and its importance subsequently increased even further. However, the US share of Belize's trade peaked in the early 1990s and then declined. The latest figures suggest that the US is now responsible for only one-third of merchandise imports and exports and it is likely to account for a similar share of service trade.[62]

This may still seem a high figure, but it means that two-thirds of Belizean foreign trade is with countries whose currency is not the US dollar. Furthermore, the currencies of most of these countries fluctuate against the US dollar. Thus, what matters for Belize is the weighted average of its currency against those of all its trade partners–not just the US. This is the Nominal Effective Exchange Rate and it becomes, when adjusted for the difference

---

[60] Both judicial challenges were led by Michael Ashcroft's associates, leading to the media coining the phrase "Ashcroft Alliance".

[61] See Central Bank of Belize (2011), p. ii.

[62] Figures on merchandise trade, including the CFZ, from Statistical Institute of Belize (2011a). The exact share of service trade is not known, but the US accounts for around one-third of visitors to Belize.

Figure 6.5: Real effective exchange rate (2005=100)

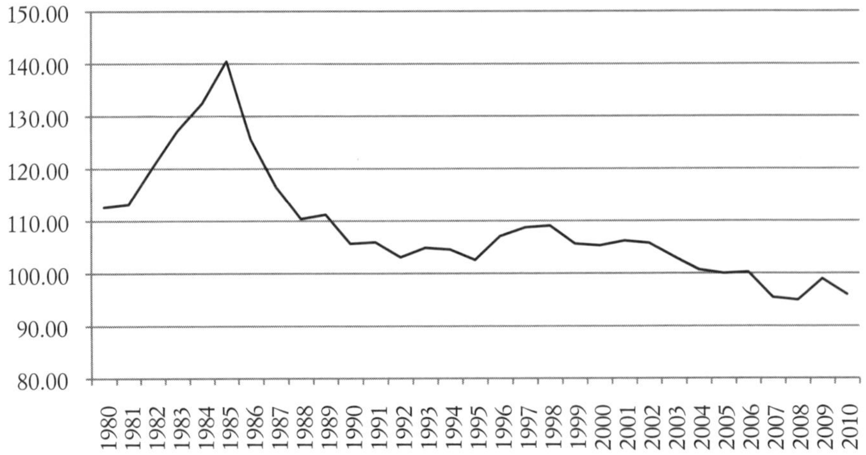

Source: WDI.

in price changes between Belize and its trade partners, the Real Effective Exchange Rate (REER).

The Belizean REER, unlike the peg to the US dollar, is not fixed. When it appreciates, it means that Belize becomes less competitive. When it depreciates, it means that Belize has become more competitive. It is therefore crucial for the economic health of the country. Yet the Central Bank of Belize has no control over many of the variables that determine the REER.

Figure 6.5 shows what has happened to the REER since independence. In the first few years there was a sharp appreciation, implying that Belize was losing competitiveness. This had nothing to do with Belize and everything to do with the strengthening of the US dollar against other currencies. Since 1985, however, the REER has slowly depreciated as the dollar has fallen in value against other currencies while Belizean inflation has remained lower than its main trade partners.

This benign trend in the REER since 1985 might explain why there is so little debate about it in Belize. Furthermore, it can be argued that the US dollar is likely to remain weak while inflation should remain low. It is, however, notoriously difficult to predict exchange rates and there are questions about how "low" Belizean inflation really is. It is measured by the Consumer Price Index (CPI), which in turn is based on a weighted average of a sample of goods and services. These weights were based on 1990 until they were finally updated in 2011,[63] so that for many years they may not

---

[63] See International Monetary Fund (2011).

have been truly representative of household expenditure in Belize.[64] Furthermore, governments of all persuasions have become skilled at targeting particular items of expenditure in order to lower measured inflation.

An example of this is the negligible increase in the CPI in 2010.[65] This very low figure was achieved despite a sharp increase during the year in the General Sales Tax (GST) and price increases for gasoline and diesel at the pump of 21.5 per cent and 25 per cent respectively. The Central Bank of Belize, however, commented:[66] "The modest uptick [in the CPI] occurred as price hikes in the fuel intensive categories of the index were countered by the targeted tax relief initiatives of the government .... Price pressures that were expected to emanate from the 2.5 percentage points increase in the GST to 12.5% in April were substantially mitigated by the government's decision to zero rate basic food items and selected household durables."

It is understandable that governments act in this way to protect households. However, the CPI is also used to approximate the annual change in business costs when calculating the REER. These costs may well be significantly higher. Furthermore, the fluctuations in the value of the REER suggest that Belize's boast of a fixed exchange rate is rather misleading. If the US share of Belize's external trade continues to fall, as may well happen, it will be even harder to achieve exchange rate stability–as measured by the REER–in the future.

Belize is a small open economy and it can be argued that the exchange rate peg has served the country well. By avoiding devaluation, Belize has escaped the fate of Guyana, Jamaica, Nicaragua, Suriname and many others where exchange rate collapse led to very high rates of inflation. Furthermore, it is widely assumed that it would be suicidal for any political party when in government to devalue. However, there are other exchange rate pegs available, including to a basket of currencies, and at some point in the future it may be necessary to change.

In addition to maintaining stability of the exchange rate against the US dollar, the Central Bank of Belize has responsibility for monetary stability. This was almost virgin territory for Belize when the Bank began operations in 1982. When the Belize (British Honduras) dollar came into existence for the first time in 1894, monetary stability was guaranteed by a currency board that required 100 per cent backing by sterling of any notes and coins issued. The Belize Monetary Authority, established in 1976, was able to take a slightly more active role. However, the monetary system that the Central Bank was asked to regulate and supervise in 1982 was still extremely primitive.

---

[64] For the weights themselves, see Statistical Institute of Belize, *Belize Consumer Price Index Basket* (Nov. 1990 = 100).

[65] The Central Bank of Belize first estimated the increase at 0.9%, but this was later revised down to zero. See World Bank (2011), Table 1.

[66] See Central Bank of Belize (2011), pp. 40-1.

Figure 6.6: Ratio of money supply (M2) to GDP (%), 1980–2010

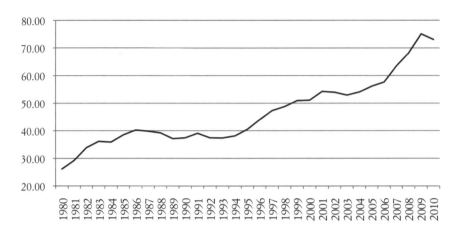

Source: WDI.

All this changed rapidly after independence as Belize acquired a modern financial system. The most significant change was the steady "financial deepening" of the country, as the ratio of the money supply (broadly defined) to GDP rose from around one-quarter at the time of independence to nearly three-quarters thirty years later (see Figure 6.6).[67] Indeed, the money supply expanded in every single year until 2010, when there was a small contraction. This is all the more remarkable in view of the fact that the annual change in the money supply is heavily influenced by the change in net foreign assets, which has fluctuated greatly in Belize from year to year and has often been negative.[68]

Such a rapid growth in the money supply (it has averaged more than ten per cent each year) would normally imply high rates of inflation. This has not happened–at least as measured by the CPI–and this is due to the structural changes that have taken place in Belize since independence. These include a decline in subsistence farming and barter, more people living in

---

[67] The money supply can be narrowly defined (current accounts, notes and coins only–M1) or broadly defined (to include time and saving deposits–M2). Whichever definition is used, "financial deepening" refers to the ratio of the money supply to GDP.

[68] Broad money, i.e., M2, represents the liabilities of the consolidated banking system and is therefore equal by definition to the sum of the banks' domestic and foreign assets. Thus, the change in M2 is equal to the change in net domestic assets ("money of internal origin") and the change in net foreign assets ("money of external origin"). In Belize the change in money of external origin has often been negative, which makes the growth in the money supply in almost every year all the more notable.

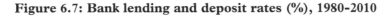

Figure 6.7: Bank lending and deposit rates (%), 1980-2010

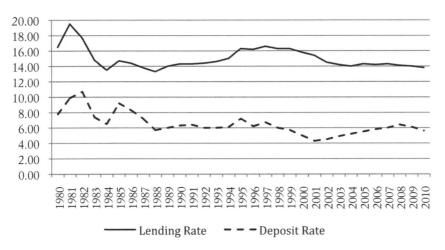

Source: Central Bank of Belize (2011a).

urban areas, growth of credit unions, the expansion of banks and ATMs as well as interest rates on time and savings deposits that have been higher than inflation.

One feature of the monetary system that has not changed, however, has been the enormous spread between lending and deposit rates by banks (see Figure 6.7). The high spread in 1980 could be attributed to the "shallow" financial system under the colonial currency board system, but the spreads have persisted and have become a source of major concern to the authorities as high lending rates by banks undermine investment and make the return on capital needed by new firms extremely challenging.[69]

There are many explanations given for the high spreads.[70] However, the most compelling is the oligopolistic nature of the banking system where one bank (the Belize Bank) accounts for nearly 40 per cent of all deposits and loans.[71] This makes the Belize Bank the market leader and allows it to set rates that other financial institutions are only too happy to follow. And, as the market leader, the Belize Bank has been able to pass on to its customers the increased costs associated with the rise in non-performing loans after 2006.[72]

---

[69] There was a significant decline in lending rates in 2011, but deposit rates fell as well leaving the spread roughly the same as it was before.

[70] Two studies have recently focused on the causes of high spreads in Belize. See Pérez (2011) and Martin and Manzano (2010), Chapter 3.

[71] This was the position at 31 December 2010. See Central Bank of Belize (2011b).

[72] These jumped sharply, as the economy slowed down and eventually went into recession in 2009.

Figure 6.8: Public revenue as percentage of GDP, 1980-2010

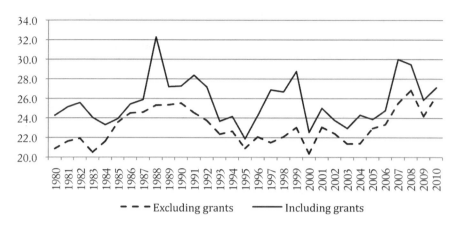

Sources: WDI and Central Bank of Belize (2011a).

The Belize Bank, renamed as such after the purchase of the Royal Bank of Canada by Michael Ashcroft, has been the main beneficiary of the tax concessions given to Public Investment Companies (PICs) by the International Business Companies Act in 1990. These tax concessions, although no longer as generous as they once were,[73] allowed the bank to build market share at the expense of its competitors through aggressive promotion of its services. The dominant market position it acquired then enabled it to maintain the high spread between borrowing and lending rates that should have declined sharply with financial deepening. The high spreads in Belize are therefore a direct consequence of the generous tax concessions granted in 1990 and which are not due to expire in the case of the Belize Bank until 2020.

Tax concessions have an impact on government revenue, which brings us to fiscal policy in Belize. Governments know only too well that fiscal policy can undermine a fixed exchange rate despite the best efforts of central banks to pursue monetary stability. Thus, the gap in Belize between public revenue and expenditure–the central government surplus/deficit–has been subject to careful scrutiny.[74]

Public revenue in Belize comes mainly from indirect taxation. This used to be derived largely from taxes on external trade. However, concessions on import duties to numerous companies, coupled with zero tariffs on imports from CARICOM, have reduced the importance of this source of

---

[73] In February 2005, "commercial banks" tax rates increased from 4% to 8% for PICs and from 10% to 15% for non-PICs. Taxation for PICs rose from 8% to 12% in January 2009. See Pérez (2011), p. 22.

[74] See, for example, Martin and Manzano (2010), Chapter 2.

Figure 6.9: Central government surplus/deficit as percentage of GDP, 1980-2010

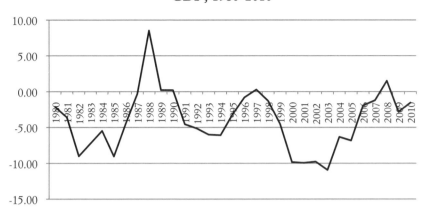

Source: WDI and Central Bank of Belize (2011a).

income. The main source of revenue is now taxes on goods and services closely followed by taxes on income and profits. There are also non-tax revenue streams, which normally represent a little over ten per cent of the total. These sources of revenue, when expressed as a percentage of GDP, have averaged around 23 per cent (see Figure 6.8). In addition, Belize–as a developing country–has received grants each year, raising average revenue to nearly 26 per cent of GDP (see Figure 6.8).

What is surprising about Figure 6.8 is that there has been no strong tendency for revenue to increase as a share of GDP despite the growth of GDP since independence. This is in contrast to what normally happens as countries become richer. This might not matter if public expenditure, including investment, had moved in line with revenue. However, as in all democracies, public expenditure has been subject to strong upward pressure (especially before elections) so that deficits on public spending have been the normal practice.

The central government surplus/deficit as a percentage of GDP since 1980 is shown in Figure 6.9, where it can be seen that deficits have been common. The deficit at the time of independence could be attributed to the impact of the recession on public revenue, but the large deficits in some years in the 1990s and between 2000 and 2006 could not be explained away-so easily. These were years of high public investment, which were particularly important when the PUP was in power.[75]

---

[75] The World Bank became so exercised by this that it cancelled its programme for Belize in 2001 on the grounds of "fiscal and governance concerns". It re-established its programme in 2011. See World Bank (2011), p. 2, n.1.

Figure 6.10: Public external debt/GDP ratio (%), 1980-2010

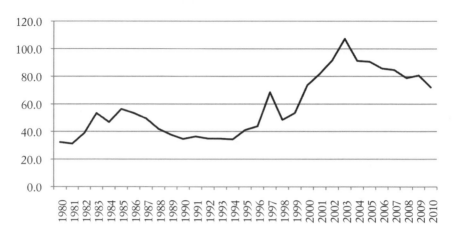

Source: WDI.

The deficits have had to be financed and the central government has resorted to both internal and external borrowing to meet its requirements, although the main source has been external.[76] This led to a big increase in public sector external indebtedness. In addition, the central government guaranteed the borrowing of public sector institutions leading to a further increase in the public external debt. The most important case was borrowing by the Development Finance Corporation (DFC) after 1998 when loans were made unwisely, and in some cases corruptly, to companies and individuals with political connections.[77]

The ratio of public sector external debt to GDP was kept below 60 per cent until the late 1990s (see Figure 6.10). This is the ratio that is often regarded as prudent, as it avoids the need for a high proportion of public expenditure to be spent on external debt servicing. However, by 2003 the ratio was above 100 per cent and external debt servicing became increasingly onerous for Belize. As Belize struggled to meet its external obligations, there was even a risk of devaluation. Belize was forced to restructure its external public debt in 2006, but the instrument used (the "super bond") is like a ticking bomb as it carries an interest rate that increases over time.[78]

---

[76] The public sector external debt at the end of 2010 was BZ$2,018 million; the public sector internal debt on the same date was BZ$368 million. See Central Bank of Belize (2011), Tables A.29 and A.30.

[77] As a result, the DFC was declared insolvent in 2004. See Martin and Manzano (2010), pp. 9-10. It reopened for business in 2009 with support from the Caribbean Development Bank.

[78] The interest rate started at 4.25%; it rose to 6.0% in 2010 and to 8.5% in 2012. The principal will start to be repaid in 2019 with the debt being paid off by 2029.

Still, Belize did succeed in reducing the ratio of external public debt to GDP and it had fallen below 80 per cent by 2010.

Fiscal policy has been the weakest part of the macroeconomic framework in Belize since independence and it invites the question of whether it could have been improved. There is no denying that there are numerous fiscal concessions for companies. Indeed, it is hard to find a company that is paying the full range of taxes that in theory apply to firms, since most qualify for concessions under either the Fiscal Incentives Act, the Export Processing Zone Act, the Commercial Free Zone Act or–in the case of the Belize Bank–the International Business Companies Act.[79] In addition, Belize collects very little from cruise ship visitors and the high tax threshold for individuals (BZ$20,000) means that most pay no income tax at all.

The suspicion that Belize is "under-taxed" is confirmed by international comparisons. If we limit ourselves to the 28 countries of the Caribbean and compare countries in 2005, regression analysis suggests that Belizean revenue was nearly 30 per cent below what might have been expected on the basis of population and GDP per head.[80] This amounts to BZ$140 million, which would have been sufficient in that year to double the size of the education budget. Even if the comparison is made only with other CARICOM countries, Belize still appears to be under-taxed by a large margin.[81]

Reducing tax concessions for firms will not be easy, since they have come to expect them. Yet there is really no alternative unless Belizean governments are prepared to restrain public spending at a time when the electorate is calling for more expenditure on defence, health, education, social security and infrastructure. Of course, many of these tax concessions would be easier to remove if Belize were able to act in unison with other countries. Building a consensus among regional governments in support of ending tax concessions in Central America and the Caribbean is long overdue and Belize will need to play its part in achieving this. The performance of the Belize economy since independence has therefore been very mixed. Macroeconomic stability has been preserved with low rates of inflation and responsible monetary policies. GDP growth has been in line with the Caribbean average and slightly above the rate of growth in Central America. However, the proportion of households living in pov-

---

[79] For more details, see Martin and Manzano (2010), Chapter 2. See also Jenkins and Kuo (2006).

[80] Authors' calculations using data on GDP and population in Bulmer-Thomas (2012) and data on revenue from national sources.

[81] We recognize that this is a controversial result, especially when so many Belizeans complain about being "over-taxed". However, fiscal concessions shrink the tax base and mean that those (companies and individuals) who do not enjoy them must pay more. Thus, the tax rate in Belize is high because the tax base is low.

erty has increased while the rate of unemployment has remained stubbornly high. Furthermore, income distribution has deteriorated and a smaller share of GDP stays in the country. Finally, fiscal policy has at times been reckless, leading to a big increase in public external indebtedness that the country can ill afford.

It was fashionable in the past to argue that a faster rate of growth of GDP would solve all these problems, but such confidence is rare today. Instead, it is increasingly recognized that the growth model itself is flawed as it relies too heavily on tax concessions that prevent the state from providing good quality public services while concentrating income and wealth in a relatively small number of hands.

It is perhaps invidious to focus on one individual, but it is undeniable that the flawed growth model in Belize has taken shape during the period when Michael Ashcroft has been such a dominant force.[82] No single person has been more assiduous in fighting for the fiscal concessions that have contributed to the failures of the growth model as well as leading to an oligopolistic banking system. In this he was helped by the British government as well as an army of highly-paid lawyers and some Belizean politicians. If Belize is to move to a more successful development model in the future, one that combines growth with equity, it will have to be very careful to avoid these errors of the past.

---

[82] We are not alone in thinking this. A recent publication stated: "The influence on the political parties and governments of Belize by the British billionaire Lord Michael Ashcroft, former [Deputy] Chairman of the British Conservative Party, has been inordinate. The unprecedented decision by the UDP Government ... to nationalize his firm, Belize Telemedia Ltd., triggered major litigation, finally resulting in the Government's decision to amend the Belizean Constitution to preserve 51% ownership of public utilities–water, electricity–and telecommunications under government control. Lord Ashcroft's "backlash" is expected to be seen in his financing of the election campaign of the People's United Party. This has been reported to have played a pivotal role in PUP's landslide victory in the 1998 General Elections." See Gibson and Palacio (2011), p. 20, n.27.

7. Conclusions

This book covers over 350 years of economic history in Belize. This is a long period by any standards and the country today bears little resemblance to the early settlement in the 17th century. Yet certain themes recur frequently, suggesting that it is possible to draw a number of conclusions. Some of these are positive, but others are negative. We will begin with the positive ones.

The most important is that Belize has survived against what have been at times overwhelming odds. The illegal logwood settlement in the century before the 1763 Treaty of Paris received little attention from Great Britain, was given no protection and excited much less British interest than the settlements on the Mosquito Shore and in the Bay Islands. Yet today Belize is an independent country with membership of the United Nations, while the former British Settlement of Mosquitia has been absorbed into Nicaragua and the former Bay Islands colony is part of Honduras.

The threat to survival did not end with the Treaty of Paris. Anglo-Spanish rivalry many times threatened Belize with extinction until it was replaced in the 19th century by territorial claims from Guatemala and Mexico. The former seemed less threatening than the latter at first, since the 1859 Anglo-Guatemalan Treaty appeared to have settled the western boundary while the colonial government in Belize risked the wrath of the Mexican authorities by appearing to side with the rebels in the *Guerra de Castas*. In the end, however, it was Mexico that became the "good" neighbour following the 1893 treaty that settled the frontier.

The Guatemalan claim since the late 1930s has not been the only threat to survival that Belize has had to endure. The wave of immigration from Central America starting in the 1980s could easily have overwhelmed the country, while the "colonisation" by North Americans of parts of Belize –notably Placencia and Ambergris Caye–provides a real test of state sovereignty in areas where Belizeans are in danger of becoming a minority. Yet the history of the country suggests that Belize will cope with these challenges and will continue to survive as an independent country.

Belize has also been successful at dealing with more powerful countries than itself. When Belize became a British settlement after the Treaty of Paris, the small population that had run its own affairs had to deal with the administrative machinery of a large imperial state. Yet Belize learnt an important lesson early on: small nations can often secure their interests against large countries because of the asymmetry of priorities. In other words, what is very important for Belize is often of minor interest to the outside power. Belize used this asymmetry to great effect before it became a colony and did so also on a few occasions during the colonial period.[1]

This lesson has also been important for dealing with the US, which in the 20th century replaced the UK as the most important foreign power for Belize. When the US is determined to have its way, there is little that Belize can do to stop it–however unfair the treatment. A good example is US pressure to interdict drugs trafficking, which has sometimes trampled on Belizean sovereignty. Yet there have been occasions when an issue was of great importance to Belize but of minor importance to the US and the smaller country has prevailed. Arguably, much the same could be said about the relationship with Mexico.

Asymmetry has not, of course, helped Belize in its relationship with Guatemala. It is true that the territorial and maritime limits of the country are more important to Belize than they are to Guatemala. Yet they are sufficiently important for Guatemala that Belize has struggled to secure its position and has yet to persuade its larger and more powerful neighbour of the sanctity of these limits.

One of the defining features of Belize during the period covered by this book has been its size. It has almost the lowest population of any country on the mainland of the Americas, while in territorial terms it is among the smallest countries.[2] Yet Belize has coped admirably with what might have been a severe disadvantage. The small size of the population does cause some problems, but Belizeans have not let territorial or demographic size undermine their ambitions.

Indeed, Belize compares favorably with other countries in Central America that have much bigger populations. Its income per head is above the average for the region and it has much better social indicators than many of them. Its income per head is not as high as that of Costa Rica or Panama, and this should be a source of concern, but compared with the other four countries (El Salvador, Guatemala, Honduras and Nicaragua) socio-economic indicators in Belize are very healthy.

---

[1] See Shoman (2010).
[2] Only French Guiana has a smaller population. El Salvador, with a much bigger population, is a similar territorial size.

Part of the reason for this is that Belize has generally avoided the macro-economic excesses and exchange rate instability from which its neighbours have suffered on occasions. Guatemala, for example, experienced high rates of inflation for several decades before the peso was replaced by the quetzal in 1923. Honduras suffered one of the worst debt crises in Latin America following a fraudulent railway loan in the 1860s. Nicaragua experienced hyper-inflation in the 1980s.

Belize, by contrast, has operated an exchange rate policy since 1894 that has been a model of sobriety. That was the year when the first Belize (British Honduran) dollar came into existence. Although it was devalued at the end of 1949, a fixed exchange rate policy (this time to the pound sterling) continued to be pursued. And when in 1976 the peg was restored to the US dollar, it was done in a way that avoided devaluation and inflationary consequences. Thus, Belize has enjoyed the benefits of a low inflation environment over a long period that started even before 1894. Indeed, it is fair to say that Belize has never suffered a long period of high inflation.

This is important because inflation is a tax that redistributes income from the poor to the rich. The reason is that the rich are much better than the poor at avoiding the inflation tax, because they have many more options when it comes to protecting themselves. This is one reason why Brazil, where inflation was very high for fifty years after the Second World War, acquired such a terrible reputation for income inequality. The poor could not escape the impact of the inflation tax and suffered accordingly.[3]

Belize, by contrast, has not had very high levels of household income inequality, although it has had high levels of wealth inequality as a result of the unequal distribution of land permitted by the colonial authorities. The moderate levels of income inequality are not only due to low inflation, but have also been due to the difficulty of accumulating private capital in a small country where investment opportunities have been limited.[4] This may now be changing, so it would be unwise to assume that Belize will always have low levels of income inequality.[5] Indeed, income and wealth inequality have clearly been rising in the last decade.

Belize has also coped admirably with high rates of migration–both inward and outward–in the last two centuries. After the end of forced migra-

---

[3] It is no coincidence that income distribution in Brazil started to improve after the mid-1990s when inflation reached much more modest levels.

[4] Marshall Bennett, Robert Sydney Turton and many other wealthy Belizeans expanded their fortunes by accumulating capital outside the country after they had become rich in Belize.

[5] Michael Ashcroft and a number of US and Canadian capitalists invested in Belize after they had already become wealthy from their activities elsewhere, suggesting that the opportunities for private capital accumulation are now much greater than they were.

tion through slavery, the Belize population was one of the fastest growing in the world as a result of inward migration from the neighbouring republics. This was followed at the end of the 19th century by a long period of outward migration, which started with the departure of many workers to help construct the Panama Canal.

Outward migration continues, although the rate has been declining in the last three decades.[6] It has been matched since the 1980s by high levels of inward migration from Central America and, in the last few years, from other parts of the world as well.[7] The acceptance by Belizeans of migration –inward and outward–as a relatively normal process is in sharp contrast to the hysterical way in which it is treated in many other countries.

These are some of the "positives" that the economic history of Belize teaches us. They suggest that there are reasons to be confident about the long-term. At a time of deep introspection by Belizeans and doubts about the future, it is worth remembering them. However, they are matched by several "negatives" that do need to be addressed if Belize is to fulfill its potential and become a more prosperous, fair and just society.

Belize is a small country that has always depended on exports. The "inward-looking" development model favoured by Latin American republics in the half century before 1980 was never attractive to Belize because it could not be expected to provide a decent standard of living for the citizens. The domestic market has always been too small to support a large number of firms selling only to Belizeans. Instead, Belize from the days of the earliest settlement has focused on finding those goods or services with which it could compete in the world market.

The first commodity was logwood and this dominated the economy during the century of illegal settlement. As prices fell, the attraction of logwood declined and Belize looked to other activities. The answer was found first in mahogany and later in the entrepôt trade with Central America. In both cases the Belizean response to the change in relative prices and new market opportunities was swift and effective.

From the mid-19th century onwards, however, the Belizean response has been slow and ineffective. The decline in mahogany prices, which coincided with the start of the colonial period in the 1860s, did not bring about a much-needed shift of resources to other (non-forest) exports. Instead, Belize shifted back to logwood so that forest products continued to dominate

---

[6] See Table 6.7.

[7] According to the 2009 Poverty Assessment Report, only 44% of immigrants in the previous three years were from Central America and Mexico compared with 23% from North America and Europe and 33% from Latin America, the Caribbean, Africa and Asia. See Government of Belize (2011), Table 2.4, p. 15.

the export list. Indeed, one of the most successful non-traditional exports before 1900 was chicle–itself a forest product.

The "forestocracy" exercised such a grip on society and the colonial administration that a sustained shift to agricultural exports would not come about until the 1950s. This, of course, was just at the time when agricultural exports were facing high levels of discrimination in world markets and falling prices. Belizean agricultural exports, especially sugar, came to depend on various tariff and quota preferences that could not be expected to last forever. Indeed, the preferences would in due course be eroded and will probably disappear at some point in the near future.

Neighbouring countries in Central America faced the same threats to agricultural exports in the 1950s. However, they reacted differently and chose instead to develop a modern manufacturing sector. As in Belize, the domestic market was too small to justify this move so it was done at the regional level. This led to the Central American Common Market (CACM), launched in 1960, and it brought about a sharp rise in intra-regional exports–especially of manufactured goods–among the member states.

Guatemalan opposition ruled out Belizean participation in CACM, so this option was not available even if Belizeans had wanted to join and the colonial government had permitted it. However, there were other options. This was, after all, the moment when Caribbean countries started shifting away from agricultural exports to services–especially tourism.[8] Indeed, already by the mid-1960s a number of small Caribbean countries–including the Bahamas, Cayman Islands, Netherlands Antilles and the US Virgin Islands–had become much more dependent on service than commodity exports.

Belize was slow to follow suit, believing instead that rising agricultural exports would be sufficient to sustain the development of the economy. However, the decline in forestry exports was very rapid and agricultural exports could not fully compensate. It was not until the 1980s that Belize started to develop a modern tourist industry, by which time most Caribbean countries had gained a huge advantage in terms of infrastructure, marketing and branding.

Just as Belize entered the tourist industry, many Caribbean countries started to diversify their service exports so that they would no longer be so dependent on travel. The new exports were mainly financial and business services, although they also diversified their travel exports as well to include music festivals, international conference facilities, health tourism and–above all–cruise shipping. By the time Belize entered these markets, however, the international environment

---

[8] Some Caribbean countries also shifted into mining and petroleum exports at this time. Belize explored for oil in the 1950s, but without success.

had become much more competitive and in some cases even hostile. A good example has been the difficulties Belize has faced in establishing an offshore financial industry. The pioneers in this field in the Caribbean had been the Bahamas and the Netherlands Antilles, but they had been joined in the 1960s by the Cayman Islands, British Virgin Islands, Turks & Caicos Islands and several others. Concern among OECD countries at the potential loss of tax revenue from these "tax havens" led to a severe backlash–just as Belize was trying to enter this market. Long-established participants, such as the Cayman Islands, have been able to adapt. However, the offshore industry in Belize did not have enough time to establish itself fully before the rules were tightened.[9]

Another example is cruise shipping. By the time this activity started in Belize in the 1990s, it was firmly established elsewhere. The industry was already dominated by a small number of firms and Belize had little or no bargaining power in dealing with the large established companies. Time and again these shipping lines have used their influence to force Belize to accept arrangements that offer only marginal benefits to the domestic economy and very little tax revenue to the government.

Belize, therefore, has been slow to diversify its exports as market conditions have changed. It has not been "ahead of the curve". On the contrary, it has usually been a laggard and has suffered accordingly. It was clear from the 1860s that Belize needed to diversify out of forest products. It was clear from the 1950s that Belize needed to encourage tourism. And it should have been clear since the 1980s that Belize needed to promote non-tourism service exports.

A second problem–fiscal concessions–has also been of long-standing. The British settlement before the colonial period ran its own affairs through the Public Assembly. Revenue needed to be raised, but taxes would clearly have fallen disproportionately on the richer members of society represented in the Assembly. Not surprisingly, they kept tax to a minimum so that revenue per head was far lower in this period than might have been expected from the level of Belizean exports per head.

This "under-taxation" should have ended with the launch of the colony of British Honduras in 1862, but it did not. The best opportunity was provided by the introduction of a land tax in 1867, but the forestocracy–especially the Belize Estate & Produce Company–did everything in its power to reduce its impact. The land tax never raised much revenue and a great opportunity was missed under colonialism to provide the resources that could have given Belize a decent system of infrastructure, education and health.

---

[9] The offshore financial industry in Belize survived the OECD onslaught, but it contributes very little to the domestic economy. Much the same can be said of the shipping register and other "offshore" activities.

Sadly, fiscal concessions did not end with internal self-government in 1964 or with independence in 1981. The propensity of all governments since the end of colonialism to offer tax exemptions to preferred interest groups or individuals has been very damaging. The tax base has shrunk and this has meant that tax rates have had to be raised for those unable to escape. The result is that most Belizeans feel they are "over-taxed", although international comparisons make clear that Belize is "under-taxed" by around 30 per cent for a country of its size and income per head.[10]

A third problem has been the cavalier approach to environmental resources. This may sound strange to those familiar with the public image of Belize as a land of "pristine" forests and an "unspoilt" barrier reef. Yet the reality is rather different. The forestocracy never practiced sustainable development and the rate of timber felling was restrained only by the cost of extraction at a time of low world prices. Indeed, when timber prices were high in the 1920s, the rate of extraction reached its maximum despite the almost complete absence of replanting.

Governments since independence have created many national parks and provided the legislation for sustainable development. This is very welcome. However, the resources have never been provided to ensure compliance and the relevant minister has too much discretion. Illegal activities in the national parks have been commonplace and in some cases–notably the Vaca Forest Reserve, the Chiquibul National Park, the Caracol Archaeological Reserve and the Columbia River Forest Reserve–have become worse over time. The result is that Belizean forests are far from pristine.

The rate of deforestation in Belize is in fact very serious. According to the most reliable studies, the forest cover fell from 75.9 per cent in 1980 to 62.7 per cent in 2010.[11] This means a loss of 25,000 acres every year. Furthermore, the rate of decline (0.6 per cent per year) may be speeding up as a result of the activities of illegal migrants crossing the border from Guatemala. Satellite imagery of the border area reveals the rapid advance of illegal activities in recent years.[12]

The barrier reef has suffered from the impact of temperature change –due in part to global warming. Yet it has also suffered from human-made activity. Maritime national parks and marine reserves have been under-resourced and there have been too many exceptions allowed to the rules designed to protect the reef. There is still insufficient recognition in Belize of the extremely fragile nature of the coastal eco-system. Coastal mangrove areas in particular have been at risk.

[10] See Chapter 6.
[11] See Cherrington et al. (2010).
[12] See Gibson and Palacio (2011), pp. 35-37.

Many countries now apply environmental accounting to adjust the GDP figures for damage to, and loss of, natural resources.[13] Invariably, these adjustments imply that the "true" rate of growth of the economy was less than the published figures. GDP growth rates take no account of declines in biodiversity, deforestation and erosion of coastal areas. If the Belizean national accounts were adjusted in this way, as they should be, the rate of growth would be lower. This may not sound very appealing to those responsible, yet it is the most powerful way of drawing public attention to the need for stronger measures to protect the environment.

Belize has often presented itself as a "bridge" between the Caribbean and Central America. Potentially, this is a very attractive role and one to which the country has every right to aspire. In truth, however, Belize has been more like an island separated from both. The connections have been minimal and the claim to provide a bridge has been somewhat exaggerated.

Until the dying days of the Spanish empire, it was impossible for Belize to have any meaningful contact with the neighbours except through contraband. When trade restrictions were lifted, Belizean merchants did in fact respond quickly and for a brief period (c.1820-c.1850) Belize was a bridge between Central America and the Caribbean based on the entrepôt trade. Indeed, Marshall Bennett and a few other merchants took advantage of the situation to relocate their business interests to Central America while keeping their connections to Belize and the Caribbean (especially Jamaica).

This was the only time, however, that Belize played a bridging role. The main problem after the decline of the entrepôt trade was the absence of transport ties. Schemes to establish infrastructure links with Central America were blocked during the colonial period. It is easy to blame this on the contentious Article VII of the 1859 Anglo-Guatemalan Treaty, but this is misleading. Article VII should have provided the perfect opportunity for a road or railway connecting Belize and Guatemala in the 19th century that might have put the two countries on a very different trajectory. Instead, the colonial authorities used Article VII as an excuse for doing nothing, since they were always concerned that their own infrastructure schemes might not meet the terms of the treaty.

The links with Guatemala therefore steadily withered away after 1850– especially after the Guatemalan currency was abandoned in 1894 by Belize as legal tender. The links were only kept alive by the logging operations of Belizean companies across the frontier and these ended in the 1940s following the closure of the border by Guatemala. There was a brief effort by the PUP leadership to revive links after 1950, but these declined when

---

[13] This has been done for Costa Rica by the country's Centro Científico Tropical and the Washington-based World Resources Institute.

President Arbenz was overthrown in 1954 and the governments that followed proved to be even more intransigent on the territorial issue.

Belize also grew apart from the rest of Central America despite the heroic efforts of George Price to build closer relations. The major developments in Central American regional integration after 1960 passed Belize by and the country's decision in 2000 to join SICA (Sistema de Integración Centroamericana) was too little and too late. Despite the support for Belizean independence from Central American republics (except Guatemala) and inward migration since 1980, Belize is still largely decoupled from the region with very little trade. In truth, the neighbouring states do not look to Belize to provide a bridge to the outside world.

Yet Belize is not fully integrated into the Caribbean either despite the decision in 1973 to join CARICOM (Caribbean Community) while still a colony. There is very little trade with the other member states in either goods or services, even less intra-regional investment and the transport links are dismal. The Caribbean–inside or outside CARICOM–does not look to Belize to provide a bridge to Central America and makes its own arrangements.

Countries often exaggerate their ability to play the role of a "bridge" between two regions. Belize is no exception, but much more could and should have been done in both directions. It is a legitimate ambition for Belize to seek to play this role, but much more thought needs to be put into how it might be achieved. Indeed, the Dominican Republic has probably been more successful than Belize at providing a link between the Caribbean and Central America, since its private investors and government have been active in both areas. Perhaps lessons can be learnt from the Dominican experience.

Belize may compare favorably with several Central American states on a variety of socio-economic indicators, but it does much worse in comparisons with most countries in the Caribbean. Belize is bound by geography to Central America, but by history and culture to the Caribbean. Thus, the comparisons with the Caribbean are legitimate and they do not reflect well on the country.

Belize was ranked first among the Caribbean countries in 1820 in terms of exports per head–a position it held for another twenty years at least. Its rapid decline–both absolute and relative–coincided with the 120 years of colonialism. Yet independence has not reversed this. The absolute decline has ended and the relative decline has not gone further, but Belize is still in the bottom quartile when compared with the countries of the Caribbean on most socio-economic indicators.

The best known of these is Gross Domestic Product (GDP) per head and it is very disappointing to learn that Belize's ranking in the Caribbean today on this metric is roughly the same as in 1981–the year of independence. Yet Belize can do much better. Size should not be an obstacle since many Caribbean countries are even smaller than Belize–in both population and territory–and yet have much higher GDP per head.

Belize should set itself the ambition of reaching in one generation an income per head that puts it in the middle of all Caribbean countries. This would make it the median country rather than one in the bottom quartile. It should also seek to close the gap with Costa Rica and Panama in Central America. These are not impossible targets, but they do require the adoption of a long-term development strategy rather than focusing exclusively on the short-term.

This will also require a major critique of the growth model adopted since independence. This model has been implemented by both main political parties in government. There have been differences in the approach, especially on fiscal prudence and control of public utilities, but there has been consensus on many issues. These include exchange rate policy, export promotion and a key role for the private sector. Above all, there has been consensus on the need to achieve a fast rate of growth in order to meet the demands of the electorate.

As we saw in Chapter 6, however, the model has delivered only a modest increase in GDP per head since 1980 averaging 2.2 per cent annually. Specifically, GDP per head at 2000 prices rose from US$2,011 to US$3,877 in 2010. At one level this might look impressive–after all it means that GDP per head at constant prices nearly doubled. Yet this does not tell the full story. First, a much higher proportion (as much as 15 per cent) now accrues to foreigners–not Belizeans. This lowers the figure in 2010 to US$3,295. Secondly, income inequality has almost certainly worsened so that the median income will not have risen as much as implied by the GDP per head figure.[14] Thirdly, these figures take no account of environmental destruction.

Thus, the model pursued since independence has delivered only a modest increase in income. At the same time, income distribution has deteriorated and unemployment has increased. Combined with the rise of violence and the threats to personal security, part of which can be attributed to the international drugs trade, it is not surprising that so many Belizeans are concerned about the future.

There are no simple answers, but there are clearly some pitfalls that need to be avoided. The emphasis on maximizing growth at all costs produced

---

[14] The median income is the one that separates the population into two halves; 50% receive less than the median and 50% more. If the rich receive a much higher share of income, then *ceteris paribus* the median will fall.

major imbalances in the Belizean economy that have still not been fully corrected. External public debt remains very high and servicing it drains scarce resources from the public purse. Belize needs to establish what growth is sustainable and not try to exceed it whatever the temptations.

The long-term sustainability of the Belizean growth rate depends on many things. One of the most important is the rate of investment and this is heavily influenced by the cost of borrowing. This, as we saw in Chapter 6, is very high in Belize. This makes it very difficult for those reliant on domestic sources of finance to find profitable opportunities. However, it is less of a problem for those with access to cheap finance in other parts of the world. If the best opportunities for investment are not all to be taken by foreigners, then Belize has to tackle the problem of its high borrowing costs as a matter of urgency.

Another determinant of the long-term growth rate is the skill level of the labour force. For far too long there was an assumption in Belize that the workforce was sufficiently skilled, since the educational level of the population was higher than in neighbouring countries. Belize, however, has to compete in an international market place where the quality and quantity of education is rising all the time. There is now recognition in Belize that the skill level of the workforce is not adequate and that investment in education is crucial.

Belize must also aim for a long-run growth rate that is consistent with the sustainability of its natural resources. This does not mean that no deforestation should ever take place, as–outside the national parks–there are legitimate projects. Yet these do need to be matched by appropriate conservation measures and replanting schemes. It is also easy to forget that Belize's attraction as a tourist destination is very largely based on its natural resources. If these continue to decline, tourism may go the same way. If Belize is to do all this, it must first learn the lessons from its own economic history.

We have tried in this book to identify what has happened in the last 350 years and to show where things have gone wrong and what might have been done differently. Not everyone will agree with our conclusions, which at times may seem harsh. Yet we remain optimistic. Belize is not a large country and the opportunities to plot a different course are often easier to grasp when a country is small. Many countries in other parts of the world have succeeded in doing this and there is no reason why Belize should not join them. We hope that this book will be seen as a contribution towards that important goal.

Appendix 1: Translations

It is said that a brave and enterprising Scottish buccaneer, called Peter Wallace, inspired by the riches said to have been secured by others on certain notorious expeditions, resolved together with the toughest of his companions to find a place in which they could build a fort with the aim of using it to carry out acts of piracy and return safely. As this took place in the middle of the 17th century, the Yucatan coast was almost uninhabited by Spaniards–the only fort they controlled (at Bacalar) having been destroyed by the pirate Abraham [Blauvelt] and by an uprising of the Maya in the area. Wallace made a careful study of the bays and reefs ... and disembarked with 80 pirates, who at once constructed a few huts surrounded by a pallisade and a simple fort. (p.21 fn.18)

Map of the Balyz, New and Hondo Rivers in the Province of Guatemala and Gulf of Honduras together with the Province of Yucatan, in which are shown the creeks, lagoons and canals and their navigability; the site of the fort of Salamanca de Bacalar, the road that leads from there to Merida, the Peten Itza lake and part of the road that is depopulated until the last town in Yucatan. (p.30 fn.66)

Map of the Bay of Honduras, the British Settlement, Indian villages on the coast of Valis, navigability of the coast for ships with the main anchorages, water sources and reefs, carried out by order of his Most Illustrious Sr. Martin de Mayorga, President and Captain-General of the Kingdom of Guatemala. (p.30 fn.67)

Record of the permission to cut logwood given to the English on the Walis, New and Hondo Rivers in the Province of Campeche; measures to be taken in the areas granted and the new concessions given under the most recent peace treaties. (p.30 fn.69)

Appendix 2: The Belize Estate & Produce Company[1]

Following the introduction in the UK in 1856 of a law permitting limited liability, many companies rushed to take advantage. The only Belize firm to do so was James Hyde & Co., which in 1859 became the British Honduras Company and was registered in London. The Directors of James Hyde & Co. included James Hyde, James Bartlett Hyde and John Hodge. The first two were established Baymen, while the latter was a London merchant who had become the settlement's agent in 1848.[2]

From the moment of its creation, the British Honduras Company was a major landowner. However, it was not the only one. The other large land-owning companies, which were not registered in London, were Young Toledo & Co., Carmichael Vidal & Co. and Sheldon Byass & Co. All these firms had UK partners and had used their access to British financial markets to purchase land in the two decades before Belize became a colony.[3]

The fall in mahogany prices accelerated from the 1860s onwards and many of these firms fell into difficulties. Even the British Honduras Company was forced to sell and its assets fell into the hands of new owners in 1875, who renamed the company the Belize Estate & Produce Company (BEC). A few years later, in 1880, Young Toledo & Co. went into liquidation and BEC issued debentures to acquire a large slice of its former rival's landholdings. At this point it must have owned at least half of all private land in the colony. However, it then sold some land of its own and in 1882 reimbursed the debenture holders. From this time onwards BEC was the undisputed largest land-owner in Belize with more than one-third of all private land (see Table 4.1).

The Directors of BEC were all based in the UK, so they were not even expatriates.[4] An analysis of the Board reveals the presence of two or three members of the Hoare family at all times–until they sold their shares in 1947 and BEC became a subsidiary of the multinational J. Glicksten & Sons Ltd.[5] It then passed into the hands of the International Timber Company (ITC) in the 1970s. This company, shortly before merging with Montague L. Meyer to become Meyer International, sold BEC together with its other tropical timber operations to F.W. Bellote, a financier from Georgia, USA. The price was US$4.7 million.[6]

---

[1] The research for this Appendix was done mainly from records provided by Companies House in London using a CD-ROM made available to the authors.
[2] See Bolland and Shoman (1977), pp.77-83.
[3] See Bolland (1977), pp.186-87.
[4] It did, of course, have a local manager who was either an expatriate or a Creole.
[5] See Bolland and Shoman (1977), p.107. By 1968 the landholdings of BEC had been reduced to 872,412 acres as a result of land sales. See Petch (1986), p.1008.
[6] See Petch (1986), p.1009.

After internal self-government in 1964, the land tax was increased significantly on undeveloped land. By 1982 unpaid taxes on land held by BEC were estimated at around US$2 million and Bellote decided to sell. The buyer was Barry Bowen, a Belizean entrepreneur, who paid US$7 million (this included responsibility for the unpaid taxes). The deal was financed in part by a loan for US$4.8 million from Banco Metropolitano S.A. in Panama.

Bowen's ambitious plans for converting BEC's lands into income-generating assets were not supported by other investors–in part because of environmental concerns. He therefore faced difficulties in servicing the loan. In a major court case in Belize in 1985, the Supreme Court ruled against the Attorney-General, making Bowen alone responsible for the debt.[7] Bowen had to find a solution quickly or face bankruptcy.

The answer was found in a sale of BEC's lands (by now reduced to 686,186 acres) for US$6 million. The Coca Cola Co. and two Houston businessmen (Walter Mischer and Paul Howell) bought 50,000 acres each. Bowen retained 50,000 for his holding company (Hillbank Agroindustry Ltd.), while the remainder was split on a 30:30:40 basis between the three. Finally, lands in the New River lagoon area were given to the government to pay BZ$800,000 in arrears.[8]

Coca Cola was unable to develop the land for citrus, as originally intended, due to opposition from environmental groups. They therefore gave some of their land to Programme for Belize (a Non-Governmental Organization–NGO) in 1990 and a further tranche was given in 1992. Barry Bowen also donated part of his remaining holding to the same NGO. Finally, BEC was dissolved in 1994.

The period when the BEC was a major force in Belize was from 1875 until the Second World War. These were the years when the Hoare family effectively controlled the company through their presence on the Board and their large shareholding. The Hoare family Directors included two who were Members of Parliament and one who was a Director of the Bank of England. One of the two MPs, Sir Samuel Hoare, was in the British government for many years and served as Foreign Secretary in 1935. As the Hoare family also controlled one of the most important private banks in the UK, the Directors included several bankers as well.

The authorised (and paid-up) capital of BEC at first was £45,000 made up of 4,500 shares at £10 each. The paid-up capital was increased to £60,000 in 1907 and it remained at this level until 1920. This was an exceptional year for all commodity exporters and the Board took advantage of this by issuing

---

[7] The Belize government argued that BEC should be forfeited in view of unpaid taxes.

[8] See Petch (1986), p.1014.

Figure A.2.1: BEC shareholding, 1920 (%)

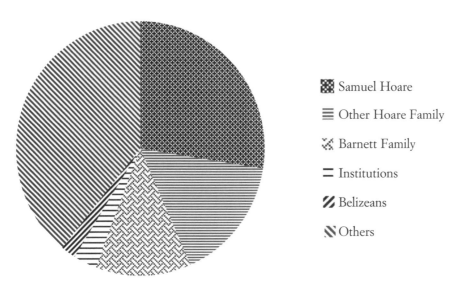

▓ Samuel Hoare

≡ Other Hoare Family

⚔ Barnett Family

= Institutions

⧄ Belizeans

◤ Others

Source: See footnote 1.

new stock from reserves to all shareholders at the rate of 1:1. This meant, in effect, paying a dividend of 100 per cent on the existing shares, although the Board then authorised an additional dividend payment of 2.5 per cent on the new shares!

The need to seek stock market approval for this increase in capital meant that the shareholding in 1920 had to be reported in detail. From this we learn (see Figure 4.A.1) that Sir Samuel Hoare owned 27.5 per cent, that other members of the Hoare family owned a further 15.8 per cent and the closely related Barnett family 12.5 per cent. These three holdings were more than sufficient to control the company. Institutional shareholders, in sharp contrast to the normal pattern today, were insignificant. There were also three Belizeans on the share register, of whom the most important by far was Robert Sydney Turton.[9] BEC was very profitable with the declared dividend normally fluctuating between 10 and 25 per cent.[10] The impact of this on the Belize economy was considerable as almost all of it was paid to shareholders in the UK. Expressed as a percentage of domestic exports the annual dividend paid by

[9] This is ironic, as Turton was allied to the US companies that competed with BEC for political and economic influence. He was, however, a very shrewd businessman. See Grant (1994).

[10] This is expressed as a percentage of the paid-up capital. Each share had a nominal value of £10, but the yield would depend on the market price of the shares.

BEC averaged 3 to 4 per cent, although it reached nearly eight per cent in 1894-95. The year 1920, however, would prove to be the high point and no dividend was declared between 1926 and 1932.

There were several key moments when BEC used its power to influence policy decisively in its favour. This it could easily do since its local manager was invariably an elected or nominated member of the legislature and its Directors in the UK had unprecedented access to the Colonial Office.[11] The first was its opposition to the land tax, which ensured that the tax rate was always low. Indeed, when the Governor took advantage of Treasury control in the 1930s to raise the tax sharply, BEC refused to pay and was "rewarded" when the tax rate reverted to its previous level without the company having to pay any additional tax.[12]

The second was its opposition to any major reform of the labour laws. When this was mooted by one of the colony's governors, BEC would always intervene to make sure the change either did not happen or was much less than originally planned. It also opposed the sale or lease of Crown lands in small plots and almost never sold its own land to small farmers, although it did rent them. And its support for infrastructure development was luke-warm, unless the proposed project passed through company land.[13]

Finally, BEC used its influence in 1932 to ensure that the loan from the UK Treasury to Belize favoured the company.[14] Some 20 per cent of this loan was given to BEC to allow it to construct a sawmill in the south of the country–this at a time when the country was still crippled by hurricane damage with many people rendered homeless. At the time, Sir Samuel Hoare was a member of the Cabinet with close ties to the Colonial Secretary.

This was perhaps the last time that BEC would have a major influence on policy. The failure of its local manager to retain his seat on the Legislative Council a few years later was a sign of the times. The Second World War also damaged the company and dividends were slashed. After the Hoare family sold out in 1947, the new owners were content to rely on land sales in large blocks to wealthy foreigners. By now the valuable timber had been extracted and the land was held mainly for speculative purposes.[15] By the time BEC was purchased by Barry Bowen, its landholdings were much reduced.

---

[11] One letter from the Hoare family to the British Colonial Secretary begins 'My Dear Leo'. See Ashdown (1979), p.183.
[12] See Ashdown (1979), pp.217-8.
[13] See Bolland (1977), p.193.
[14] See Ashdown (1979), p.210.
[15] See Bolland and Shoman (1977), p.108.

Appendix 3: Sources for Chapter 5

The material for this chapter comes mainly from four sources:

For the economic history of the 19th century, the published material is extensive and those cited in the notes to this chapter represent a minimal selection.

The National Archives in London house a full record of the Governor's annual reports and can be found at CO/123.

The Royal Botanic Gardens Kew Library and Archives house three volumes of particular interest to the Belize Botanic Station. These include the Botanic Station Reports 1900-1911 and two volumes of correspondence that are cited fully in the notes to this chapter. This material covers the establishment of the garden and gives considerable insight into Kew's relationship with the Colonial Office. In addition it covers relations with the United Fruit Company. The correspondence in these volumes is handwritten and had to be copied by hand and then transferred to a personal computer so they could be read and a narrative extracted.

The Belize Archives Department at Belmopan houses a full collection of Botanic Station Reports 1900-1917. In addition, they hold Minute Papers that cover the winding up of the Belize Botanic Station at Bolton Bank as well as the details of some of the day-to-day maintenance and staff matters. There is also a separate record of plans.

Appendix 4: Gate rules for Belize Botanic Station

Belize. September 1st, 1896.

1. For visits of pleasure and instruction, as well as for the sale of plants, open daily to the public from 6 a.m. to 6 p.m.

2. Admission free.

3. Application for seeds or plants to be made to the superintendent.

4. Visitors are requested not to tread on grass borders but to walk on paths provided for this purpose.

5. On entry and exit visitors are invited to close the gate.

6. It is forbidden to touch any plant, flower or fruit.

7. Presentations of seeds and plants to the gardens are invited.

8. No dogs are admitted.

9. In furtherance of the objects of the Gardens the encouragement and co-operation of the public invited.

By Order,

The Superintendent

Appendix 5: Native plant specimens sent and determined at Kew

Belotia grewioefolia, A. Rich
Luhea sp.
Gowania domingensis L.
Bauhinia porrecta Sw.
Combretum farinosum, H.B.K.
Eugenia Fieldingi, Berg.
Heterotrochum octonum D.C.
Muriria rhoiphoefolia, Tricena
Myginda Sp.
Psychotria sp.
Ageratum salicifolium, Hemsl.
Zexmenia trachylepsis
Wedelia sp.
Aphelandra acutifolia, Nees
Belopernoe, sp.
Th'yrascantus sp.
Dianthera tryotoides, Mart
Euphorbia eriabtha, Benth.
Dalechampia tilifolia, Lam.
Dalechampia sp.
Hiliconia brevispatha, Hook
Spathiphylum Fendlerii, Schate
Hypolytrum sylvestris, Kunth.
Tripsacum dactyloides, L.
Rheedia sp.
Heteropterys beechyana, A. Jess.
Gurania levyana, Cogn.
Psycholia sp.
Oleganthese oxylepsis, Benth.
Begonia sp.
Coruntia piradata , L.
Dalechampia scandens, L.
Phyllanthus glaucesens HBK
Dorstenia contrayeva, L.
Laelia digbyana, Benth.
Pitcairnia puncea, Beer.
Asplenium celtifolium, Kuntz.
Asplenium trifolialum, Sw.
Toenitas lanceolatum, R. Br.
Cycoches chlorochilon
Cycoches rossianum, Rolfe.
Gymnopodium floribundum, Rolfe. (A new genus discovered by
Campbell - see Hooker's Icones Plantarum (Vol VII Part IV).

Source: Botanic Station Report 1897-99
Note: Names as given.

Appendix 6: List of economic plants and fruit trees under cultivation at the Botanic Station in 1909

COMMON NAME	BOTANICAL NAME	PRODUCT
Hennequen	Agave sisalana	Fibre
Bowstring hemp	Sanseviera guineensis	Fibre
Sandal wood	Santalum album	Wood
Breadfruit	Artocarpus incisa	Fruit
Jackfruit	Artocarpus integrifolia	Fruit
Jackfruit (large Indian var.)	Artocarpus integrifolia	Fruit
Arrowroot	Maranta arundinacea	Starch
Pineapple	Ananas sativa	Fruit
Pineapple (smooth)	Ananas sativa	Fruit
Grape Black (Hamburgh var.)	Vitis uvifera	Fruit
Grape white Muscat	Vitis uvifera	Fruit
Lime, common	Citrus acida	Fruit
Lime, spineless	Citrus acida	Fruit
Lemon, ponderosa	Citrus limonum	Fruit
Lemon, Sicily	Citrus limonum	Fruit
Sour sap	Anona muricata	Fruit
Cherimoya	Anona cerimoya	Fruit
Custard apple	Anona reticulate	Fruit
Malay apple	Eugenia Malaccensis	Fruit
Myrtleberry	Eugenia Malaccensis	Fruit
Star apple	Chrysophylum caimito	Fruit
Liberian coffee	Coffea Liberica	Coffee
Maragopipe coffee	Coffea var.	Coffee
Ginger	Zingerber officinalis	Ginger
Chinese persimmon	Diospyros kaki	Fruit
Mabola	Diospyros discolour	Fruit
Avocado	Persea gratissima	Fruit
Kolanut	Cola acuminate	Cola
Vanilla	Vanilla planifolia	Vanilla
Rubber	Hevea brasilensis	Rubber
Rubber, native	Castilloa elastica	Rubber
Rubber, West African	Futuma elastica	Rubber
Kananga	Cananga odorata	Perfume
Coconut	Cocos nucifera	
Loquat	Erybotyra japonica	Fruit
Cotton	Gossipium var.	
Figs white var.	Ficus carica	Fruit
Figs black var.	Ficus carica	Fruit
Carambola	Averrhoa carambola	Fruit
Gimbling	Phyllanthus disichus	
Monkey apple	Moquilia platypus	Fruit, timber

Peach, red Ceylon var.	Amygdalus persica	Fruit
Peach, Waldo	Amygdalus persica	Fruit
Plum, Terrel	Prunus domestica	Fruit
Plum, How var.	Prunus domestica	Fruit
Cocoa, Forestero var.	Theobroma cacoa	
Cocoa, alligator var.	Theobroma pentaphylla	
Cocoa, native var.	Theobroma sp.	
Turmeric ginger	Curcuma longa	Turmeric
Screw pine	Pandanus utilis	Hat straw
Genep	Melecoca bijuga	Fruit
Lemon eucalyptus	Eucalyptus citrifolia	Oil
Divi-Divi	Caesalpina corearia	Tannin pod
Orange, var. Majorca	Citrus aurantium	
Orange, var. Ruby	Citrus aurantium	
Orange, var. Tardiff	Citrus aurantium	
Orange, var. Pineapple	Citrus aurantium	
Orange, var. (Washington nav)	Citrus aurantium	
Mango, var. Cambodiana	Mangifera indica	
Mango, var. Carlin	Mangifera indica	
Mango, var. Sandersha	Mangifera indica	
Mango, var. Malgoba	Mangifera indica	
Mango, var. No. 11	Mangifera indica	
Mango, var. Black	Mangifera indica	
Mango,(var. Peter Trinidad)	Mangifera indica	
Mango, var. Gordon	Mangifera indica	
Mango, var. Julie	Mangifera indica	
Genepa	Genepa Americana	
Peanut	Arachis hypogaea	Nut
Mahua	Bassia latifolia	Oil
Sugarcane	Saccharum officinarum	Sugar
Sugarcane, var. B. 208		
Sugarcane, var. D. 295		
Sugarcane, var. Naga		
Sugarcane, var. Ribbon		
African Oil Palm	Elaeis guineensis	
Plum	Flacourtia ramontchi	
Nutmeg	Myristica fragrans	Nutmeg
Guava	Psidium guava	
Plantain	Musa paraisica	
Banana	Musa sapientum	
Banana, var. diinese	Musa cavandishii	
Banana, var. Red	Musa discolour	
Corn	Zea mays	
Coca	Erythroxylon coca	Cocaine

Source: Botanic Station Report 1909
Note: Names as given.

Appendix 7: List of specimens in the herbarium of the Belize Botanic Station

No.	Botanical name	Where Collected
5	Brassavola Grandiflora	Belize
2	Epidendron Chocleatum	Punta Gorda
4	Epidendron Nocturnum	Belize
6	Epidendron Alatum	Orange Walk
7	sps. not identified	Belize
12	sps. not identified	Orange Walk
11	Maxillaria Tenuifolia	Belize
3	Oncidium Carthaginense	Belize
9	Oncidium Cobeleta	Belize
10	Oncidium Sphacelatum	Belize
8	Ponera Striata	Belize
1	Sobralia sp.	El Cayo
34	Altenanthera Ficoidea	Belize
39	Bauhinia Porrecta	Orange Walk
46	Brysonima Crassifolea	Belize
16	Clematis Dioca	Orange Walk
36	Combretum Erianthum	Orange Walk
49	Chrysobalanus Elipticus	Belize
43	Coutobea Spicata	Manatee
25	Dioscoria Capillaris	Orange Walk
14	Eustoma Exaltum	Orange Walk
37	Erythrina Coralodendrum	Orange Walk
52	Eugenia sp.	Belize
62	Eichornera Azurea	Belize
51	Gliricidia Maculata	Belize
17	Hamelia Patens	Belize
24	Hydrolea Spinosa	Belize
28	Heteropterys Beecheyana	Orange Walk
31	Hibiscus Abelmoschus	Tower Hill
47	Helecteris Guazumioefolia	Belize
19	Jacquemontea	Belize
50	Jaquinea Aristatata	Belize
35	Lippia Guinata	Belize
23	Mimosea sp.	Belize
32	Melanthora Deltoides	Tower Hill
42	Marsyplanthes tryptinide	Manatee
45	Miconia Ciliata	Manatee
57	Morinda Citrifolia	Government House
60	Mourira Parvifolia	Old River
61	Maranta Arundinacea sp.	Orange Walk
18	Nectandra Senguinea	Belize River

41	Opismenus Coliaceus	Orange Walk
15	Passiflora Foetida	Orange Walk
30	Panicum Devaricatum	Tower Hill
26	Panilinia Velutena	Orange Walk
30	Polypremum procumbens	Tower Hill
58	Passiflora Vespertilis	Botanic Centre
38	Ruselia Turnifora	Botanic Centre
55	Rhabdadenia ehrenbergi	Bolton Bank
21	Sida Duinosa	Orange Walk
2	Solanum Nudum	Temash River
3	Selaginella Flabellata	Botanic Centre
33	Thevetia Nitida	Temash River
40	Tabebium sp	Government House
64	Triphasia Trifoliates	Belize
48	Tetrapteris sp	Belize
53	Tabernaemontan littorali	Belize
56	Terminalia Ruceras	Bolton Bank
63	Xiphidium Flaribundum	Orange Walk

Appendix 8: List of tables and figures

Tables

Figures

Appendix 9: List of Abbreviations

ACP	African, Caribbean and Pacific
ATMs	Automated Teller Machines
bd ft	board feet
BBS	Belize Botanic Station
BEC	Belize Estate & Produce Company
BTL	Belize Telemedia Ltd.
BZ$	Belize dollar
CACM	Central American Common Market
CARICOM	Caribbean Community
CARIFORUM	Caribbean Forum
CBI	Caribbean Basin Initiative
CBR	Crude Birth Rate
CDR	Crude Death Rate
CFZ	Corozal Free Zone
CO	Colonial Office
CSA	Commonwealth Sugar Agreement
CSO	Central Statistical Office
DFC	Development Finance Corporation
DFI	Direct Foreign Investment
DLOC	Digital Library of the Caribbean
EC	European Community
ECLAC	Economic Commission for Latin America & the Caribbean
EEC	European Economic Community
EPA	Economic Partnership Agreement
EU	European Union
GDP	Gross Domestic Product
GNI	Gross National Income
GST	General Sales Tax
IBC	International Business Company
IDB	Inter-American Development Bank
IMF	International Monetary Fund
ITC	International Timber Company
JSTOR	Journal Storage
NAFTA	North American Free Trade Agreement
NGO	Non-Governmental Organization
OAS	Organization of American States

OECD	Organization for Economic Co-operation and Development
PICs	Public Investment Companies
PTAs	Preferential Trade Agreements
PUP	People's United Party
REER	Real Effective Exchange Rate
UDP	United Democratic Party
UFCO	United Fruit Company
UK	United Kingdom
UN	United Nations
UNDP	United Nations Development Programme
UNYITS	United Nations Yearbook of International Trade Statistics
UPCA	United Provinces of Central America
USA	United States of America
WB	World Bank
WDI	World Development Indicators

References

Official Sources

BRITISH HONDURAS COLONIAL REPORTS. London: HMSO. (Published each year from 1889 to 1966).

CENTRAL BANK OF BELIZE. (2011). *Twenty-ninth annual report & statement of accounts for the year ending 31 December 2010.* Belize City.

CENTRAL BANK OF BELIZE. (2011a). *Statistical digest 2010.* Belize City.

CENTRAL BANK OF BELIZE. (2011b). *Quarterly Financial Information on Commercial Banks.* Belize City.

CENTRAL STATISTICAL OFFICE. (1987). *Belize Abstract of Statistics.* Belmopan.

COLONIAL DEPARTMENT. (1836). *Honduras: Account of the expenses of the government of Honduras defrayed by taxes raised on the inhabitants of that settlement, from the beginning of the year 1824 down to the present period, so far as the same can be made* out. London: House of Commons.

EVANS (SIR GEOFFREY) COMMISSION. (1948). *Report of the British Guiana and British Honduras Settlement Commission.* London, England: HMSO.

GOVERNMENT OF BELIZE. (2004). *2002 Country Poverty Assessment.* Belmopan, Belize: Government Printers.

GOVERNMENT OF BELIZE. (2011). *2009 Country Poverty Assessment.* Belmopan, Belize: Government Printers.

INTERNATIONAL MONETARY FUND. (2011). *Belize 2011 Article IV Consultation.* Country Report No. 11/340. Washington, DC: IMF.

STATISTICAL ABSTRACT FOR THE PRINCIPAL AND OTHER FOREIGN COUNTRIES. (various years). London, England: HMSO.

STATISTICAL INSTITUTE OF BELIZE. (2011). *Main Results of 2010 Population and Housing Census.* Belmopan, Belize. (Available from: http://www.statisticsbelize.org.bz/)

STATISTICAL INSTITUTE OF BELIZE. (2011a). *External Trade Bulletin.* Belmopan, Belize. (Available from: http://www.statisticsbelize.org.bz/)

STATISTICAL TABLES RELATING TO THE COLONIAL AND OTHER POSSESSIONS OF THE UNITED KINGDOM. (various years). London, England: HMSO.

UNITED NATIONS. (various). *Yearbook of International Trade Statistics.* New York, NY: UN.

UNITED NATIONS DEVELOPMENT PROGRAMME. (2010). *Human Development Report.* New York, NY: UN.

WORLD BANK. (2011). *Country Partnership Strategy for Belize. Report No. 63504-BZ.* Washington DC.

Secondary Sources

ANCONA, E. (1889). Historia de Yucatán, desde la época más remota hasta nuestros días. Barcelona: Imprenta de J. J. Roviralta.

ANTOCHIW, M., & BRETON, A. (1992). Catálogo Cartográfico de Belice (1511-1880). San José, Costa Rica and Mexico, D.F.: Bureau Régional de Coopération en Amérique Centrale, Centre d'Etudes Mexicaines et Centraméricaines.

ASHDOWN, P. (1979). *Race, class and the unofficial majority in British Honduras, 1890–1949.* (Unpublished doctoral dissertation). University of Sussex, Brighton, UK.

ASHDOWN, P. (1985). The growth of Black consciousness in Belize 1914–1919: The Background to the Ex-Servicemen's Riot of 1919. *BELCAST Journal of Belizean Affairs*, 2(2), pp.1–5.

ASHDOWN, P. (1986). Race riot, class warfare and coup d'état: The ex-servicemen's riot of July 1919. *BELCAST Journal of Belizean Affairs*, **3**(1 & 2), 8–14.

ASHDOWN, P. (1986a). The colonial administrators of Belize: Sir Alfred Moloney (1891–1897). *Belizean Studies*, 14(2), 1–10.

ASTURIAS, F. (1925). *Belice.* Sociedad de Geografia e Historia de Guatemala. Guatemala,C.A. Availablefrom:http://ufdc.ufl.edu/UF00075400/00001/21j)

ASTURIAS, F. (1941). Belice. Guatemala, Centro América: Tipografía Nacional de Guatemala.

ATKINS, J. (1735). *A voyage to Guinea, Brasil and the West Indies.* London: C. Ward and R. Chandler.

ATKINS, J. (1970). *A voyage to Guinea, Brazil and the West Indies in His Majesty's ships, The "Swallow" and "Weymouth".* London: Cass.

BAILEY, T. A. (1964). *A diplomatic history of the American people.* Englewood Cliffs, NJ: Prentice-Hall.

BANCROFT, H. H. (1883). *History of Central America.* San Francisco: A. L. Bancroft.

BENNETT, J. A. (2008). *Education in Belize: A historical perspective.* Belize City, Belize: Angelus Press.

BOLLAND, O. N. (1977). *The formation of a colonial society: Belize, from conquest to crown colony.* Baltimore: Johns Hopkins University Press.

BOLLAND, O. N. (1988). *Colonialism and resistance in Belize: Essays in historical sociology.* Benque Viejo del Carmen, Belize: Cubola Productions.

BOLLAND, O. N., & MOBERG, M. (1995). Development and national identity: creolization, immigration, and ethnic conflict in Belize. *International Journal of Comparative Race and Ethnic Studies, 2*(2), 1-18.

BOLLAND, O. N., & SHOMAN, A. (1977). *Land in Belize, 1765–1871.* Mona, Jamaica: Institute of Social and Economic Research, University of the West Indies.

BRIDGES, G. W. (1828). *The annals of Jamaica.* London: John Murray.

BRIDGEWATER, S. (2011). *A natural history of Belize: Inside the Maya Forest.* Austin: University of Texas Press.

BRIEF SKETCH OF BRITISH HONDURAS. (1963). Belize, 1963. Also published in 1927, 1928, 1939, 1944, 1948, 1952, 1954 and 1958.

BRISTOWE, L., & WRIGHT, P. (1890). *The handbook of British Honduras for 1889–90.* Edinburgh: Blackwood.

BROCKWAY, L. (1979). *Science and colonial expansion: The role of the British Royal Botanic Gardens.* New York, NY: Academic Press.

BULMER-THOMAS, V. (2012). *The economic history of the Caribbean since the Napoleonic Wars.* New York, NY: Cambridge University Press.

BURDON, J. A. (1931). *Archives of British Honduras.* Volume I. London: Sifton, Praed & Co., Ltd.

BURDON, J. A. (1934). *Archives of British Honduras.* Volume II. London: Sifton, Praed & Co., Ltd.

BURDON, J. A. (1936). *Archives of British Honduras.* Volume III. London: Sifton, Praed & Co., Ltd.

BURNS, A. (1949). *Colonial civil servant.* London: G. Allen & Unwin.

CAIGER, S. L. (1951). *British Honduras: Past and present.* London: G. Allen & Unwin.

CALDERÓN QUIJANO, J. A. (1944). *Belice, 1663(?) -1821: Historia de los establecimientos británicos del Río Valis hasta la independencia de Hispanoamérica.* Sevilla: s.n.

CANNY, N. (Ed.). (1998). *The Oxford history of the British Empire: Vol. 1: The Origins of Empire.* Oxford, UK: Oxford University Press.

CAREY JONES, N. S. (1953). *The pattern of a dependent economy: The national income of British Honduras.* Cambridge, UK: Cambridge University Press.

CASTAÑEDA, G. A. (1969). *Belikin: Descripción monográfica de veintidós mil novecientos kilómetros cuadrados de centroamericanidad irredenta. Centenario de la usurpación, 1859-1959.* Guatemala, Central America. (Available from Open Library: http://openlibrary.org/books/OL16609560M/Belikin)

CAVE, R. (1976). Printing in nineteenth-century Belize. *The Library Quarterly 46*(1), 20-37.

CHALONER AND FLEMING, MAHOGANY AND TIMBER BROKERS. (1851). *The mahogany tree: Its botanical characters, qualities and uses. With a map and illustrations. And an appendix, etc.* Liverpool: Rockliff & Son; London: Effingham Wilson.

CHAMBERLAIN, R. S. (1948). *The conquest and colonization of Yucatan, 1517-1550.* Washington DC: Carnegie Institution.

CHARLEVOIX, P.-F.-X. (1733). *Histoire de l'isle Espagnole ou de S. Domingue: Ecrite particulierement sur des memoires manuscrits du P. Jean-Baptiste le Pers, Jesuite, missionnaire à Saint Domingue, & sur les pieces originales, qui se conservent au Dépôt de la marine.* Amsterdam: Chez François L'Honoré. (Available from: https://market.android.com/details?id=book-HgcOAAAAQAAJ&hl=en)

CHERRINGTON, E., EK, E., CHO, P., HOWELL, B. F., HERNANDEZ, B. E., ANDERSON, E. R., . . . ERWIN, D. E. (2010). *Forest Cover and Deforestation in Belize: 1980-2010.* Panama: Cathalac: Centro del Agua del Trópico Húmedo para América Latina y El Caribe.

CLEGERN, W. M. (1967). *British Honduras: Colonial dead end, 1859-1900.* Baton Rouge: Louisiana State University Press.

THE COLONY OF BRITISH HONDURAS: ITS HISTORY, TRADE, AND NATURAL RESOURCES. (1867). Presented to the Directors and Shareholders of The British Honduras Company, Limited, by their manager. Foreign and Commonwealth Office Collection, London.

CONZEMIUS, E. (1932). *Ethnographical survey of the Miskito and Sumu Indians of Honduras and Nicaragua.* Washington: U.S. Govt. Printing Office.

COOK, J., & HAAS, M. F. (1935). *Remarks on a passage from the river Balise: In the bay of Honduras, to Merida: the capital of the province of Jucatan in the Spanish West Indies.* New Orleans, LA: Midameres Press.

CRAIG, A. (1969). *Logwood as a factor in the settlement of British Honduras. Caribbean Studies,* 9(1), 53-62.

DAMPIER, W. (1699). *Voyages and descriptions: In three parts: to which is added a general index to both volumes.* London: Printed for James Knapton.

DAMPIER, W. (1931). *Voyages and discoveries.* London, England: The Argonaut Press.

DAVIDSON, W. V. (1974). *Historical geography of the Bay Islands, Honduras: Anglo-Hispanic conflict in the western Caribbean.* Birmingham, AL: Southern University Press.

DAWSON, F.G. (1983*). William Pitt's settlement at Black River on the Mosquito Shore: A challenge to Spain in Central America, 1732-87. The Hispanic American Historical Review,* 63(4), 677-706.

DAWSON, F.G. (1998). The evacuation of the Mosquito Shore and the English who stayed behind, 1786-1800. *The Americas,* 55(1), 63-89.

DESMOND, R. (1995). *Kew:The history of the Royal Botanic Gardens.* London: Harvill Press with the Royal Botanic Gardens, Kew.

DOBSON, N. (1973). *A history of Belize.* Port of Spain, Trinidad &Tobago: Longman Caribbean.

DOZIER, C. L. (1985). *Nicaragua's Mosquito Shore: The years of British and American presence.* Tuscaloosa, AL: University of Alabama Press.

DUMOND, D. E. (1997). *The machete and the cross: Campesino rebellion in Yucatan.* Lincoln, NE: University of Nebraska Press.

DUNLOP, W.R. (1921). *Report on the economic and natural features of British Honduras in relation to agriculture.* London, England: Crown Agents.

DU TERTRE, J. B. (1667). *Histoire Générale Des Antilles habitées par les françois.* Paris, France: T. Iolly.

ELLIOTT, J. H. (2006). *Empires of the Atlantic world: Britain and Spain in America, 1492-1830.* New Haven: Yale University Press.

ENCALADA, N. & AWE, J. (2010). *St. George's Caye: The birthplace of a nation.* Belmopan, Belize: NICH, Occasional Publication No.1.

EVERITT, J. (1986). The growth and development of Belize City. *Journal of Latin American Studies,* 18(1), 75-111.

EXQUEMELIN, A. O. (1976). *The buccaneers of America: A true account of the most remarkable assaults committed of late years upon the coast of the West Indies by the buccaneers of Jamaica and Tortuga, both English and French. Wherein are contained more especially the unparalleled exploits of Sir Henry Morgan.* Williamstown, MA: Corner House.

FAIRLIE, S. (1965). Dyestuffs of the Eighteenth Century. *Economic History Review, 17,* 490-92.

FAIRWEATHER, D. N. A. (1970). *A short history of the volunteer forces of British Honduras.* Belize City, Belize: s.n.

FANCOURT, C. S. J. (1854). *The history of Yucatan: From its discovery to the close of the seventeenth century.* London, England: John Murray.

FERRAND, A. (1880). *Lettres de la Presidente Ferrand au Baron de Breteuil, suivies de l'Histoire des Amours de Cléante et de Bélise et des poésies d'Antoine Ferrand, revues sur les éditions originales, augmentées des variantes, de ... notes ... et précédées d'une notice biographique par E. Asse.* Paris, France: Charpentier.

FLOYD, T. S. (1967). *The Anglo-Spanish struggle for Mosquitia.* Albuquerque, NM: University of New Mexico Press.

GAGE, T. (1648). *The English-American, his travail by sea and land: or, A new survey of the West-India's: Containing a journal of three thousand and three hundred miles within the main land of America ... : also, a new and exact discovery of the Spanish navigation to those parts ... with a grammar, or some few rudiments of the Indian tongue, called, Poconchi, or Pocoman.* London, England: Printed by R. Cotes.

GARCÍA BAUER, C. (1958). *La controversia sobre el territorio de Belice: Y el procedimiento ex-aequo et bono.* Guatemala, Central America: Editorial Universitaria.

GARCÍA LORCA, F. (1957). *Amour de Don Perlimplin & de Bélise dans leur jardin: alleluia érotique en troix tableaux et un prologue traduit de l'espagnol par Jean-Marie Souto.* Lyon, France: A l'Arbalète.

GARCÍA PELAEZ, F. P. (1851). *Memorias para la historia del antiguo reino de Guatemala.* Guatemala, C. A.: Tipografía Nacional de Guatemala.

GIBBS, A. R. (1883). *British Honduras: An historical and descriptive account of the colony from its settlement, 1670.* London: S. Low, Marston, Searle & Rivington.

GIBSON, D. & PALACIO, J. (2011). *Belizean Strategic Culture.* Miami: Florida International University.

GOMBAULD, J. O. (1657). *Les epigrammes de Gombauld: Divisées en trois livres.* Paris, France: Augustin Courbé.

GONZÁLEZ, N. L. S. (1988). *Sojourners of the Caribbean: Ethnogenesis and ethnohistory of the Garifuna.* Urbana, IL: University of Illinois Press.

GRAHAM, E. (2011*). Maya Christians and their churches in sixteenth-century Belize.* Tallahassee, FL: University Press of Florida.

GRANT, C. H. (1976). *The making of modern Belize: Politics, society, & British colonialism in Central America.* Cambridge, England: Cambridge University Press.

GRANT, L. A. (1994). *The life of Robert Sidney Turton.* Belize: National Library Service.

HARING, C. H. (1910). *The buccaneers in the West Indies in the XVII century.* New York, NY: Dutton.

HARLOW, V. T. (1923). *The voyages of Captain William Jackson (1642-1645).* London, England: Offices of the Society.

HENDERSON, G. (1809). *An account of the British settlement of Honduras: being a view of its commercial and agricultural resources, soil, climate, natural history, &c.: to which are added, sketches of the manners and customs of the Mosquito Indians, preceded by the journal of a voyage to the Mosquito shore.* London, England: C. and R. Baldwin.

HENDERSON, G. (1811). *An account of the British settlement of Honduras: being a view of its commercial and agricultural resources, soil, climate, natural history, &c.: to which are added, sketches of the manners and customs of the Mosquito Indians, preceded by the journal of a voyage to the Mosquito shore* (2nd ed.). London: C. and R. Baldwin.

HEWITT, A. & STEVENS, C. (1981). The Second Lomé Convention. In C. Stevens (Ed.), *EEC and the Third World: A survey.* London, England: Hodder and Stoughton.

HOBHOUSE, H. (1999). *Seeds of Change: Six plants that transformed mankind* (Revised ed.). London, England: Macmillan Publishers Ltd.

HONDURAS ALMANACK. (1826). Belize, 1826. Also published in 1827, 1828, 1829, 1830 and 1839.

HONDURAS GAZETTE. (1826/9). Belize: James Cruickshank. Published weekly in Belize and available on Google books (http://books.google.com/).

HUMMEL, C. (1921). *Report on the Forests of British Honduras, with suggestions for a far reaching forest policy.* London, England: Colonial Research Committee.

HUMPHREYS, R. A. (1961). *The diplomatic history of British Honduras, 1638–1901.* London, England: Oxford University Press.

IYO, A., TZALAM, F., & HUMPHREYS, F. (2007). *Belize, new vision: African and Mayan Civilizations.* Belize City: Angelus Press.

JENKINS, G. & KUO, C.-Y. (2006). *Fiscal Adjustment for Sustainable Growth in Belize.* Washington, DC: Inter-American Development Bank.

JOLLY, K. & MCRAE, E. (2003). *The environment of Belize: Our life support system.* Benque Viejo del Carmen, Belize: Cubola Productions.

JONES, G. D. (1989). *Maya resistance to Spanish rule: Time and history on a colonial frontier.* Albuquerque, NM: University of New Mexico Press.

JONES, G. D. (1998). *The conquest of the last Maya kingdom.* Stanford, CA: Stanford University Press.

JONES, O. L. (1994). *Guatemala in the Spanish colonial period.* Norman, OK: University of Oklahoma Press.

JOSEPH, G. (1974). British Loggers and Spanish Governors: The Logwood Trade and Its Settlements in the Yucatan Peninsula, Part I. *Caribbean Studies, 14*(2), 7-37.

JOSEPH, G. (1976). British loggers and Spanish governors: The logwood trade and its settlements in the Yucatan Peninsula: Part II. *Caribbean Studies, 15*(4), 43-52.

KING, E. (1991). *Belize 1798, the road to glory: The battle of St. George's Caye: a novel history of Belize.* Belize City, Belize: Tropical Books.

KUPPERMAN, K. O. (1993). *Providence Island, 1630-1641: The other Puritan colony.* Cambridge, England: Cambridge University Press.

LANGLOIS, M. (1926). *Louis XIV et la cour. D'après trois témois nouveaux: Bélise, Beauvillier, Chamillart.* Paris. A. Michel.

LAUTERPACHT, E., SCHWEBEL, S., ROSENNE, S. & ORREGO VICUÑA, F. (2002). *Legal Opinion on Guatemala's Territorial Claim to Belize*, Belmopan, Belize: Government Printers. (Available from http://vandeplaspublishing. com/store/product.php?productid=28&cat=10&page=1)

LEONARD, T. M. (1985). *Central America and United States policies, 1820s-1980s: A guide to issues and references.* Claremont, CA: Regina Books.

LEONARD, T. M. (1995). Relaciones entre Guatemala y Estados Unidos. In M. J. Luján and A. Herrarte, (Eds.), *Historia general de Guatemala. Tomo IV. Desde la República Federal hasta 1898.* Guatemala: Asociación de Amigos del País, Fundación para la Cultura y el Desarrollo.

LESLIE, R. (Ed.). (2008). *A History of Belize: Nation in the making.* Benque Viejo del Carmen: Cubola Productions.

LOW, G. A. (1824). *The Belise merchants unmasked, or, A review of their late proceedings against Poyais: From information and authentic documents gained on the spot, during a visit to those parts in the months of August and September, 1823.* London: Printed for the authors, and sold by Effingham Wilson.

MALONEY, A. (1896). Botanical Enterprise in British Honduras. *Bulletin of Miscellaneous Information, Royal Gardens, Kew, 113-114*, 101-5.

MARTIN, R. M. (1834). *History of the British Colonies Vol. II. Possessions in the West Indies.* London, England: Cochrane and McCrone.

MARTIN, D. & MANZANO, O. (2010). *Towards a Sustainable and Efficient State: The Development Agenda of Belize.* Washington, DC: Inter-American Development Bank.

MCCRACKEN, D. P. (1997). *Gardens of empire: Botanical institutions of the Victorian British empire.* London, England: Leicester University Press.

MCLEISH, J. (1926). *British activities in Yucatan and on the Moskito Shore in the eighteenth century.* (Unpublished MA thesis). London, England: University of London.

MEANS, P. A. (1917). *History of the Spanish conquest of Yucatan and of the Itzas.* Cambridge, MA: The Museum.

METZGEN, M. S. & CAIN, H. E. C. (1925). *The handbook of British Honduras, comprising historical, statistical and general information concerning the colony.* London, England: Crown Agents for the Colonies.

MOBERG, M. (1992). *Citrus, strategy, and class: The politics of development in Southern Belize.* Iowa City, IA: University of Iowa Press.

MOBERG, M. (1997). *Myths of ethnicity and nation: Immigration, work, and identity in the Belize banana industry.* Knoxville, TN: University of Tennessee Press.

MOBERG, M. (2003). Responsible men and sharp yankees: The United Fruit Company, resident elites, and colonial state in British Honduras. In S. Striffler & M. Moberg (Eds.), *Banana wars: Power, production, and history in the Americas* (145-147). Durham, NC: Duke University Press.

MORDECAI, J. (1968). *Federation of the West Indies.* Evanston, IL: Northwestern University Press.

MORRIS, D. (1883). *The colony of British Honduras: Its resources and prospects; with particular reference to its indigenous plants and economic productions.* London, England: E. Stanford.

MUSGRAVE, T. & MUSGRAVE, W. (2000). *An empire of plants: People and plants that changed the world.* London, England: Cassell.

NAYLOR, R. A. (1988). *Influencia británica en el comercio centroamericano durante las primeras décadas de la independencia: 1821-1851.* Antigua, Guatemala: Centro de Investigaciones Regionales de Mesoamérica.

NAYLOR, R. A. (1989). *Penny ante imperialism: The Mosquito Shore and the Bay of Honduras, 1600-1914:A case study in British informal empire.* Rutherford, NJ: Fairleigh Dickinson University Press.

NAYLOR, R. A. (1995). *Los Británicos en la Economía Centroamericana: El Comercio Anglobeliceño.* In M. J. Luján and A. Herrarte, (Eds.), *Historia general de Guatemala. Tomo IV. Desde la República Federal hasta 1898.* Guatemala: Asociación de Amigos del País, Fundación para la Cultura y el Desarrollo.

NEWTON, A. P. (1914). *The colonising activities of the English Puritans: The last phase of the Elizabethan struggle with Spain.* New Haven, CT: Yale University.

OFFEN, K. (2000). British Logwood Extraction from the Mosquitia: The Origin of a Myth, *Hispanic American Historical Review, 80, 1, pp.113-35.*

ORTIZ, F. (1940). *Contrapunteo cubano del tabaco y el azúcar: (advertencia de sus contrastes agrarios, económicos, históricos y sociales, su etnografía y su transculturación).* La Habana, Cuba: J. Montero.

PALMER, R. R. (1950). *A history of the modern world.* New York, NY: Knopf.

PARES, R. (1956). *Yankees and Creoles: The trade between North America and the West Indies before the American Revolution.* Cambridge, MA: Harvard University Press.

PARKER, F. D. (1964). *The Central American Republics.* London, England: Oxford University Press.

PENDERGAST, D., JONES, G. & GRAHAM, E. (1993). Locating Spanish colonial towns in the Maya lowlands: A case study from Belize. *Latin American Antiquity, 4,* 59–73.

PENICHE, F. (1869). Belice. *Sociedad Mexicana de Geografía, Boletín, 2da ep.*(i), 217-9.

PÉREZ, P. (2011). *Determinants of interest rate spreads in Belize.* Belize City, Belize: Central Bank of Belize.

PERKINS, D. (1941). *Hands off: A history of the Monroe doctrine.* Boston, MA: Little, Brown and Company.

PERKINS, D. (1947). *The United States and the Caribbean.* Cambridge, MA: Harvard Univ. Press.

PETCH, T. (1986). Dependency, Land and Oranges in Belize. *Third World Quarterly, 8*(3), 1002-1019.

PIM, A. (1934). *British Honduras, financial and economic position* (cmd 4586). London, England: HMSO.

REED, N. A. (1964). *The Caste War of Yucatan.* Stanford, CA: Stanford University Press.

RODRÍGUEZ, M. (1964). *A Palmerstonian diplomat in Central America: Frederick Chatfield, Esq.* Tucson, AZ: University of Arizona Press.

ROSSANO, G. (1969). Down to the Bay: New York shippers and the Central American logwood trade, 1748-1761. *New York History, 70*(3), 229-250.

SCHIEBINGER, L. (2004). *Plants and empire: Colonial bioprospecting in the Atlantic World.* Cambridge, MA: Harvard University Press.

SHOMAN, A. (1973). The birth of the Nationalist Movement in Belize, 1950–1954. *Journal of Belizean Affairs, 2,* 3–40.

SHOMAN, A. (1994). *13 Chapters of a history of Belize.* Belize City, Belize: Angelus Press.

SHOMAN, A. (2010). *Belize's independence and decolonization in Latin America: Guatemala, Britain, and the UN.* New York, NY: Palgrave Macmillan.

SHOMAN, A. (2011). *13 Chapters of a history of Belize* (2nd ed.). Belize City: Angelus Press.

SIERRA, J. (1849). Ojeada sobre el establecimiento británico de Belice y reflexiones sobre su futura influencia. *El Fénix, 62*(5). Campeche, Mexico.

SIMMONS, D. C. (2001). *Confederate settlements in British Honduras.* Jefferson, NC: McFarland.

SMITH, G. (2011). *George Price: A life revealed–the authorised biography.* Kingston, Jamaica: Ian Randle Publishers.

SOCIÉTÉ ANGLO-FRANÇAISE DE HONDURAS. (1857). *Notice sur les acajous de la Baie de Honduras.* Paris, France: imp. de Ch. de Mourgues frères.

SQUIER, E. G. (1855). *Notes on Central America: Particularly the states of Honduras and San Salvador: Their geography, topography, climate, population, resources, productions, etc., etc., and the proposed Honduras inter-oceanic railway.* New York, NY: Harper & Bros.

SQUIER, E. G. (1858). *The states of Central America: Their geography, topography, climate, population, resources, productions, commerce, political organization, aborigines, etc., etc., comprising chapters on Honduras, San Salvador, Nicaragua, Costa Rica, Guatemala, Belize, the Bay Islands, the Mosquito Shore, and the Honduras inter-oceanic railway.* New York, NY: Harper & Bros.

STANDLEY, P. C., & RECORD, S. J. (1936). *The forests and flora of British Honduras.* Chicago, IL: Field Museum of Natural History.

STEPHENS, J. L. (1841). *Incidents of travel in Central America, Chiapas, and Yucatan.* New York, NY: Harper & Bros.

STONE, D. (1932). *Some Spanish Entradas, 1524-1695.* Tulane University, LA: Middle American Research Series, No. 4.

STRAUGHAN, J. (n.d.). *Emigration from Belize since 1981.* Unpublished Paper available on website of University of Vermont.

SUTTON, D., HUGHES, A. & BULMER-THOMAS, B. (2000). Recent records of pteridophytes for Belize, Central America. *Bulletin of the Natural History Museum London, 30*(2), 81-99.

THOMPSON, J. E. S. (1972). *The Maya of Belize: Historical chapters since Columbus.* Belmopan, Belize: Government Printing Office.

THOMPSON, J. E. S. (1988). *The Maya of Belize: Historical chapters since Columbus* (reprint of 1972 edition). Benque Viejo del Carmen, Belize: Cubola Productions.

THURSTON, A., & PUGH, R. B. (1995). *Records of the Colonial Office, Dominions Office, Commonwealth Relations Office, and Commonwealth Office.* London, England: HMSO.

TROLLOPE, F. M. (1832). *Domestic manners of the Americans.* London, England: Whittaker, Treacher.

URING, N. (1726). *A history of the voyages and travels of Capt. Nathaniel Uring.* London: Printed by W. Wilkins for J. Peele.

URING, N. (1928). *The voyages and travels of Captain Nathaniel Uring: With a new draught of the Bay of Honduras.* London, England: Cassell and Co.

WADDELL, D. A. G. (1961). *British Honduras: A historical and contemporary survey.* London, England: Oxford University Press.

WASHBURN, W. E. (1975). *The Indian in America.* New York, NY: Harper & Row.

WASHBURN, W. E. (1995). *Red man's land/white man's law: The past and present status of the American Indian.* Norman, OK: University of Oklahoma Press.

WATTS, D. (1987). *The West Indies: Patterns of development, culture, and environmental change since 1492.* Cambridge, England: Cambridge University Press.

WILLIAMS, M. W. (1916). *Anglo-American Isthmian diplomacy, 1815-1915.* Washington: American Historical Association.

WILSON, A. (1936). The Logwood Trade in the Seventeenth and Eighteenth Centuries. In D. C McKay (Ed.), *Essays in the history of modern Europe.* New York, NY: Harper Brothers.

WINZERLING, E. O. (1946). *The beginning of British Honduras, 1506-1765.* New York, NY: North River Press.

WOODWARD, R.L. (1985). Central America from Independence to c.1870. In Bethell, L. (ed.), *The Cambridge History of Latin America. Vol. III. From Independence to c.1870.* New York: Cambridge University Press, pp.471-506.

WRIGHT, H. (1912), *Hevea Brasiliensis or Para Rubber.* London: MacLaren and Sons.

XIMENEZ, F. (1930). *Historia de la Provincia de San Vicente de Chiapa y Guatemala. Tomo II.* Guatemala, C.A.: Tipografía Nacional de Guatemala.

Additional Digital Sources

BIBLIOTHÈQUE NATIONALE FRANÇAISE. http://gallica.bnf.fr/

CARIBBEAN CENTRE FOR MONEY AND FINANCE. http://www.ccmfuwi.org/

CARIBBEAN COMMUNITY (CARICOM) SECRETARIAT. http://www.caricom.org/

CARIBBEAN DEVELOPMENT BANK (CDB). http://www.caribank.org/

CARIBBEAN TOURISM ORGANIZATION (CTO). http://www.onecaribbean.org/

CENTRAL BANK OF BELIZE. https://www.centralbank.org.bz/

DIGITAL LIBRARY OF THE CARIBBEAN. http://www.dloc.com/

ECONOMIC COMMISSION FOR LATIN AMERICA AND THE CARIBBEAN (ECLAC/CEPAL). http://www.eclac.org/

FOUNDATION FOR THE ADVANCEMENT OF MESOAMERICAN STUDIES.
   http://www.famsi.org/reports/96072/index.html/
GOOGLE BOOKS. http://books.google.com/
INTERNATIONAL LABOUR ORGANIZATION (ILO). MINIMUM WAGE DATA-
   BASE. http://www.ilo.org/travaildatabase/servlet/minimumwages/
JSTOR. http://www.jstor.org/
PARLIAMENTARY PAPERS. http://www.portculis.parliament.uk/
PORTAL DE ARCHIVOS ESPAÑOLES. (http://pares.mcu.es/).
STATISTICAL INSTITUTE OF BELIZE. http://www.statisticsbelize.org.bz/
UNITED NATIONS, WORLD TOURISM ORGANIZATION. http://unwto.org/en
UNITED NATIONS DATA (UND). http://data.un.org/
UNITED NATIONS NATIONAL ACCOUNTS (UNNA). ttp://unstats.un.org/
   unsd/snaama/Introduction.asp
WORLD BANK. *World Development Indicators* (WDI). http://data.worldbank.
   org/

Index